Feminist Anthropology

Feminist Anthropology

Past, Present, and Future

EDITED BY PAMELA L. GELLER
AND MIRANDA K. STOCKETT

PENN

University of Pennsylvania Press

Philadelphia

10   9   8   7   6   5   4   3   2   1

Published by
University of Pennsylvania Press
Philadelphia, Pennsylvania 19104-4112

Library of Congress Cataloging-in-Publication Data

Feminist anthropology : past, present, and future / edited by Pamela L. Geller and
Miranda K. Stockett.
    p.   cm.

ISBN: 978-0-812-22005-6

Includes bibliographical references and index.
    1. Feminist anthropology.   I. Geller, Pamela L.   II. Stockett, Miranda K.
GN33.8 .F443   2006
301.082—dc 22   2006042130

To our families

Contents

Foreword: Taking Stock—The Transformation of Feminist Theorizing in Anthropology

LOUISE LAMPHERE

Over thirty years have passed since the publication of *Woman, Culture, and Society* (Rosaldo and Lamphere 1974) and *Toward an Anthropology of Women* (Reiter 1975)—two volumes that signaled the renewed interest in feminism and women within anthropology. By the publication of *Gender at the Crossroads of Knowledge* (di Leonardo 1991a) seventeen years later, the emphasis had shifted to gender rather than women, and archaeologists, linguists, and biological anthropologists had begun to theorize about gender difference. With this volume, we have come to another point of assessment, one where archaeologists and biological anthropologists are the center of new approaches to the study of gender from a feminist point of view.

In some respects feminist anthropology looks very different than it did thirty years ago. The number of feminist anthropologists has increased and the kinds of scholars producing feminist anthropology have multiplied. The contributors to Rosaldo and Lamphere's and Reiter's volumes are nearing retirement age, and some, like Shelly Rosaldo, Lois Paul, and Carol McCormack, have died. At least two new cohorts of feminist scholars have conducted field research (those writing in the 1980s and early 1990s and those who have just now begun to publish) and both have changed feminist theory. More of these are minority women, men (both minority and white), women raised in non-Western traditions, and self-identified gay and lesbian anthropologists. The emphasis has shifted. Gone is the interest in sweeping universals. Writing about gender has replaced writing about women. Within cultural anthropology more attention is paid to history, to analysis of single cultures, and to multisited ethnography in a globalizing world.

Despite these changes, there are several striking continuities in feminist anthropological thinking over the past three decades. As we have moved from an interest in women to an analysis of gender and then to a focus on difference and identity, we have still retained an interest in critically evaluating the relationships between men and women, understanding the nature of power, and connecting political economy and culture. We have adopted a new language, however, much of it derived from the work of Michel Foucault and Judith Butler. This new language offers possibilities for more nuanced and productive ways of thinking about gender and, as the chapters in this book demonstrate, for creating dialogue and arenas of common interest among archaeologists, biological anthropologists, and cultural anthropologists.

Feminist anthropology has always been about critique—critical appraisal of the social structures and cultural ideologies that shape women's lives and reformulation of the theoretical apparatus that anthropologists have used to understand these structures and cultural notions. At first our focus was on the categories and theories of male anthropologists (often white, American or European). Malinowski (1984[1922], 1929) missed the importance of women's funerary exchanges in the Trobriands, as Annette Weiner's work has shown (Weiner 1976). Evans-Pritchard (1940, 1951) did not see the crucial role of women as dispute settlers and as replacements for men in the institution of woman/woman marriage (Gluckman 1955; Gough 1971). Archaeologists and biological anthropologists elevated Man the Hunter over Woman the Gatherer as the inventor of culture in human history (Lee and Devore 1968). Feminist anthropologists in the 1970s criticized these androcentric theories and went on to provide new frameworks for analyzing women's roles (Tanner and Zihlman 1976; Tanner 1981). Equally important in this process was the making visible of women's activities, the exploration of their sources of informal and even formal power, and the analysis of their economic contributions to a wide variety of societies.

During the 1980s and 1990s our critique more often turned to the categories that feminist anthropologists have been using in an effort to build a more nuanced theory of gender. Not only have we discarded dualisms and turned to more historical and localized analysis (the universalizing particularity called for by Henrietta Moore 1994, 17), but we have become wary of essentialism, preferring to examine the productivity of gender, the cultural construction of sexuality, and the importance of understanding heteronormativity as it has skewed our thinking about social arrangements. In all this, the initial feminist attention to variability, to issues of power, and to the forces of social change are still evident but recast in different terms. The chapters in this volume continue this critical approach taking care to interrogate categories of analysis, but reaching toward an analysis that brings together individual agency, the analysis of the body, the production of gender difference, and political economies in which these are embedded. The contributors to this volume represent current work in archaeology, cultural anthropology, and biological anthropology and thus build on the diversity within anthropology that has emerged over the past thirty years as feminist anthropology has grown through reclaiming our past, teaching new generations of students, and becoming more diverse.

Diversifying Feminist Anthropology

One of the most central trends in broadening and diversifying feminist anthropology has been historical. Not only have we acknowledged the importance of nineteenth-century women anthropologists (e.g., Alice Fletcher, Matilda Coxe Stevenson), but we have rediscovered a feminist legacy within anthropology that goes back to the early writing of Elsie Clews Parsons. This has led to a reevaluation of the work and lives of Parsons and her colleagues Ruth Benedict and Margaret Mead and to a reclaiming of Zora Neale Hurston and Ruth Landes as feminist foremothers.

Discovering this legacy has been part of the larger process of documenting the contributions of women anthropologists, in general, from Nancy Lurie's history of the nineteenth-century Women's Anthropological Society (Lurie 1966) to the publication of *Women Anthropologists: A Biographical Dictionary*. This collection of profiles of women anthropologists spans one hundred years from Erminie Smith, born in 1836, to Eva Hunt, born in 1934 (Gacs et al. 1988). Another source of the new scholarship on women anthropologists is the collection of papers from the Daughters of the Desert conference, *Hidden Scholars* (Parezo 1993). It examines the impact of women's research and applied anthropology on the study of Native Americans in the American Southwest. Adding to these sources that emphasize white women anthropologists has been the new scholarship on the contributions of minority women, many of whom did not have Ph.D.s or spent much of their careers in minority institutions or outside traditional academic departments. We now view Zora Neale Hurston, Katherine Dunham, Ella DeLoria, Christine Quintasket (Morning Star), Catherine Bond Day, Irene Diggs, Manet Fowler, and Vera Green as pioneering women in anthropology (Finn 1995; Harrison and Harrison 1999). Not all the women anthropologists celebrated in these books were feminists nor did they all focus on the study of women's lives, but they were models of professional women who conducted research, taught students, or brought perspectives from non-Western cultures to the public at large.

Hand in hand with "finding" minority and white women as pioneers in anthropology has been the incorporation of more minority women into our graduate programs and teaching positions within the academy. Many of these women have contributed to the growing scholarship on women and gender. Johnetta Cole's collection *All American Women* (1986) featured feminist writing and the biographical sketches of minority and working class women, as well as white women. More recent African American feminists have contributed to our understanding of the impact of globalization and neoliberalism on women's lives in the Caribbean (Bolles 1996; Harrison 1997), collected the narrative histories of women (McClaurin 1996), documented the impact of poverty and women's strategies (Mullings and Wali 2001) and explored gender relationships in African cultures (Shaw 1995). The forging of Black feminist anthropology is well documented in the personal statements and research documented in *Black Feminist Anthropology* (McClaurin 2001). Among Chicano/Latina women who have studied women's lives are Patricia Zavella (1987), Iris Lopez (1997), and Ruth Behar (1993). Bea Medicine's innovative scholarship on Lakota women warriors (1983) and Nancy Mithlo's research on Native American women artists are examples of anthropological contributions by Native American women (1993).

Another aspect of diversity has been the flowering of gay and lesbian anthropology. In the 1970s, this research was initiated by Ester Newton through her research on female impersonators (1972), Ellen Lewin with her study *Lesbian Mothers* (1993), and Elizabeth Kennedy through her innovative oral histories of lesbian women in Buffalo, New York (Kennedy and Davis 1994). Ellen Lewin and William Leap have published a collection focusing on lesbian/gay relations in the field (1996) and one emphasizing the impact of gay/lesbian theorizing on cultural anthropology (2002). In this volume, the chapters by Evelyn Blackwood and Thomas Dowson expand this research by exploring how our very assumptions of gender relations come out of a pervasive heteronormativity—the inability to see family relations as anything other than based on the heterosexual couple—and the unwillingness to view archaeological evidence outside of our modern notions of masculinity and femininity. Both bring the insights of queer theory to feminist anthropology, a relationship that continues to be a productive one.

Constructing a New Pedagogy

Building on the critical vision that feminist anthropologists have brought to their research, many scholars have sought to transform the content of their courses and their interaction with students in the classroom. To this end, the Association for Feminist Anthropology (AFA) initiated a project where feminist anthropologists worked with textbook authors to include more material on women and gender in their introductory textbooks. In addition, Sandra Morgen and other AFA members, under the auspices of the American Anthropological Association, published a collection on *Gender and Anthropology: Critical Reviews for Research and Teaching* (Morgen 1989a). This volume included conceptual essays, specific curricular suggestions, and a list of resources for over nineteen topics within feminist anthropology. The essays ranged from overviews of subfields (Archaeology, Biosocial Anthropology, Primate Studies, Linguistics) to updates relevant to teaching of feminist research in different regions of the world (Africa, Latin America, the Middle East, Southeast Asia, the United States). There were also essays on gender and public policy, development, and sexuality. The purpose of the book was to help teachers of undergraduate anthropology courses incorporate the new scholarship on women and gender into their courses.

Julia Hendon and Ann Kakaliouras, in their contributions to this collection, further advance feminist curricular reform. They put forth the view that a feminist pedagogy in anthropology involves problematizing accepted anthropological concepts and theories, engaging students in dialogue (rather than seeing them as receptacles of knowledge), and asking students to interrogate their own hidden assumptions and values. Unlike earlier literature, which tended to make programmatic suggestions about curriculum revision, the chapters by Hendon and Kakaliouras recount their successes and failures, so readers learn how they dealt with student reactions to feminism, evolutionary theory, and concepts of race—all notoriously fraught topics in the twenty-first-century undergraduate classroom. Since these chapters focus on biological anthropology and archaeology where there is scant literature on actual feminist teaching practice, they are welcome additions.

Forging a New Theoretical Language

One of the major preoccupations of *Woman, Culture, and Society* (Rosaldo and Lamphere 1974) and *Toward an Anthropology of Women* (Reiter 1975) was variability, both within and between cultures. In the Rosaldo and Lamphere collection, the chapters by Karen Sacks and Peggy Sanday built cross-cultural frameworks for examining women's status in a wide variety of non-Western societies. Other chapters (for example, those by Nancy Tanner and Joan Bamberger) made comparisons of women's domestic, political, or cultural position within a cultural or geographic area (Southeast Asia, lowland South America). Several contributions examined women within one culture, giving us a sense of how individual women or women in different structural positions or social

settings pursued their own goals (Stack), attained and exercised power
(Hoffer), or used ties with other women to build women's associations
that represented their interests (Leis). The chapters in the Reiter volume covered variability within women's situations using case studies on
a particular aspect of women's status (from small populations like the
Kung San in Botswana and the Iroquois of upstate New York to poor
and rural women in China and Columbia). There were also broad comparative contributions about women's role in gathering, the origin of
the family, and the possibility of matriarchal societies. As later collections became more focused on gender, they too continued to emphasize
variability through both case studies of gender relations in one society
and articles that featured comparative data (Collier and Yanagisako
1987a; Ortner and Whitehead 1981a). Variability remains an important
component of this volume as well, drawing our attention to gender differences in past societies (Joyce, Perry and Potter, Walrath, Dowson) as
well as to contemporary ones (Blackwood, Moore).

A second theme was what we would now call agency. In their chapters
in *Woman, Culture, and Society*, Jane Collier and Margery Wolf viewed
women as active agents (Rosaldo and Lamphere 1974, 89–96, 157–72).
Women were the worms in the apple that constituted the patrilineage.
In Taiwan, for example, women built uterine families within large patriarchal Taiwanese households to eke out a place for themselves and
build loyal sons whom they could influence. By pursing their own goals
they often contributed to the break-up of these family groups. My own
research (1974, 1977), as well as that of Carol Stack (1974) examined
women's strategies and tactics to gain power within families, to combat
poverty and raise their children, and to resist management coercion
and forge a space for worker autonomy in the workplace. The term
agency is a broader one than that of strategy and entails a theory of producing a self in relation to others in contexts and thus has been more
widely adopted by feminist anthropologists including the authors in this
collection (e.g., Moore, Joyce, Kus, Perry and Potter).

A third theme is power. Feminist anthropology's emphasis on women's
status, on sexual asymmetry, and on the possibility of egalitarian societies has always implied an analysis of power. In the 1970s, feminists
drew on either Weberian or Marxist definitions of power. For example,
Michelle Rosaldo's analysis (Rosaldo and Lamphere 1974, 117–42),
based on Weber's classic exposition, centered on the distinction between power and culturally legitimated authority, making the point that
men held positions of authority, but women exercised informal power.
In contrast, Karen Sacks emphasized a definition of power centered on
the control of productive resources and argued women are social adults
equal to men in foraging and some horticultural societies in contrast to

state societies where they become wife's ward (losing not only control over productive resources but also marital and political rights) (Rosaldo and Lamphere 1974, 207–22). The work of Foucault has revolutionized the ways in which feminists think about power, viewing power as productive and capillary, yet as always entailing resistance. Power through Foucaultian notions of the panopticon powerfully shapes the self and inscribes habits of self-policing and states of subjugation forming "docile bodies" (Foucault 1977). It is this analysis of power that has shaped many of the contributions to this collection (see chapters by Moore, Joyce, Perry and Potter).

This volume not only builds on these older, yet evolving, themes but adds new fields of interest and frameworks. A new theme that was barely identified in the 1970s is the focus on the gendered body. Through the work of Judith Butler (1990, 1993), feminists have come to see gender not only as constructed, but performed. This emphasis on the body is a particularly helpful avenue for bringing the approaches of archaeology and biological anthropology into conversation with cultural anthropology. It offers a way of connecting gender performance, the materiality of the body and by extension its material products (the data that archaeologists utilize). We can see this explicitly in Rosemary Joyce's chapter that argues for "Making Bodies Matter" in feminist archaeology, an approach she uses in her own exploration of gendered bodies as seen in Classic Maya art. Elizabeth Perry and James Potter apply the same conceptual framework to the performance and transgression of gender norms in the ancestral southwest. Finally, Dana Walrath, a biological anthropologist, brings feminist insights to paleoanthropology, reexamining assumptions about a flawed female reproductive biology that created risks for unattended childbirth in humans. She suggests discarding this approach (with its emphasis on the "obstetrical dilemma") and instead viewing sexual dimorphism and human evolution in a more gender neutral way without the assumptions of male competition and female constraint.

Two final themes and ones that are the focus of this collection—identity and difference—are an outgrowth of the new ways of looking at variability, agency, and power. As Miranda Stockett and Pamela Geller suggest in their introduction, the emphasis on identity and difference is a way to more clearly analyze the multiple positions that men and women hold within various societies. Gender difference intersects with race, class, age, and other social locations, and individual identities are built through social interactions shaped by these variables. But to engage with this intersectional approach, one must have a broader, more dynamic framework, one that places a Foucauldian analysis of power and individual agency at the center of the construction of difference and identity.

Conclusion

Thus there are strong undercurrents of continuity within feminist anthropology over the past three decades as well as new topics of analysis.
As I have emphasized, much of the language through which feminist
theory is now conveyed has changed. Fifteen years ago, Micaela di
Leonardo brought together a group of feminist essays that focused
squarely on gender and balanced an analysis of culture with a focus on
political economy, while rejecting the solipsistic "navel gazing" aspects
of postmodernism/poststructuralism. This approach acknowledged the
importance of history and social context and emphasized that gender
relations are embedded, that is, intertwined with race/ethnicity, age, religion, sexual preference, nationality, and other social categories. Yet,
like postmodern theorists, di Leonardo and her colleagues recognized
that anthropological knowledge is partial and the positions of anthropologists and their subjects are profoundly shaped by one's social location. This volume takes the di Leonardo collection one step further.
While many of the chapters still hold on to the important emphases on
both culture and political economy, the stress, particularly for archaeologists, is on the materiality of social relations and gendered bodies. The
focus on difference, identity, and a Foucaultian notion of power also entails a more dynamic and processual analysis. Authors are much more
interested in the production of gender. Negotiation and performance
are key terms here. Use of these terms takes us away from presumptions
of innate biological identity or essentialism and emphasizes the creation
of the subject through the exercise of power and the ongoing performative nature of gender difference. Bodily difference is produced rather
than already being there. The creation of the subject, the production of
agency, and the negotiation of difference are all phrases that capture
the dynamic and fluid aspects of social relationships that previous work
had not adequately explored. Feminist anthropology may now be a diverse and disparate body of knowledge, but the chapters in this volume
demonstrate new linkages across the subfields of cultural anthropology,
archaeology, and biological anthropology, and a new willingness to critique our analytical concepts as well as to share the insights of feminist
pedagogical practice.

Introduction

Feminist Anthropology: Perspectives on Our Past, Present, and Future

MIRANDA K. STOCKETT AND PAMELA L. GELLER

> *The only true voyage of discovery is not to go to new places, but to have other eyes*
>
> —Marcel Proust, *Remembrance of Things Past*

Today, we as anthropologists find ourselves standing at a confluence in the anthropological highways and byways of feminist practice and theory. Micaela di Leonardo's (1991) earlier, and largely sociocultural, visit to similar crossroads transpired more than a decade ago, and since this time much fostering and fragmenting have occurred in feminist anthropology. We feel that the time has come to take stock once again. In this vein, we consider past, present, and possible future permutations of feminist scholarship in anthropology. We begin by reflecting upon feminist inroads made in the field of anthropology by means of a critical historical review highlighting pivotal works that have contributed to the social sciences' feminist corpus, as well as those that have run contra to the mainstream thinking of the time.

The conclusions that we draw from our discussion of feminist scholarship are twofold. First, many of our subdisciplines have become somewhat quiescent in their focus on women and women's experiences. As our history stresses, this immobility reflects a continuing reliance upon binary oppositions, the assumption that gender primarily structures identity in societies through space and time, and the conflation of gender with women. We suggest that these assumptions rely upon heteronormative formulations of social and sexual relations that belie feminist claims of critical revisionism. It is, however, important to note that anthropology's subfields fall victim to these indiscretions to varying degrees. For example, many practitioners of sociocultural anthropology have wrestled with feminist concerns far longer, and thus have made far greater analytical headway than their colleagues in archaeology or physical anthropology. As a subdiscipline, archaeology remains characteristically tardy to develop ideas incorporated from outside the discipline, while physical anthropology has yet to even adopt some of the most rudimentary feminist insights. A small but determined group of practitioners in both of these fields, however, have encouraged conceptual changes by pushing the boundaries of so-termed third wave studies (e.g., Dowson 2000, this volume; Gilchrist 1999; Hollimon 1997; Joyce 1998, 2000, this volume; Kakaliouras, this volume; Kus 1992, this volume; E. Martin 2001; Meskell 1999; Walrath, this volume). Regardless of subfield affiliation, it is crucial that anthropologists, feminist or not, recognize the fact that feminist anthropology has more to offer than solely an emphasis on gender and sex.

Second, we conclude that feminist anthropology has indeed become highly fragmented in its foci. Rather than being a shortcoming, however, we suggest that such fragmentation is both healthy and necessary. Indeed, though seemingly disunified, current feminist approaches share both a common history and a set of political and intellectual goals that unite, rather than divide them. These goals, inspired by the political feminist critique, emphasize variable expressions of identity and foreground difference, rather than normativity. In order to support the investigation of identity and difference, feminist anthropology must naturally proliferate into myriad research agendas, questions, and interpretations. Thus, perceived fragmentation signals not the splintering and disintegration of feminist theory in anthropology, but its vigorous growth. The value of these disparate current, and hopefully future, feminist-inspired works lie in their ability to critically reenvision past anthropological projects, acknowledge the power of political agendas to make visible (or invisible) marginalized groups, and find practical applications for ephemeral theories grounded in case studies and classroom education.

In particular, we point to the emerging feminist focus on identity and difference as crucial to the anthropological endeavor. Such a project eschews an exclusive concentration on categories of women, gender, or sex, in favor of considerations of what those categories mean and how they intersect both with one another and with other relevant categories, such as age, occupation, religion, status, and so on (as exemplified by Dowson 2000; Gilchrist 1999, 2000; Joyce 1998, 2000a; Kus 1992; Meskell 1999; Schmidt and Voss, eds. 2000a; Tarlow 1999). Indeed, we identify feminist anthropology as distinct from gendered anthropology as a consequence of its broader concerns and emphasis on difference and identity. Moreover, we believe that feminist anthropology is not (and should not be) done only by women or for women. A project emphasizing both diverse foci and diverse practitioners is needed to make feminist theory more widely applicable, and practical, within the subdisciplines, discipline, and social sciences.

Surfing the Waves: Trajectories in the History of Feminist Thought

For most of history, Anonymous was a woman. (Virginia Woolf)

Bart: Boys will be boys.
Marge: I hate that kind of tautology. "The Bart of War," *The Simpsons* (Episode #312, May 18, 2003)

Social scientists have often conceived of feminist theories as occurring in waves. These are conceptualized in the progressive terms of first wave, second wave, and third wave (di Leonardo 1991; Gilchrist 1999; Meskell 1999). Though this provides a useful descriptive metaphor, its somewhat evolutionary implications may be misleading. Indeed, as we discuss later, the proponents of each wave pushed different issues to the fore, critiquing and expanding upon—without rendering obsolete—their predecessors' perspectives (see also Nelson, this volume). And, unlike real waves, these perspectives have not always followed their advance with a retreat. For example, so-termed second wave feminism, certainly the most popular perspective in archaeology and arguably the most thoroughly explored viewpoint within anthropology, continues to mature and prosper despite the advent of third wave approaches. In addition, transitions between waves have not proceeded in a chronologically linear fashion. Nonetheless, defining the constitution of these waves, as well as what distinguishes them from one another, can prove useful for clarifying and discussing overarching themes and contrasts. We recognize that wave distinctions are historical, and even generational, moments in time, but feel that they remain useful analytical devices for discussing the developmental trajectory of feminist theorizing.

First wave feminism was realized through, and defined by, political activism (di Leonardo 1991) that sought expanded civil, educational, and employment rights for women. Nancy Cott (1987), however, makes the point that the term "feminim" did not itself signal the beginning of the Women's Movement or the fight for suffrage. Rather, these battles had begun long before feminism emerged as an ideology and a watchword in the 1910s. From its inception, feminism was already burdened with a paradoxical heritage. On the one hand, it was characterized by a diversity of women (of many races, classes, and legal statuses) and goals, yet on the other, it was grounded in the supposed unity of those women and their shared quest for expanded rights (Cott 1987). This tension between women's solidarity and the reality of their multiply constituted experiences and concerns (Cott 1987, 6) has been a wellspring of conflict as well as productive legacy for feminists who champion difference and identity today.

Despite its diversity, first wave feminism has been critiqued for its perceived confinement to circles of privileged upper-middle-class Caucasian women (e.g., Barkley Brown 1989; Mohanty 1988; Spivak 1988), a class of women who, not coincidentally, were those most able to voice their views in influential public circles. While this characterization is not totally inaccurate, it nevertheless overlooks the diversity of the early feminism movement, and the roles of lower- and middle-class women, both white and African American, who were active in the pursuit of suffrage, civil, and labor rights (see Cobble 2004; Terborg-Penn 1998).

It was also during this first wave that many advances were made with regard to women's reproductive heath. These changes, while perhaps still governed by long-standing social prohibitions, also likely affected many women from disparate racial groups and socioeconomic classes. Significant among them, for example, was the establishment of Planned Parenthood by Margaret Sanger in 1919. Sanger's social reforms ultimately ensured women's reproductive choices, made birth control accessible to low-income, minority, and immigrant women, and were instrumental in reversing federal and state laws that banned the production and dissemination of literature concerned with sex, sexuality, and contraception. Characterized by a diversity of agendas—from finally winning the right to vote to championing the importance of women's reproductive health—first wave feminism also provided a powerful starting point for later advances by laying the groundwork for an attack on the androcentrism omnipresent in the academy, as well as women's lack of personal and professional equity.

By the 1960s, first wave feminists' continuing commitment to political activism began to result in the successful promotion of women's rights in the public sphere. Renewed impetus for activism and professionalism came, in part, from Betty Friedan's vocalization of "the problem that had no name." In her pathbreaking *Feminine Mystique* (1963), Friedan echoed the unspoken sentiments of many American women. Education had left women unfulfilled personally in their socially dictated roles as housewives and primary caregivers. Reaction took the form of political activism and advocacy of social change as exemplified by the 1966 formation the National Organization for Women (NOW). Nonetheless, many have noted that the experiences of middle-class, suburban, and educated housewives did not resonate with working class, poor, and nonwhite women (e.g., Boucher 2003; Cobble 2004; hooks 2000, 1–3; Tong 1998, 26). Finally, it should be emphasized that the clear priority of first wave feminism was primarily political and social rather than academic.

At this time, feminists both outside and within the academy were responding to what they perceived as sexual, reproductive, and personal oppression. However, while this agenda may have resonated personally with women in the academic community, it had little immediate impact on their scholarship.

By the 1970s, however, the fine line between the personal and professional was becoming less distinct, and the so-termed second wave began to emerge. Second wave feminist concerns grew beyond the political arena, finding theoretical and methodological niches in academic and intellectual communities (Quinn 1977; Wylie 1991). One of the major insights offered by early second wave scholars was that anthropologists, in their dedicated study of Man, had often overlooked the diversity of human experiences. Responding to these critiques, some anthropologists began to awaken to the notion of a sexually heterogeneous (or at least dualistic) humanity. No longer would it suffice to study Man and mankind. The acknowledgment of this anthropological gender bias highlighted the necessity of throwing Woman, often characterized at the time as a nomothetic group, into the melee of cultural studies. The inherent androcentrism that had pervaded the discipline since time immemorial was suddenly the frontispiece of second wave feminist critique.

Interestingly, this period in feminist theory and activism highlighted women by focusing on ideologies of patriarchy and female oppression. In the landmark volume, *Woman, Culture, and Society* (Rosaldo and Lamphere, eds. 1974), feminist-inspired anthropological research emphasized social relationships, characterizing society as the combined creation of male and female actors. It can be argued, however, that in exploring issues such as universal male dominance and female subjugation, the volume did not directly challenge entrenched gender stereotypes and androcentric biases, at least not as much within the published literature as it did within the halls of academia. Indeed, contributions to *Woman, Culture, and Society* brought many authors not peer acceptance, but difficulties in navigating both the hiring and tenure process (Lamphere, personal communication 2005). While these "seminal" feminist forays may not have toppled the androcentric heritage of anthropology (Moore 1988), they did provide a strong foundation for the development of feminist inquiry in the discipline. In particular, *Woman, Culture, and Society* implicitly challenged feminist anthropologists to address three points—notions of universality, the prevalence of binary oppositions in society, and the possibilities for variability within the former two constructions (Lamphere, personal communication 2004).

The volume's focus on universal male dominance addressed the first point, and heavy referencing of, and reliance upon, structuralist binary oppositions was also particularly prominent during this period of feminist scholarship (as per Lévi-Strauss 1969). Binary oppositions, universal and asymmetrical in their composition, illuminated gender issues while reifying female subordination and male dominance. While sexual asymmetry was attributed to cultural forces rather than biological ones, in identifying women as restricted by their childbearing and child-caring responsibilities, biology as destiny was in fact reinforced. Rosaldo (1974) asserted that despite varied cultural manifestations, the intertwined roles of mother and child-bearer restricted women to private/domestic spheres, while men's activities were enacted in public loci. In addition to a nature : culture dichtomony, Ortner (1974) also argued for this public : private dichotomy, suggesting that women were aligned with natural, immutable, and inferior qualities while man, as a cultural creation, was superior, dynamic, and innovative. Some of the most prevalent and enduring binary oppositions include culture : nature, man : woman, mind : body, gender : sex, public : private, civilized : primitive, and active : passive. We consider these dualisms as interdigitated with one another, and argue that they have been (and continue to be) employed in ways that predetermine our interpretations and conclusions about individuals and societies.

The third point, that of variability, was less prominently but no less eagerly taken up in early feminist research. Indeed, scholarship that ran contra to an understanding of universal male dominance and strict binary oppositions emphasizes that wave theory cannot always be conceptualized chronologically, and that strict lines cannot always be drawn between different waves. In the same Rosaldo and Lamphere edited volume, for example, several authors (see Sanday 1974; Sacks 1974) offered contrary viewpoints. Sanday in particular did not affirm male dominance; instead, she questioned universal statements that denied the diversity of human experiences. In certain social and cultural settings, she argued that women act as powerful forces, engaging in social complimentarity with men. That they are seen as capable of contributing to cultural continuity, cohesion, and nurturance is a theme that pervades many of Sanday's (1981, 1990a, b, 1998) writings. Similarly, Weiner's (1976) consideration of Trobriand society communicated women's unique roles within the economic exchange system; a facet of society that Malinowski (1984 [1922]) had overlooked in his original analysis.

In work published after *Woman, Culture, and Society*, investigation and ultimately deconstruction of notions of universality and binary oppositions were increasingly prioritized. In fact, the majority of early second wave investigations within sociocultural anthropology professed the deconstruction of deep-rooted assumptions and stereotypes, redirecting the analytical gaze to women and their social roles. As Lamphere (1987) pointed out, however, the sustained use of an androcentric toolkit problematized early consciousness-raising within anthropology. In other words, taking traditional male-biased viewpoints and trying to "find" women within them did little to rectify long-standing misrepresentations. Mukhopadhyay and Higgins (1988) recognized that the ethnographic explosion driven by these early feminist contributions soon served to highlight the inadequacies in the universal stance of sexual asymmetry and women's lower status. Thus, the isolating and dismantling of anthropology's male-biased epistemology has been foregrounded in subsequent feminist undertakings. For instance, the use of binary oppositions has been rightly critiqued for its reductionist, ahistorical, and static representations, as well as projecting a "Western folk model" onto the rest of the world (Collier and Yanagisako 1987b; Moore 1993). The reliance on binary oppositions may be cited as an example of problems inherent in early second wave approaches, and one that has not yet been resolved. Indeed, the use of binary constructions in anthropological research continues to mask human variability.[1] As such, recent critiques of this problem, from within both feminist anthropology and queer theory, have served as a major catalyst for the rise of third wave feminist perspectives.

While we do not wish to jettison dualisms entirely, deconstruction of them in light of their specific historical and cultural context is important. The search for shades of gray should replace our black and white understandings of cultural categorizations. To emphasize the ways dualisms were appropriated, and later critiqued, we turn to a brief consideration of how early second wave feminist scholars conceptualized and defined sex and gender. Codification of the distinction between sex and gender became a pervasive binary dichotomy in second wave feminist scholarship. Many of these scholars argued for the unchanging biological essence of sex; gender, on the other hand, came to be viewed as the symbolic and social meanings attributed to different sexes (e.g., Morgen 1989; Moore 1988; Ortner and Whitehead 1981b; J. W. Scott 1999 [1986]). Once sex and gender were divorced from one another, gender was problematized as a cultural construct while sex was naturalized (for an exception, see Collier and Yangiasako 1987b). Furthermore, the concept of gender gained almost complete analytical dominance over that of sex.

Divisions between gender and sex, and the near-abandonment of the latter as a significant variable, had a profound impact on feminist theorizing. In particular, it narrowed inquiry to gender. Gender was often uncritically conceptualized in its own dichotomous terms, man : woman, and all too frequently excluded nuanced discussions of third genders, transgendered individuals, or queers. This theoretical asymmetry has only recently begun to be rectified. The return of inquiry regarding sex and sexuality is one of the tenets of third wave feminism, which began to recenter attention on issues of sexuality, thereby complicating our understandings of gender and sex (e.g., Butler 1990, 1993; Errington 1990; Laqueur 1990). As a major contribution, such scholars underscored the idea that sex, sexuality, and gender are socioculturally constructed categories rather than natural ones; categories created through discourse, representation, and repetitive performance within the nexus of the body.

In many cases, these conceptual advances can be credited to important works authored by Judith Butler (1990, 1993) and Thomas Laqueur (1990), rhetorician and historian, respectively. Other scholars, however, were introducing similar ideas directly within anthropology. For example, Shelly Errington's (1990) concurrent distinction between Sex, sex, and gender underscores the notion that specific biological differences (e.g., genitalia, internal body temperature) may not provide a cross-cultural touchstone for sexual differences. Her conception of "sex" and "Sex," "points to something that exists [corporeally] but has no meaning outside the way it is construed within specific cultures and historical periods" (Errington 1990, 27). She emphasizes that rather than operating with preformed ideas, we must approach our subjects as situated within their unique cultural and historical contexts.

Within the subdiscipline of archaeology, similar issues have come to the fore as feminist insights are adopted. Of the conceptual incorporation and advances in archaeology, practitioners have long bemoaned a time lag. Though several major contributions have been made, archaeologists stand well behind socioculturalists in the speed of their adoption, integration, and furthering of feminist scholarship. Perhaps the earliest cohesive statement in American archaeology can be traced to Conkey and Spector's (1984) mandated investigation of gender roles, identities, and ideologies. Their call to action advocated viewing gender issues through the lens of historical shifts and cultural diversity, and suggested that the gendering of archaeology as male was no longer adequate or appropriate. By the late 1980s and early 1990s, while socioculturalists were fleshing out the nuances between sex and gender (and Sex), archaeologists were just beginning to uncover the presence of "Woman" in their reconstructions of past. Rather than presume universal male dominance, as socioculturalists did in their initial discussions, these early second wave feminist archaeologists reconstructed narratives in which women played active roles in the past as progenitors, inciters, innovators, and inventors (e.g., Brumfiel 1992; Hastorf 1991; McCafferty and McCafferty 1988; Spector 1993; Watson and Kennedy 1991).

At this time, like-minded scholars generated a proliferation of conferences and edited volumes. Notable among these was the Wedge Conference, out of which came the groundbreaking publication, *Engendering*

Archaeology (Conkey and Gero, eds. 1991; also see Claassen, ed. 1992a; Walde and Willows, 1991). Early second wave approaches foregrounded four primary concerns: (1) to validate gender as an investigative category; (2) to delimit a functional feminist methodology; (3) to reflexively consider the epistemology and academic practice of archeology in order to effect change; and (4) in light of a deconstruction of androcentric bias, to identify and interpret issues related to women and gender in the past, composed of male and female differences (Conkey and Gero 1991). Many early second wave approaches failed to heed Conkey and Gero's (1991) initial advice, tending to simply "add women and stir." While the focus of researchers' writings was largely womanist (Joyce and Claassen 1997, 1), the nature of this work was a necessary step in the transformation to a more theoretically sophisticated feminist archaeology.

In revisiting the application of gender and feminist studies to archaeology, inasmuch as its practice, representation, and interpretations are concerned, Conkey and Gero (1997) highlighted the diversity of perspectives that arose in the aftermath of their pivotal edited volume. Recognizing the challenge that material culture presents to archaeologists, they cataloged several theoretical positions that productively lend themselves to the gendering of the subfield. These included sociobiology, social constructivist critiques, evolutionary models, political economic approaches, agency theory, and performance models. Perhaps most importantly, they drew a distinction between an (en)gendered archaeology and an archaeology of gender. In the case of the former, more broadly feminist concerns, questions, critiques, and interpretations were seen as prime movers by which the discipline was reenvisioned. Conkey and Gero (1997) further suggested that this project should be a conceptual one, rather than a thematic one (as in the case of an archaeology of gender). We see this as an important recognition of the fundamental differences between feminist and gender studies, the former of which emphasizes a wide, and intertwined, range of social categories and the latter of which highlights a narrower view of the contextual roles of men and women in the past.

The issues raised by Conkey and Gero also provide an interesting point of comparison to the similar list of investigative foci implicit in the themes and topics discussed in the earlier Rosaldo and Lamphere volume (1974). The former emphasized issues of methodology, something their feminist forbearers touched on little. We suggest that this addition highlights pervasive, and not unimportant, differences between anthropology's subdisciplines, and questions the degree to which investigative concerns can always be shared among all practitioners. In particular, we may query the degree to which feminist theory may be variously applied to sociocultural study, archaeological research, and physical anthropological inquiry.

As Conkey and Gero (1997) pointed out themselves, issues of methodology, and degree of fit between theory and data, are topics often cited but little explored. We suggest, and discuss further below, that practical considerations of how much, and how well, feminist insights may be adapted to various types of data should form a central component of future scholarship.

To return to Rosaldo and Lamphere's (1974) earlier call to feminist anthropologists, we may note that later archaeological inquiries took up the challenge to investigate, and deconstruct, notions of universality, and to explore binary oppositions. Variability was also addressed, but was explored primarily as a function of gender roles. Much like early work in sociocultural studies, archaeological investigations underscored gender as a significant analytical category by highlighting it as a primary structuring principal in social relationships. Whereas sex was largely deemed an unchanging, biological given, gender was viewed as more dynamic and mediated by unique historical and cultural contexts. In this way, gender and sex were taken as binary oppositions. Within archaeology and physical anthropology, investigators have been slower than their sociocultural colleagues to relinquish the notion of "sex" as a static biological category distinct from gender. Gilchrist (1999, 14) has recently acknowledged that the "collapsing of [sex : gender] categories remains problematic, since our interrogations frequently begin with biological sexing of human skeletons, without the benefit of direct observation or engagement with embodied individuals." Likewise, this observation might also provide insight into physical anthropologists' reticence to embrace feminist perspectives. We would argue that it is through a focus on identity and difference, which characterizes more recent third wave inclined studies, that such an obstacle might begin to be addressed.

We suggest that third wave feminism can be viewed as the first feminist push in anthropology to situate variability at its heart and to foreground the role of difference. Characterized by intellectual and practical stimulus from, among others, lesbian feminists, feminists of color, and feminists from developing nations (e.g., Abu-Lughod 1990; Behar and Gordon, 1995; del Valle, 1993; Weston 1998), third wave feminism affirms cultural and human variability, calling attention to emic constructs, multivocality and difference, as opposed to (in)equality and hierarchy. "Woman," long utilized in academic and public discourse as a homogeneous category, is completely cast aside. The ways in which factors of ethnicity, status, and age influence the category and experience of woman are no longer assumed within anthropological research. More importantly, the categories of sex and sexuality are exploded, and the many ways they structure identity are explored (e.g., Dowson 2000; Joyce 2000b; Meskell 2000; Schmidt and Voss 2000b; Voss 2000).

Indeed, as third wave feminists locate intersections of age, race, ethnicity, sexual preference, religion, class, and gender, the latter comes to be considered as a component of relative importance within identity construction, rather than an identity in and of itself. Likewise, third wave feminists are open to masculinist approaches, in which case is taken not to essentialize the male subject (Brode 1987; Connell 1995; Gutmann 1997; Knapp 1998a, b). Through these and other perspectives, feminist anthropologists have come to embrace the different variables that contribute to the construction of identity.

From Past, into Present, and Toward the Future

Look not mournfully into the Past. It comes not back again. Wisely improve the Present. In is thine. Go forth to meet the shadowy Future, without fear, and a manly heart. (Henry Wadsworth Longfellow)

In light of such a history, how might we characterize the present and envision the future of anthropological feminism? From the foundations of third wave feminism, as discussed above, current scholarship is turning its gaze to ever-broader topics. In particular, strong interests in nationalism, race, ethnicity, and the body are manifest in the current literature, though contributions by sociocultural and medical anthropologists notably predominate over those of archaeologists or physical anthropologists (e.g., McClaurin 2001; O'Donnell 2004; Rapp 2001; Reischer and Koo 2004; Schildkrout 2004; Skokic 2001; Yuval-Davis 2003). Intersecting with issues of globalization and marginality such foci speak to, in many cases, relevant concerns of the modern world and its fractious interactions. Considered alongside feminist archaeological interests in gender roles, age, agency, and identity, this diversity of interests across the subdisciplines raises the specter of fragmentation, and feminist anthropology's present may be argued to lack the coherence of a unified viewpoint. Yet we contend that such fragmentation is both healthy and much more cohesive in spirit than many recognize. The inspiration for research addressing such varied topics derives, we believe, from a shared concern with difference and identity.

In particular, we see power as a critical component, insofar as it is exerted upon and derives from the construction and expression of identity through the recognition (and reaction to) difference. Here, difference is taken to mean social differences that lend themselves to the constitution of identity. Indeed, the very act of identification necessitates the recognition of similarity and difference. Furthermore, the construction and enactment of identity, whether self or social, occurs through discourses and actions that are often structured by contexts of power that are sociohistorically generated. As a result, in a given context some identities may be embraced while others are rejected or marginalized. We see the intersection of power, difference, and identity as the place at which many feminist anthropologists are now situating their research, be it to explore the consequences of these intersections, reframe our theoretical understandings of them, or critique the past androcentric lens through which they have been viewed and interpreted. These interests stem, most particularly, from feminism's political heritage, in which efforts are made to empower and make visible those previously marginalized. We suggest that in recognizing the crucial juncture of power, difference and identity, feminists stand on common ground regardless of their specific point of inquiry. Additionally, by moving beyond (but still incorporating) traditional foci such as gender, feminist approaches to identity and difference greatly expand the intellectual and practical relevance of feminist anthropology itself.

In light of this, we look ahead to highlight three additional threads that we see as important to formulations of feminist analysis in all sub-disciplines of anthropology. These are (1) a critical reenvisioning of past interpretations; (2) an accentuation of feminism's, and anthropology's, inherently practical and political aspects; and (3) a critique of heteronormative assumptions about society. We see these three arenas of investigation as interrelated in their shared emphasis on exploring variability in time and space, and on stressing difference. All of these foci may serve to move researchers beyond probing categorizations within society, such as "gender" and "sex," and query instead the assumptions behind those categories and the interconnections between them. We argue that, in doing so, they may push anthropological inquiry toward a more textured and richer understanding of the expression, or suppression, of difference and the construction of identities.

Critical Reenvisioning

One important facet of current feminist scholarship involves radically reinterpreting previous theoretical formulations. Rewriting and reconsidering traditional interpretations from a feminist engendered perspective has, actually, had a long-standing place at the fore of many of feminism's waves. In particular, we identify archaeologists, some building upon the work of primatologists, and many upon the work of socioculturalists (e.g., Lee 1968, 1980), as having challenged deeply gendered notions, such as "Man the Hunter" (Washburn and Lancaster 1968) and "Man the Provisioner" (Lovejoy 1981). By emphasizing "Woman the Gatherer" (Conkey and Williams 1991; Hayden 1992; Slocum 1975; Tanner and Zihlman 1976; Zihlman 1981) and "Woman the Domesticator" (Watson and Kennedy 1991), researchers attributed agency to females as well as presented an alternative (re)envisioning of humanity's past. As discussed previously, such efforts characterize some of the revolutionary advances of early second wave feminist concerns.

While these provide a beginning point, much work remains to be done with regard to critically reassessing the utility of previous theories and the legitimacy of resultant interpretations. We suggest that the power of revisionist work lies in its ability to transform deeply entrenched perceptions about who and what constitute various social categories, and how differing social roles are enacted, embraced, or contested within a myriad of sociohistorical contexts. Contributors to this volume begin such a project, taking to task long-entrenched heteronormative assumptions about the family, questioning the utility of Judith Butler's work, seeking practical, personal, professional, and political applications for feminist theoretical stances, and attempting to forge dialogue between students and teachers, researchers and the public, and—not insignificantly—between feminists themselves. These are several diverse ways in which feminist-inspired theory may ultimately transform and diversify our understanding of human identity and human experience. They also provide a model for future feminist reformulations of static and quiescent understandings of society in the past and present.

More broadly speaking, this thread of inquiry relates directly to something long a part of feminist movements and feminist scholarship—critique and revision. Born in anthropology alongside of the postprocessual critique (Conkey and Gero 1997; Gilchrist 1999), current feminist anthropology has its roots in a position based upon questioning assumptions. Though many previous suppositions have now been demonstrated as flawed, the role of critique and revision remains essential to the growth of scholarship, be it anthropological, feminist, or otherwise. Without critique, change cannot occur, biases cannot be identified, and assumptions cannot be laid bare. Without revision, critique leads to little but compliance, and nothing but attack. Radically reformulating old interpretations with insights drawn from the observation of politically constructed differences and the practice of identity will continue to enrich our understanding of society and invigorate our discipline.

Political Agendas and Practical Accessibility

Another major avenue of feminist anthropological work relates to practice and politics. These two agendas are united in their emphasis on connecting anthropological research to real world concerns. As our history has illustrated, whether tacitly or explicitly, all feminist inquiry in anthropology is owed to a politically motivated heritage. In particular, emphasizing the exposure of structures of inequality and the valuation of oppressed or marginalized identity groups is derived particularly from political feminism and, more recently, influences from queer theorists. This activist heritage pervades investigation of all manner of identities and differences, from agency to sexuality and race to gender. Opposing the oppression of marginalized groups and the degradation of their experiences continues to underlie the work of many scholars today. Whether addressing the role of women as toolmakers in past societies, or studying the social marking of rites of passage among age cohorts, feminist anthropologists are all motivated on some level by the belief that a homogenous and normative view of society is lacking and exclusionary.

This perspective, acknowledged or not, derives from the hard-made, and as yet unwon, political movement of marginalized and oppressed interest groups, including feminists among many others. Additionally, while the political impetus behind feminism is implicated in the ways that we approach our research and pose our questions, it also speaks to the practical—and inherently political—aspects of being a woman professional in a male-dominated field. Feminist anthropology must continue to focus upon practical goals such as professional equity for women and other disenfranchised groups, an agenda set forth by both first and second wave feminists that has yet to be fulfilled.

The political underpinnings of the feminist movement are made visible to varying degrees in feminist scholarship. But they can also be seen in practical considerations of the dissemination of knowledge to the public, and in issues of pedagogy in undergraduate and graduate settings. Though we spend much time focusing upon our role as theoreticians, anthropologists are also researchers and teachers. The latter two roles, in many ways, are a more dominant part of both our intellectual and professional lives than is our role as theorists. As researchers, we must constantly and critically assess the degree of fit between our theories and our data. For some, even the most ethereal theoretical formulations may be grounded in ethnography or particularly rich sets of archaeological data, but for others, only limited questions may be investigated. Though we may wish to explore the nature of sexuality or performativity in archaeological datasets, for example, those data may not always permit such nuanced interpretations. This does not mean, however, that these and other identities or constructions of difference may not have existed or ever be materially visible. It only means that we must always honestly address the juncture between our theories and our data. It is crucial for the advancement and wider acceptance of our ideas that we present an analytically strong feminist anthropology alongside a theoretically innovative one.

Furthermore, as practitioners and teachers, we have a responsibility to make our investigations accessible and intelligible to the public sphere. After all, it is this wider segment of society who makes our research possible, and for whom we purport to conduct that research. The classroom is a particularly potent politico-practical venue for feminist critique and reformulation. Furthermore, it is through feminist pedagogy that instructors can initiate or further alternative ways of learning about and knowing one's world. Locating the experiential and the participatory at the center of students' education can work to diminish the authoritarian voice of traditional scientific research. But we are still left with difficult questions such as, how do we educate and entertain while at once supplementing and competing with the plethora of information made available by diverse media, such as documentaries, textbooks, the Discovery Channel, the Learning Channel, and Hollywood movies? How do we balance our research interests with those of other academics and those of lay people? How do we address issues of accessibility and the inherent academic scorn that is often applied to those who endeavor to reach larger audiences? These questions, we argue, are among the most important challenges that anthropology's practitioners will meet in the near future.

Feminist anthropology, with its focus on people and experience, the expression of identities, the construction of narratives, and the exploration of difference, is particularly well suited to take up these burdens. Indeed, we must also bear in mind that many segments of the wider society we purport to educate also constitute our research subjects. Assessing the degree to which our anthropological endeavors should be designed to educate, aid, or even alter the lives of our subjects is a topic of great importance. Applied feminist anthropology need not become mired in cultural relativism, but rather strive to contend with inequities driven by social differences, gender representing just one variable, in both Western and non-Western settings.

Queer Theory Meets Feminist Theory: Debunking the Myths of Heteronormativity

Finally, we advocate that greater attention should be given to an avenue of inquiry recently splintering out from the generative core of both feminist and queer theories—the study of heternormativity. The relationship between queer theory and feminist theory has not always been an easy one, and in fact, Butler (in Osborne and Segal 1994) notes that a certain degree of antifeminist thought resonates in queer theory. Many

queer theorists cite feminist anthropology's long-standing, implicit reliance on the binary man : woman in its investigations of sex and gender
as exclusive and heterosexist. This critique is, indeed, well aimed as the
study of homosexuality, third (or multiple) genders, and transgressive
identity, while present in feminist anthropology, have never become
part of its mainstream. Some, in fact, have rebutted that this characterization "has been reduced to almost a caricature" (Weed 1997, 3). For as
Butler (in Osborne and Segal 1994) notes, a study of sexuality cannot be
separated from an understanding of gender. Indeed, more recent emphases that shatter old assumptions and investigate difference provide a
space in which feminist anthropologists and queer theorists might reconcile.

The study of heteronormativity is one juncture where productive
overlap might occur between queer theory and feminist theory. Heternormativity is the assumption that heterosexuality and its resultant social institutions are the normative sociosexual structures in all societies.
Blackwood articulates heteronormative notions' damaging effects,

heteronormativity works to erase women's agency in households and kin
groups. More importantly, it works to misrepresent the textures and structures
not only of domestic relations but also of gendered social relations that weave
the fabric of daily life. Finally, heteronormativity works to erase same-sex relationships, sustaining the illusion that these relationships have no meaning or
significance for understanding kinship and "family." (2002, 12)

Interrogating heternormativity may affect the way researchers view the
construction of ethnographic narrative and past identities, illuminating
powerful and pervasive biases and assumptions. Heteronormative perspectives underscore the need to reconfigure kinship studies, as well as
highlight the ways in which politically charged issues may reveal stereotypes previously shrouded in the cloak of intellectual truisms. Through
addressing the concerns of marginalized groups within modern society,
identities of difference are granted space on the academic stage, henceforth challenging past interpretations and reinvigorating future ones.

Both revisionist approaches and critiques of heteronormativity highlight the importance of acknowledging and speaking to political agendas. Investigations of identity are greatly enriched when structures of
political oppression are exposed. These investigations are similarly
more honestly framed when the equally political motivations behind
them are disclosed. Recognizing that regimes of power help to define
human identity is only valuable if we as scholars in turn acknowledge
our political motivations to expose and critique mechanisms of oppression, assumption, and bias. This is an important aspect of feminist-
inspired scholarship, and one which has underlain the field since its

inception as a political movement. As argued here, political agendas may also revolve around finding ways to make the insights of feminist-inspired scholarship more practical—both in the context of our own research and in terms of disseminating our finds in professional, lay, and classroom settings.

Conclusions

Feminist anthropology is characterized by both cohesion and variation. Within feminism's many fragmentations, researchers address seemingly disconnected topics. Despite wide-ranging coverage, these researchers are united in their politically motivated commitment to investigating identity and interrogating difference. Within this rubric, the practical and personal experiences of being a scholar and teacher are addressed as frequently as the construction of broad frameworks for investigating past and present identities through a lens of difference. It should be clear from our previous discussion of feminism's many branches that a massive proliferation of perspectives has occurred since the early days of the feminist movement. Can these disparate perspectives be considered a cohesive body of theory guiding a cumulative effort in research?

We would suggest that despite its diverse trajectories, and differential rates of adoption within various subdisciplines, feminist theories all share several underlying traits that unite them in meaningful ways. First, and shared with many theoretical perspectives within anthropology, the social sciences, and humanities, is an emphasis upon the critical reassessment of traditional, entrenched, and normative assumptions that pervade many aspects of academic research. The importance of a critical deconstructionism (and reconstructionism) is underscored by decades of research by postprocessualists, postmodernists, hermeneuticists, phenomenologists, feminists, queer theorists, masculinists, and many other -ists. Tackling old models, traditional interpretations, and biased assumptions is an approach shared by many feminists, harkening to a common heritage of questioning, critiquing, and reenvisioning.

Related to this is the legacy of first wave feminist political agendas. These made possible and continue to pervade, permit inquiry, and provide a space for the joining of feminism with other related perspectives, such as agency theory and queer theory. Whether working to rectify inherent biases in the academy, or expose androcentric and heteronormative assumptions underlying research, these perspectives are motivated by a belief that structures of power have obscured the social experiences of many. The perspective that difference, rather than normativity, most strongly characterizes and defines the composition of social life underlies much of feminist scholarly work today. Those shades of gray existing between the center and margins of society are the places at which culture, society, and identity are best scrutinized and understood.

It is interesting to note that because political feminism was directed toward addressing women's historic misrepresentation and exploitation, and became an academic tool for rectifying both overt and covert abuses within and without the academy, it has also been seen as exclusionary, the purview of women only. While anthropology's incorporation of feminist-inspired theories has been successful in its illumination of androcentric discourse and practice, and women's varied experiences, the widely held view that feminism's political agenda is exclusionary presents a major obstacle to its reception and wide application within the discipline. This may be due, at least in part, to the early and persistent equation of feminist anthropology with the study of gender. As we see it, the problem is not with feminist analyses of gender, but rather that the language of feminism appears to have become inextricably bound to gender.

Spheres of discourse within feminist-inspired anthropology continue to successfully highlight women's experiences and gender issues. Despite the value of such studies, they have come to be viewed as the sole focus of this corpus of scholarship. It is this perception, and the resultant belief that feminist anthropology is strictly associated with women and female gender issues, that we view as a hindrance to the wider incorporation of feminist insights into anthropology. This problem stems particularly from the notion that the concept of gender is a more relevant category for women than for men, and the subsequent claim by many practitioners of anthropology that such an approach is not relevant to their lives or research. We hope that the preceding history, and discussion of feminist foci on identity and difference, has revealed this viewpoint to be untenable. Ultimately, we advocate a feminist-inspired project that does not focus exclusively on categories of women, gender, or sex, but more broadly on difference and identity.

In focusing on identity, and highlighting the role of difference, feminist anthropology addresses the negotiation of variously competing, or complementary, constructs such as age, sex, sexuality, religion, status, quotidian practice, and gender, as well as many other factors. This focus makes space for scholars with widely disparate interests, and thus is of import to all of the anthropological subdisciplines. As feminist anthropologists look to the future, we urge them to further consider the individual, the diverse, the ambiguous, and the personal, and to consider them within their larger social, cultural, and historical settings. By shifting our lens of inquiry from gender and women to identity and difference, we broaden and invigorate feminist theory immensely, making it a theoretical perspective with great applicability for all anthropologists.

Such a framework provides space for those interested in debunking heteronormative myths, those dedicated to bringing feminist perspectives to classroom teaching, those desiring to reframe old questions in a new light, and to those who advocate for political movements and activism. These seemingly disparate goals and perspectives are united in their application of feminist-inspired ideas and critiques, as well as their focus on the importance of investigating and championing identity. Ultimately, it is the interpretive search for identities and differences that enriches our understanding of human experience. Indeed, it is not in spite of, but because of its richly textured diversity of perspectives, that feminist theories provide a wonderfully varied but still cohesive framework from which all anthropologists, social scientists, and humanists may draw insight into the workings and meanings of the human condition.

Part I
The Past and Future Impact of Feminist Theorizing

Chapter 1
The Future of Gender or the End of a Brilliant Career?

HENRIETTA L. MOORE

In recent years, analyses of gender have moved away from a focus on dichotomous models toward a concern with multiply constituted locations—identity, embodiment, and subjectivity. The privileged position of gender as an analytical category, its epistemic privilege, has been questioned and its connection to identity politics undermined (cf. Bordo 1993; Benhabib et al. 1995; Brewer 1993; Young 1994). Gender can no longer be analyzed as distinct from other forms of difference. The lived experience of gender is that it is already class, already race or ethnicity, there is no means of extracting gender from race or class or any of the other differences through which people construct a sense of self and engage with the world. Gender, once so strongly linked to sex as a category of analysis, now has an uneasy relation with sexuality, and feminist theory finds queer theory an unhappy bedfellow (cf. Abelove et al. 1993; Jagose 1996; Moore 1996; B. Martin 1994; Sedgwick 1990; Warner 1993; Weed and Schor 1997). Gender and sexuality are both seen as contested areas of cultural production and negotiation, and yet both are seen as determinedly and deterministically ambiguous and multiplicitous. Gender is said to be no longer a category, but something experienced and analyzed as sets of performative practices (cf. Butler 1990, 1993). Queer theory builds on this insight to argue that we need a more sustained critique of what constitutes identity, and that sexuality has an ambiguity that gender does not. Ambiguity and plurality are the new forms of essentialism, and everywhere in the academy—and also outside it—this is seen as unambiguously a good thing. One consequence of this is a certain naturalization of ambiguity and plurality both in the academy and in popular discourse, and the analytical models of the academy mimic rather than criticize this process, describe rather than analyze it, endorse rather than critique it.

Does this matter with regard to the analysis of gender? It certainly

seems strange given that the core of feminist scholarship has traditionally been the attempt to undermine and critique processes of naturalization and reification with regard to gender, and other forms of
difference. Perhaps these resonances between academic models and
popular discourses can be accounted for ethnographically, in the sense
that the models aim to be "true to life." Certainly, we need some way of
linking gender as an analytic category to the experience of gender as a
lived experience, but will we achieve this through the deconstruction of
gender as a category of analysis? Has gender as a category of lived experience actually become less important to people? And if not, why are we
abandoning it in the academy? It might be worth asking whether gender
should still be an important category of analysis in academic theorizing
and, if so, what should be its link to feminist politics? Do multiplicity
and ambiguity solve the problems either of analysis or of politics?

Categories of Analysis: Revolution or Crisis?

Postmodernism, in defining itself against modernism, repudiated not
only grand narratives and the boundaries, categories, essences, and histories on which they were based, but through its critique of Enlightenment reason, it also rejected the unitary subject of humanism (cf.
Lovibond 1989; Lyotard 1984; Soper 1990). This has had a profound effect both on our descriptions of our worlds and on our descriptions of
ourselves. Nowhere has this been more evident perhaps than in work on
gender, sexuality, and identity where scholars have moved definitively
away from the notion of the self-identified and self-identificatory subject
to ideas about multiply constituted subjects, and their multiple, contra-
dictory, and conflicting forms of subjectification. In terms of the history
of feminist thought this can be briefly summarized as a move from analyzing the differences between women and men, to focusing on the
differences among women, to identifying the differences within each
woman. Multiple forms of difference, such as race, class, gender, ethnicity, and sexuality were initially analyzed as additive, then as serial, and
ultimately as mutually constitutive. The emphasis now is not so much on
the differences between identities, as on the fact that difference is the
condition for the possibility of identity, its constitutive limit (cf. Moore
1994). Identity and difference are thus mutually imbricated.

Within this narrative, the career of gender has clear parallels with
other concepts and analytical terms in the social sciences. Terms like
"society," "community," "self," "culture," "class," and "race" have all been
subjected to equally rigorous debate and deconstruction. One clear analytical thrust has to do with boundaries and the insight that race, class,
and gender, for example, cannot be specified independently of each

other. Hence the proposition that race is just one modality in which class is lived (cf. Gilroy 1987; Ortner 2003). This mode of interconnection is true of the intersections between other forms of difference also. The philosophical breakthrough here was a deceptively simple one: forms of difference may be perceived categorically, but they are lived relationally and relationships are by definition mutually constituted (Moore 1994, chap 1). However, changes in the way we understand key terms and concepts in the social sciences are not the unadorned product of philosophical critique. The world of the social scientist is bound up with its subjects and objects of study. Two consequences follow: one, that changes in theoretical thinking in the social sciences have historically been connected to wider political movements; and two, that the terms and concepts of the social sciences form part of the relation that people have to their lived worlds. Good examples of the first point include the relationship between feminist theory and queer theory, and the black consciousness, feminist, and gay movements. Clear exemplars of the second are provided by terms such as "capitalism," "globalization," and "society." When studying globalization, for example, the patterns and configurations that social scientists find of interest are determined as much by the manner in which the heads of multinationals understand the term "globalization" and act on it, as they are by the philosophical entailments of social science analytical constructs (Moore 2004).

Terms such as capitalism and globalization are concept-metaphors (cf. Moore 1997) and they retain indeterminate status both as theoretical abstractions and as a set of processes, experiences, and connections in the world. This is true for social scientists and for ordinary individuals. A notion of the global is now part of most people's imagined and lived worlds. This simple fact sets up—or perhaps is played out according to—a series of apparent antinomies between theory and praxis, the symbolic and the material, culture and politics. These antinomies are, of course, false. Concepts such as the global, capitalism, and society have been changing in response to mass migration, global consumerism, transnational communities, mass media, flexible capital, and the electronic economy. However, whatever the material changes that have been driving our changing understanding of these terms, it is also the case that changes in the way these terms, entities, or processes are perceived have also been propelling further change in material conditions. One clear example here is global capitalism itself. Scholars are struggling to make sense both of increasing global diversity and increasing integration, and trying to find ways of imagining and modeling the pluralistic, multifaceted, and labile nature of contemporary capitalism (cf. Comaroff and Comaroff 2000; Giddens 1994; F. Jameson 1991; Lash and Urry 1987; Robertson 1992). The result is that the notion of capitalism within the academy and outside it has changed dramatically, and yet since it is impossible to adequately specify in any comprehensive or complete way the referents of the terms capitalism or globalization, they continue to function as abstractions that guide our imaginative relation to lived worlds.

From this perspective the symbolic is always and already the material, there is no sense in which culture and economy can be separated as frames of analysis or action. Across the social sciences, there is now a shared perception that cultural production and issues of identity are at the core of a new political economy. Culture has become increasingly commodified, and it has also become the vehicle through which diversification is replicated by and through global processes, experiences, and interconnections. Culture is no longer, if it ever was, fixed and bounded (cf. Gupta and Ferguson 1992). As workplaces, organizations, communities, and institutions have become less relevant to identity formation—or become only a part of it—people's sense of space and place has shifted (cf. Sennett 1998). The result is that processes of subjectivity and subjectification have become increasingly bound up with images, aspirations, identifications, lifestyles, and forms of consumerism that are not necessarily based on locale, but on interconnection, and forms of space/time compression (cf. Appadurai 1996). In this compressed and newly imagined world, economic profit is won through the commodification of difference, cultural production and innovation are at the basis of the economic system, and what is offered for sale are lifestyles themselves (F. Jameson 1998, 67).

If the production of everyday life is bound up not only with new forms of capitalism, but with the global itself, then older ideas about society, culture, self, and identity clearly will not hold. These are no longer bounded units or entities, but contested fields of signification and interconnection, as well as flows of people, ideas, images, and goods. The pretheoretical assumptions underlying notions of society, community, and culture in the social sciences are brought into question, and they become ever more pressingly landscapes that are navigated by agents who both experience and constitute them, in part, from their own sense of what these landscapes offer (Appadurai 1996, 32–33). Appadurai sees globalization in terms of a cannibalization of sameness and difference (Appadurai 1996, 37). Another example of their mutually constitutive nature.

If sameness and difference feed off each other in the way we think not only about the gendered subject, but also the multiple, dispersed, and fragmented world in which that subject lives, what kind of relation does this subject have to the world they inhabit? One curious paradox here is that while we endlessly reiterate the importance of historicizing gender, race, and class as categories of analysis, praxis, and experience, there are times when contemporary social science shows little evidence of an ability to historicize itself. This may be because of its increasingly problematic relationship to the political and to politics tout court. However, we have to recognize that our current imaginative fictions about subjects and their worlds are bound up with our own experience as social scientists of living in that world. As Marilyn Strathern has remarked, it seems unlikely that what is imagined as fragmentation actually comes from a world of fragments, any more than the traditional notion of culture or society came from a world that was a coherent totality (M. Strathern 1992, 22). Fragmentation, multiplicity, ambiguity, diaspora, and disjuncture are one way of imagining people and their lives, one way of acting on, experiencing, and living in those lives, but not the only one. For all of this, people still live in communities, inhabit spaces, feel themselves to be acting agents, take control over their lives, and experience intimacy, and consistency and inhabit life projects. We need to ask ourselves what fragmentation, ambiguity, and multiplicity are doing for us in the social sciences, and for people in their lives.

Gender and Politics

One line of thought here raises the question of whether postmodernist accounts of multiplicity and ambiguity can ever be effectively linked to projects of social and economic transformation. Various scholars have suggested that postmodern theorizing is more a description of our world than a critical reflection on it, and yet others have suggested that postmodern theory is predominantly a preoccupation of Western, white elites with little relevance for those suffering violence, immizeration, and discrimination (cf. Fraser and Nicholson 1988; Lovibond 1989; Mohanty et al. 1991). More sophisticated accounts have interrogated the obvious links between forms of theorizing and the material conditions in which they find favor and purchase. David Rieff, for example, wonders whether multiculturalists realize how often their phrases such as "cultural diversity," "difference," and "the need to do away with boundaries" resemble the discourse of the modern capitalist corporation. He argues that multinationals are possibly more eager to overthrow singular views of culture and its associated subject, "the white, European, male," than the multiculturalists imagine, since these ideas stand in the way of capturing new nonwhite, non-European, nonmale, nonheterosexual consumers (Rieff 1993). Difference itself has become a commodity (cf. Dirlik 1994). Slavoj Žižek argues that the shifting identities and multiple subjectivities of postmodern theory are an obstacle to real social transformation. Rather than subverting contemporary capitalism, postmodern theories of a subject divided by race, gender, and class are possible only in the context of contemporary global capitalism (Žižek 1999).

These critiques alert us once again to the complex recursive relationship between social science theorizing and the world it analyses. This has had particular significance for theories of gender, as well as those of race and class. One persistent question has been the relationship between theories of gender and sexuality and feminist politics. If current theories of difference undermine the political cohesiveness of the category woman and thus subvert identity politics, what relationship can exist between theory and politics? In other words, what is the basis for feminist politics if women are no longer a group? This question has been answered by feminists in many ways, but its force remains, and it is most pressing in situations pertaining to the matter of the relationship between difference and equality. In this regard, various commentators have remarked that postmodern theories of gender, class, and race are merely cultural, that is, they have no clear relation to social and political transformation based on economic equality (cf. Butler 1997c; Fraser 1998). In consequence, theories of difference give rise to a politics that seeks "recognition" and "social justice" for various identified and self-identified groups, but without seeking radical reform of capitalism (cf. Fraser 1997; Phillips 1997, 1999). What is at stake here, some argue, is that gender and class are no longer crucial to the functioning of the political economy. Marxism linked production and reproduction in ways that argued that both were essential to the functions of capitalism, but with the demise of Marxist theory and politics, and the abandonment of the project of economic equality by the Left in the West, it is not clear how gender or class link to the reproduction of labor power or political consciousness (cf. Lash and Urry 1987). Thus, what was once seen as a question of how gender was involved in the reproduction of political economy is now seen as a problem about recognition and social justice. This is true of other forms of difference.

In her writings, Nancy Fraser has made a distinction between injustices of distribution and injustices of recognition (Fraser 1997, 1998, 2000). Both cause harm and both have material affects. To be misrecognized is to be prevented through instutionalized patterns of interpretation and evaluation from participating as a full partner and peer in social life. Misrecognition is a status injury, but an injury that while dependent on cultural and social evaluations, has a material affect on people's lives. Misrecognition may or may not be accompanied by maldistribution, and vice versa, but in order to determine this it is necessary to analyze the relationship between economic resources and structures of prestige and status (Fraser 1997, chap. 1). Fraser's analysis is useful because it demonstrates that forms of misrecognition are not merely "cultural" or "symbolic," but are tied up with institutions, social practices, and economic resources, including immigration law, tax law, social welfare, employment policies, and equal opportunities legislation. The cultural constructions of forms of personhood and entitlement matter and can bring about economic harm. Fraser's argument is that recognizing both misrecognition and maldistribution in society are important because an improvement in the latter would not necessarily bring about an amelioration in the former. Social inequality and economic inequality are both part of political economy, but how they are connected and how forms of determination work is something that has to be investigated and not assumed. Fraser further argues that the relationship between recognition and distribution is something that has to take account of the nature of contemporary capitalism because of the way that in contemporary capitalism gender and sexuality are increasingly disconnected from the family and from the imperatives of production and reproduction.

In her more recent writing, Fraser has sounded more pessimistic, acknowledging that questions of recognition are increasingly eclipsing issues of redistributive justice rather than working alongside them, and that in the context of complex multicultural societies identity politics can enhance separatism, intolerance, and authoritarianism (Fraser 2000). In the following sections, I take Fraser's concerns a stage further by exploring the problematic links between the reification of identities, choice, and autonomy in popular discourses and in contemporary social science theorizing.

The Individual and Individualism

Ideas about choice and autonomy not only underpin modern ideas about intimate lives, family relationships, and personal aspirations, but they also inform theories of subjectivity and agency, particularly with regard to gender and sexuality. A number of scholars have investigated the relationship between changing family structures, romantic love, and intimacy and modernization (cf. Giddens 1992; Luhmann 1986). Historically, romance and love are associated with an increasing capacity to exercise choice on the part of individuals, a process that began in earnest in the West in the eighteenth century and finds its apogee in the late twentieth and early twenty-first century. Whatever the details of this historical narrative of transformation, it is clear that there have been considerable changes in the way people experience their sense of self, think of themselves as agents, and act as family members over this period of time. Elizabeth Beck-Gernsheim (1998) argues that in the West the reflexive-modernity characteristic of the late twentieth century has emphasized individuality and autonomy from family structures and life-plans. While it is easy to overdraw the distinction between modern and traditional societies on these matters, it is nonetheless clear that a focus on sensation, personal experience, choice, autonomy, and lives and lifestyles realized through aspiration is on many people's minds. One has only to look at the vast market in magazines, health advice, relationship counseling, therapy, and "how-to" books. All giving advice on how to handle relationships, selves, families, bodies, and sex lives. This process is clearly one that is inflected by race and class, as well as religion, sexual preference, and ethnicity. There are clear struggles over meaning and power as these trends are strongly resisted by religious groups, cultural groups, and other interest groups.

What is evident is that contemporary capitalism provides flexible spaces within which interests collide, coalesce, and diverge. Some scholars see this process as one of fragmentation and disjuncture. However, romance and love as cultural forms, and as aspects of self-aspiration and self-realization—and like gender and sexuality—have never been free of political economy. With industrialization, as Luhmann (1986) argues, the discourse on love and its various products opened up the possibility of relationships between strangers, between people who were not tied to family, kinship, place, and locale in their choice of partner. Thus, parallel to changes in the market and forms of capitalism came not only forms of labor, association, and mobility, but also a parallel market in emotion, in choice, and in the commodification of self. However, this process is not a static or finished one. The current concern with sensation, the individual quest for pleasurable experiences, for new ways of living and being, for a form of self-realization that occludes the other in favor of the immediate benefits to the individual (cf. Bauman 1998, 2001; Featherstone 1991; Illouz 1998; Wouters 1998) is a narrative account of the modern self that is fiercely contested by those who argue for a return to family values, the importance of culture and tradition, and the primacy of religious faith. But, this new form of sexuality based on sex and sensation is also closely linked to political economy to lifestyle choice and consumer rationality. Bodies themselves have become objects of consumption and so have selves. This is the context in which theories of gender emphasizing creativity, performance, the noncorrespondence of bodies and sexualities, and the life-project nature of gendered identities have become powerful and persuasive. It is also the moment when the analysis of gender as a category moves over to gender as performance, and ultimately gives way altogether in favor of sexuality, sexual practice, and queer theory. Having deconstructed women, feminists now deconstruct gender and end up with sex, which of course is where it all began (cf. Moore 1999).

The commodifications of selves and bodies are closely linked to questions of agency and choice. Selves, bodies, and sexualities all become life projects, aspects of self-creation and self-realization. The self-creation of late modernity is characterized by an apparent lack of limits (cf. Bauman 2000a; Lasch 1979). The illusion of a limitless world is a chimera, but one which nonetheless molds forms of self-aspiration and social responsibility with the seductive call to transcend the limits of the self.

In 1994, a sixty-two-year-old Italian woman gave birth to a son. Rosanna della Corte was postmenopausal and her baby was born from a donated ovum fertilized by her husband's sperm and implanted into her womb. Mrs. della Corte's reason for having a child was to replace her teenage son who had been killed some years before in a motorcycle accident. There were those in favor and those against, those who wondered whether a "grandmother" should bring up a baby, and those who pointed out that a man's fertility continues into old age and asked why should not a woman's? In 1997, an American woman, Arceli Keh, who had originally immigrated with her husband to the United States from the Philippines, had her first baby at the age of sixty-three. When asked why, Mrs. Keh replied, "We are working people. I only retired to have my baby!" In the United Kingdom, there are now more first-time mothers in the thirty- to thirty-four-year-old age group than in the twenty- to twenty-four age group. There has also been a 50 percent increase as compared to ten years ago in the number of women over forty having a first baby. This trend is strongest in better-educated women. When the doctor treating Mrs. Keh was asked if he had known her correct age whether he would have treated her, he replied that he probably would not have, but he also said that the age limit of fifty-five years currently set by his clinic for assisted reproduction is arbitrary. His prediction is that in the future, young women will have their eggs frozen and stored so that they can have their children between the ages of forty and fifty-five.

There is nothing new about the fantasy that technology can transcend death and create life—Mary Shelley's story of Frankenstein's monster was such a one. What characterizes late modernity is a shift in the appreciation of rights. There is a very lively debate on the question of whether an individual has the right to have a child. The issue is a complex one, but what is evident is how often the notion of right slips into a demand, and from there into an entitlement. Having a child is not like the basic right to shelter, food, and clean water, and those suffering poverty and immizeration do not have access to the technology that would make that right a realizable one in all circumstances. Never mind the fact that for most poor women around the globe controlling their own reproduction is more about the right to decide not to have a child. For those who do have the means and the access to the technology, the issue is not only choice, but also an issue of freedom. The freedom to choose—even if it involves transcending the limitations of the human body—becomes not just a right, but an entitlement. Self-realization and self-creation are the only forms of emancipation that ultimately matter: "I want to be able to choose. I am entitled to choose."

This is not just individualism, but an overdetermined form of individualization (cf. Bauman 2000b; Beck and Beck-Gernsheim 2001). "What's wrong with choice?" you might reasonably ask. Well, nothing, but what happens when choice leads to failure? The responsibility for choice, for the right decision, becomes a kind of tyranny, an ever-present threat of potential failure: "am I handling the children right"; "did I make the right decision at work"; "what if I haven't bought the right house?" The apparent similarities in choices, dilemmas, and the agonies of ordinary everyday life do not result in a set of common interests; they do not become the shared interests of citizens, they remain the anxieties of individual egos with little regard for each other (cf. Bauman 2000b). One of the most popular television shows in recent years in the United Kingdom has been an extraordinary spectacle known as *Big Brother*.

The essence of *Big Brother* is that a number of contestants of both sexes are secluded in a specially designed house that is completely cut off from the outside world. These housemates are filmed 24 hours a day and must wear their personal microphones at all times. The Diary Room is where the housemates go every Monday to nominate two people for eviction and to provide reasons. Both the visits and the nominations are compulsory, as are a series of tasks that are assigned the housemates from time to time. Edited versions of the housemates' activities are shown on television, and the full horror of all the details and goings-on are continuously streamed on the website. During the television show, incidents of house activities and excerpts from the confessional nomination scenes are interspersed with commentary from expert psychologists and others who comment on the behavior, motivation, and personalities of the housemates. However, the decision as to who to evict every week is actually taken by members of the public who select between the two housemates who have received the most eviction nominations from their fellows. Viewers register their votes by phone, text messaging, and digital TV, and then get to watch the response live on television of the unfortunate whose failure has paradoxically found favor with them.

What makes this show distinctive is that the winner, the person who remains in the house when the others have been evicted, receives approximately £70,000 in prize money ($125,000 as of October 2005). This inevitably results in a considerable amount of game playing or strategizing. Principally, this involves building alliances with some individuals who will all nominate the same people for eviction, and retaining the favor of others so that they do not nominate you. In essence, it is a strange parody of the children's playground where you gang up on people, make hurtful personal remarks, and try to make sure that others are eliminated before you are. The currency of exchange is basically deceit and spite. Like talk shows, it encourages the viewer to take pleasure in other people's suffering and in their failure to make the grade as an individual within the group. There is much rhetoric of team playing in many of the encounters, but in the end there is only one winner and each person is pitted against the others in a highly personal and personalized form of survival. The idea is that something about the participants' inner selves is being revealed and your success depends on who you are and whether you can triumph over others. Much agonizing in confessions in the Diary Room is thus reserved for the question of who to betray and when. Since all nominations for evictions have to be based on "frank and honest reasons" as laid down in the game rules, the result is a flood of personal and very critical remarks about others. Watching people being nasty about others is apparently very addictive if we are to judge by the show's enormous popularity.

There is nothing unusual in taking pleasure in the discomfiture of others. It is probably the oldest form of entertainment! But, what is remarkable about the show is the creation of a faux community where everyone is encouraged and rewarded for acting as an individual, and more importantly a selfish individual. There is, therefore, no substantive content to the notion of community because this is a community made up of separate egos in competition with each other. The viewers or public act as the imaginary parents who referee between the siblings, and the rewards for parental approval are considerable. This probably accounts in large part for the very obviously childish behavior that forms a major part of the viewers' entertainment. From a sociological point of view, the show is a kind of reflection on popular understandings of individualism and choice in the twenty-first century.

The winners of *Big Brother* and many of the participants have gone on to become minor celebrities. One recent participant found himself voted "the most handsome man in Scotland!" What this suggests is that these individuals may embody something important for their audiences with regard to the management of self. Celebrities do seem to fascinate, why has never been completely clear, but it seems likely that we do not identify with celebrities just because they are rich or famous, but because they embody some aspect of our fantasies of self-aspiration. What celebrities and our fascination with them reveal is a dramatic convergence of the public and the private. We could be like them, but in order for that to be possible we have to be reassured that they are really just like us. Thus, the "public interest" has slowly reduced in scale to the private lives of public figures. One of the most obvious manifestations of this in the United Kingdom is our continuing fascination with the details of the private lives of the Royal Family. A *Daily Mail* reporter recently gained access to the Buckingham Palace by applying for a job as a footman. This deception was justified by the editor of the *Mail* in terms of public interest, although much of the country is still quietly mystified as to whose interest was served by learning that the queen has Tupperware on the breakfast table as well as silver.

Private lives and private sentiments increasingly fill the space of public culture. Far more pages are devoted in newspapers to details on the lives of the famous, the newly famous, and the barely famous than are ever devoted to government policy on refugees, asylum, education, and economic growth. The collective interest is of little intrinsic interest compared to the fascinating lives of the famous. However, the truly famous rarely seem to be admired for their accomplishments. They are admired just for being themselves. The most salient example of this in the United Kingdom at the moment is David Beckham the footballer. The man, who is a good footballer, but not the best, and good-looking, but hardly handsome, is a worldwide celebrity.

What Beckham symbolizes is the self-help-manual aspiration "to make something of yourself." Fame is attractive not just because it is about success, but because it has become the new morality. The idealized object objectifies the purpose of life, which is the work of self-preservation and self-realization. The famous are thus exemplifications of desirable human capabilities: the ability to do it all yourself, the understanding of self as a vocation. David Beckham is David Beckham is David Beckham; that's who he is and what he does. This kind of self-realization is not only a form of survival, but more than that a form of emancipation, the very definition of freedom for the later modern individual. More than the realization of personal dreams, it is the dream of the self-made good. In this context, it is perhaps not surprising that the winner of *Big Brother* 2004 was a Portuguese transgender woman whose words on winning were, "I am now accepted by the public as a woman." The choice of contestants is, of course, cynically manipulated by the production company to ensure viewer ratings, and sensationalism is their aim. However, 74 percent of the viewing public voted for Nadia Almada. Commentators have all emphasized that what apparently captured the imagination of the audiences was her self-made nature, her personal journey toward self-aspiration, and her huge desire to be accepted. In a sense, she encapsulated that desire to be something more than ourselves, which is always the search for the true self: the freedom to be whatever we choose to be.

David Beckham has recently been the subject of a sociological study (Cashmore 2003). The analysis concluded that Beckham is emblematic, among other things, of the changing nature of masculinity (cf. Whannel 2001). According to the author of the study, Beckham, who is known to be—that is he is presented as—something of a fashion dandy given to wearing hair bands and jewelry, is also said to be a doting father, a defender of family values, and a keen lover of ballet. Nothing wrong with any of that. But, his popularity does seem to rest on the apparent ease with which he combines apparently conflicting aspects of masculinity. He is an aggressive competitor on the field, a fashion icon, a doting father, a lower-middle-class boy made good, a conspicuous consumer, and a frequenter of celebrity gala occasions. He is thus all things to all men and, presumably, to all women. He is everyone's ideal man.

Beckham's popularity says something about popular discourses on masculinity. He plays on a good deal of ambiguity in personal appearance, but no one has ever suggested he is gay. The range of possible identifications with Beckham is very broad and this accounts, in part, for his enormous popularity, but it is also part of a wider trend with regard to sexuality and identity. Queer theorists have been arguing for some time that gay identity is restricting; that what the broader lesbian, gay, bisexual, and transgender community should do is to rethink their commitment to identity. As D. Travers Scott rather pithily put it: "Homosexuality's over" (1997, 68). The talk now is of a "post-gay" thinking. What this entails is a critique of any shared "gay" or "lesbian" identity that could be used to define a community, and a strongly felt antipathy to the idea that one's identity can be defined by a label. There is a strong dissatisfaction with terms such as "gay," "lesbian," and so on, both as cultural and as political identities, but the larger disagreement is with the idea that these terms define aspects of the self or self-identity (cf. Harris 1998; Roof 1997; Sinfield 1998). The broader dissatisfaction is with the idea of fixed identities and collective politics based on those identities. People do not want to be labeled; they want to be free to choose, and to determine how they make themselves and how they want to be seen by others. This is the new morality.

This trend is not confined to activists or those involved in academic writing, but can also be seen at play in the popularity of an icon like Beckham. In the United Kingdom, a great deal of discussion about sexuality has focused on football, and a vocal number of "gay" fans are clear that they are unhappy with traditional ideas about being gay, especially the idea that gay men don't like football! They are particularly critical of ideas of gay masculinity that are based on certain ways of dressing and behaving endorsed in many gay lifestyle magazines. The desire of the moment is to be like every other man, not to be pigeonholed, to be allowed to be gay in a way that works for them as individuals and as men (cf. Fanshawe 2004). Once again the popular disagreement is with collective identities that impinge on personal identities based on choice and self-determination.

The Problem of Politics

The late modern individual might cleave to a notion of freedom as the
right to make oneself, but this freedom is an anxious one. The peren-
nial question is not just the one of "how successful am I?" but the logi-
cally prior one of "what are the rules?" The do-it-yourself life is
increasingly underpinned by social, economic, and political changes.
One of the reasons for this is that modern individuals are increasingly
dependent on the labor market and because of that they are dependent
on education, consumption, state regulations and policies, as well as on
the services that grow up via the market to deal with the contradictions
thus produced, including psychiatric and medical services, welfare provision, and the like (Beck and Beck-Gernsheim 2001). The market extends into every area of life, and as global capitalism gathers force and
speed this process becomes ever more encompassing. But, the market is
an uncertain mechanism, one that increases rather than reduces risk. As
global corporations strive for profits, they make particular demands on
their labor forces. The world of work for some is now intensely competi-
tive, characterized by flexibility and rapid changes in skills and tasks. An
increasing dependence on information and knowledge management
drives the dominance of the service sector of the economy globally. The
individuals who survive in such environments have to be very highly educated. Whereas earlier forms of industrialization were characterized by
organized labor that remained in single employment over a long period
of time, the modern work force is constantly being downsized, subject to
efficiency gains, and laid off. Those who are highly educated and who
work in the growth areas of the global economy, such as information
and communication technology, culture, film, music, and nanotechnol-
ogy, find their skills in high demand and can command high wages. But,
the situation for others is very different.

   Global capital seeks out cheap labor in emerging and developing
economies, it determines conditions of trade, and draws millions of people into processes that they can have no hope of influencing, let alone
controlling. The failure of the trade negotiations at Cancun is a very
dramatic example of this, and emphasizes the point that primary producers, and not just those who sell their labor on the market, are dramatically affected by such processes.[1] Life is therefore full of increased
risks, but risks that cannot be specified or managed. Capitalism increasingly exposes people to the forces of globalization as individuals. The
extreme conditions of uncertainty in employment and income undermine the motivation and effectiveness of collective action. More than
this though, global capitalism is increasingly exclusionary. Literally
millions of people—especially the rural poor—are irrelevant to its func-

tioning. If you can neither maintain your livelihood, nor gain a living from wage labor or from capital, then you will likely find yourself in a situation where you are cut off from traditional securities while at the same time unable to access the basic benefits and resources of modernity. Poverty is therefore changing its character and becoming a structural feature of the system and is thus utterly ineradicable.

This process characterizes not only relations between developed/ emerging and developed economies, but also within them. For example, social inequality in the United Kingdom has risen steeply and is escalating. The lifestyle of the elite is increasingly dependent on the labor of those who are prevented, whether by education level or by lack of legal status, from entering the labor force on equal terms. Professional women have come in for the sharpest criticism here being accused of maintaining their lifestyles and incomes by exploiting the labor of other women as domestic workers and nannies (cf. Ehrenreich 2001; Toynbee 2003). This is "what feminism has brought us" is the oft-repeated phrase. These domestic workers, and others like them, are maintaining themselves on the edges of the system because they have access to some work, but they are nonetheless poor. The poor, contrary to the famous phrase, are not "always with us" because research in the United Kingdom shows that about two-thirds of those households classified as poor move in and out of poverty at different stages in their lives. These shifts correspond to their changing relations to the labor market and to the state. However, below these groups of individuals are those who are unable to work and those whose legal status prevents them both from working and from claiming state benefits. Modern capitalism has no need for these individuals either as workers or as consumers, and yet their experience of and commitment to individualization is no less than that of those who are fully within the capitalist system and benefiting from it to greater or lesser degrees.

Individualization has a profound effect on identity, on ideas about the self, and on conceptions of the relationship of the individual to other individuals and to larger collective wholes, including the state. The changing nature of these ideas have been accelerated and reinforced by current socioeconomic and political changes, including the rolling back of the boundaries of the state, the retreat of welfare systems, the structural enforcement of a reliance on personal coping strategies, and the changing nature of legislation, notably in many countries the removal of or imposition of severe constraints on the right to strike. Individualization both drives and is driven by the socioeconomic and political changes that make up global capitalism, and the two are mutually reinforcing.

A recent report on attitudes to the welfare state in Britain exemplified a number of these points (Sefton 2004). The study was conducted in the context of government efforts to "promote opportunity" and "personal responsibility" as part of a move to increase the provision of privately funded and/or provided welfare services. The results for the period 1983–2002 showed that strong and sustained support for spending on health, education, and social benefits contrasted with a sharp decline in support for more spending on welfare benefits for the poor. The decline was greatest among young people (eighteen to thirty-four) and Labour Party supporters. While the composition of the Labour party in Britain has changed and become broader-based over this period, the comparative figures show that the difference in attitudes between those on the right and those on the left has narrowed considerably, and attitudes toward public spending and redistribution are less divided along ideological lines than in the 1980s. Within the category of the "poor," there was more support for spending on disabled people, pensioners, and working people on low incomes as compared to support for single parents (predominantly women) and the unemployed. What the data do demonstrate is a dramatic decline in support for the welfare state overall among younger people as opposed to older generations (the proportion who agree that benefits for the unemployed are too low and cause hardship fell by 29 percentage points between 1987 and 2002 among those aged eighteen to thirty-four, but only 16 percentage points among those aged fifty-five and over). Even more notable is that the priority attached to social security spending has fallen even among those who would benefit from it most, especially those on low incomes and the unemployed. These trends may not be permanent because attitudes toward benefit claimants tend to harden during periods of economic growth and soften during recessions, and there is no way of knowing whether the attitudes among the younger age group are transient or not. However, the study shows that attitudes toward welfare spending are changing across all social and interest groups, and that while the majority of people surveyed recognized the need to support the vulnerable, there was very little support for redistribution in general. The generally endorsed view was that "people should stand on their own feet." Ideas about self-realization and self-aspiration are changing people's attitudes toward the state, but also toward those who are seen as not striving toward those goals, notably single parents and the unemployed.

The all-pervasive nature of individualization means, however, that we need a more nuanced and reflective approach to it. It is possible to say that the culture of "everyone for themselves" means that society is doomed because we are all simply getting more selfish. However, what research shows is that different cultures of individualization exist within and between societies, that there are divergent forms of late modernity both within societies, as well as between them. There are two important trends here. One is that resistance is growing to individualization, especially individualization based on high consumerism. The most salient form of this resistance comes from religious groups and religious faiths as they take new global forms in the later modern period. In Europe, resistance to individualization is growing through the environmental and anticapitalist movements (cf. Beck and Beck-Gernsheim 2001). But, these movements are not like the collective action of an earlier period; they are not based on a collective identity, but on the idea that the individual is the unit of democracy. Thus, the ideologies that drive these movements are not collective in the sense we might be familiar with from the early twentieth century because they are not based on a shared identity, but on the idea that as individuals we have a right to a better quality of life. What this shows is that being an individual does not mean failing to care about others or about issues that affect large numbers of people, but it does show that modern politics has changed (Beck and Beck-Gernsheim 2001). What drives political action now is the right of the individual to choose quality of life, and the fact that collective bodies—particularly corporates and states—should not be allowed to threaten that quality of life. Conviction now exists in new forms, and these forms are born out of individualization and the politics of choice.

This is exemplified by a report about equality between women and men in the United Kingdom published by the Equal Opportunities Commission in 2004 (Howard and Tibballs 2004). The headline findings were that people are aware that social inequality and discrimination are widespread in the United Kingdom. They believe that society should be fairer and more tolerant, but they are deeply antithetical to notions of equality if they are based on policies aimed at producing equality of outcomes. People are comfortable with the idea of equality of opportunity and protection from discrimination, but their political and social goals are based on fairness and tolerance leading to "having the same chance in life." There is little support—from both women and men— for the idea that women are unequal in society today and both are absolutely against any form of positive discrimination, believing it is discriminatory because it gives some unfair advantages. People recognize that inequality and social prejudice exist, but are strongly opposed to strategies that involve group or collective action. Overall society is seen as being more equal, but less tolerant than in the past. Most women feel that they have experienced discrimination, but are reluctant to frame these experiences as the result of inequalities. Respondents recognized that women have less well-paid jobs and do more domestic work, but see this as a result both of personal choice and natural gender differences. Overall, women and men express a strong sense of needing to take personal responsibility for the problems they face, and to get on with life. As one man said: "Everybody can start equal but they aren't going to end up in the same place because you make different choices" (Howard and Tibballs 2004:23).

"I think feminism is as outmoded as the suffragettes," one woman said (Howard and Tibballs 2004:40). Feminism is felt to be particularly outdated. Both women and men feel that when problems occur it is up to the individual to deal with them. This accords with other research in Europe and America that shows that younger women are particularly uninterested in what they think of as the politics of resentment. Insofar as they do want to work toward better treatment for women in the workplace, or campaign on health issues and equal pay, they see this as a matter of choice. What is particularly unattractive to them is the ideology of solidarity and collective action on which an earlier feminism is based because it is seen as undermining personal choice. People expect to be able to define their own ideas and allegiances, and they are much more interested in single-issue politics than in a politics based on structural change in society. However, what research shows is that while people's commitment to family and community remain vital to their sense of self and their motivations in life, they do not want to engage in collective action to redress society's ills. There is a strong sense that the individual is the building block of society and that individuals should be responsible for addressing problems. This is manifested in a strong interest in psychological explanations for problems and in the idea that people feel that if they have problems they need to adjust themselves. Hence, the extreme popularity of self-help books, therapy, and so on. The sense is that unhappiness or frustration can be dealt with by finding advice and support and pursuing personal change.

Conclusion

In making sense of the individualization of the moment and its relationship to our theorizing, we may need to reflect more purposefully on the interconnections between philosophical critique and social criticism (cf. Fraser and Nicholson 1988). There are two important questions here. The first is, what are the assumptions of fragmentation, ambiguity, plurality, and multiplicity doing for us in the social sciences and for people in their lives? The second is, what is the nature of the link between extreme particularism as the logical entailment of a commitment to difference and the individualization underpinning contemporary discourses of the self and the social? These questions are clearly related, but in seeking to answer them we need to be attentive to historical forms and processes. The great philosophical theories of difference and their critique of liberal humanism found purchase at a moment in the twentieth century when Europe was still profoundly committed to collective politics. Whatever else we might want to claim, it is clear that postmodernism and popular individualism or individualization do not share a common origin in any simple sense. In addition, while particularism might be the logical entailment of the deconstruction of difference—"its turtles all the way down"—it does not necessarily follow that contending that difference is the condition for identity means that there is no basis for collective identities. There is, therefore, no essential logical connection between postmodernism or deconstruction and the demise of the political. We might cynically recall that both sets of theories are on the decline in the academy now and yet hyperindividualism and the disavowal of collective identities, at least in the West, seems to be going from strength to strength.

We should be conscientious here with regard to historical nuances. As I suggested earlier, hyperindividualization may be a potent force in contemporary social life and in the popular imagination, but it is also violently opposed by other competing social trends, including the return to faith. The divisions between forms of individualism and faiths, and between cosmopolitanisms and nationalisms may yet prove to be the basis for major conflict in the twenty-first century (cf. Cheah and Robbins 1998). The point I want to make in conclusion comes from a slightly different vantage point and has to do with the nature of theorizing in the social sciences. There is no doubt that the critique of liberal humanism and of the self-defining unitary subject has found its mark. We do need to be attentive to historical diversity and to critique metanarratives and avoid universalizing categories. From a political point of view as feminists, we need to acknowledge that both justification and consensus must always be fought for rather than assumed. However, there is a sense in which difference has now become the new essentialism. The grand narratives of liberal humanism have given way to the grand narratives of difference. Difference in the social sciences is now a pretheoretical assumption and that should be a call to critical self-reflection, if not a source of concern.

Why should this be so? Academic models of the moment, particularly those associated with gender and sexuality—have a disquieting tendency to mimic and find resonance with emerging forms of individualization. In one sense, this is not surprising since feminist, black, and gay scholarship are based on forms of agency linked to emancipatory politics, the desire to be free of larger determining structures, discourses, and ideologies. The notion of individual freedom is central to their imagined selves (cf. Mahmood 2001). Postmodernism finds resonances with this strand of liberal emancipatory politics because its labile, fluid nature fits well with certain aspects of the experience of individualization. While postmodern theory on the surface appears to denaturalize and de-essentialize subjects, selves, and differences, its focus on ambiguity and plurality paradoxically finds favor with the self-made nature of individual sexuality and the gendered self. It is of little consequence that many theorists—including Judith Butler (1990, 1993)—have warned against the pitfalls of voluntarism and criticized performative and meta-performative theories that appear to ignore regimes of power and their productive effects. The predominant view in the academy, as outside it, is that categories of analysis homogenize and dehistoricize, that they do not allow differences to emerge and be recognized. But, when we interrogate closely what it is that these categories are obscuring, the answers are all couched in highly individualistic forms: experience, self-identity, differences. There is a tendency in such moves for experience, self-identity, and difference to be both naturalized and essentialized, taken as "given" and foundational.

Hyperindividualization and the disavowal of social categories may be important elements of contemporary experience and the popular imagination for many groups of people around the world, but they are not the only story worth telling. There are other longer-running, larger-scale structures producing poverty, conflict, and immiseration in people's lives, and these economic, social, and political determinants also urgently need theorizing. This is not to argue for a return to the grand narratives of Western philosophy, for a conscious and conscientious politicized commitment to moral, political, and epistemological pluralism is the prerequisite for any analysis of these longer-run determinants. However, precisely because academic theories and popular discourses always contaminate each other—especially perhaps in the domains of gender and sexuality—we need both to deconstruct and to maintain the analytic categories—like gender—that help us to historicize and analyze that process of contamination.

Chapter 2
Feminist Theories of Embodiment and Anthropological Imagination: Making Bodies Matter

ROSEMARY A. JOYCE

Contemporary feminist theorizing is characterized by a rich diversity of approaches that some might see as indicative of fragmentation, but that I would argue are an index of productive engagement with the real complexity of understanding power-laden social relations organized along lines of sex differences. Different emphases in feminist theorizing help illuminate alternative feminist research questions, and without this diversity, it is unlikely that we will be effective in a comprehensive critique of the social conditions of inequality based on gender whose amelioration I take as the shared goal of feminism. I discuss here some explicitly feminist work on embodiment, explore ways in which it has informed anthropological, and particularly archaeological, practice, and suggest some of the ways that this work may contribute to continuing feminist projects in the future. Taking seriously an implication of feminist standpoint theory, that every argument is made from a specifically situated position, I begin by locating myself within anthropological and feminist perspectives.

Feminism and Anthropology

In a review of feminist theory and practice in anthropology published over a decade ago, Micaela di Leonardo (1991) characterized feminist anthropologists as sharing an assumption that gender is inextricably linked to other institutions and discourses, such as race, gender, sexuality, age, ethnicity, and class. Related to this, she argued that anthropology was then experiencing the effects of a substantive shift in wider feminist theorizing from concerns with gender identity to concerns with gender difference, a shift more widely associated with the transformation from second- to third- wave feminisms (e.g., Visweswaran 1997, 595–96). This point was reinforced by Henrietta Moore (1994) who argued that feminist anthropology needed to take account of multiple forms of difference, in an extension of her earlier, path-breaking analysis of the relations between anthropological and feminist analyses (Moore 1988). Visweswaran, di Leonardo, and Moore all pointed toward the need to consider processes of identification and disidentification in place of assuming any easy way to define gendered identities.

Feminist anthropologists who have taken these analyses to heart have proceeded to write not only about the place of women and the relations of inequality from which they suffer, but also about cross-cutting dimensions of difference that are as likely to separate women from each other as link them together. Important work of this kind has emanated from Chicana and black feminists, from feminist subaltern studies, and from queer theorists, among others (see Visweswaran 1997, 610–15).

Feminist attention to bodily difference has been part of these developments, and I argue continues to be critically needed in anthropology and especially in anthropological archaeology. Moore (1994, 12) noted that despite anthropological attention to race, gender, and other dimensions of difference, "one fixed position remained, and that was the division between sex and gender. Gender was seen as socially constructed, but underlying that idea was a notion that although gender was not determined by biology, it was the social elaboration in specific contexts of the obvious facts of biological sex difference." She traces the persistence of the naturalization of biological difference to the initial arguments in feminist anthropology that women's subordinate status was based on culturally specific reactions to universal female biological processes such as menstruation, pregnancy, and childbirth (Moore 1994, 10–11). Moore identifies two main "comparative theories" explaining the presumed universal subordination of women explored by anthropologists in the 1970s. One traced the roots of this disadvantage to a universal association of women with nature, based on an asserted closer tie to biology (exemplified by Ortner 1974). The other located the same hierarchy in women's restriction to a domestic sphere, based again on biological "facts," in this instance, assumed entailments of women's roles in reproduction (exemplified by Rosaldo 1974).

While long ago reexamined by feminist anthropologists, including those who made the original landmark arguments (Ortner and Whitehead 1981b; Rosaldo 1980), assumptions of a biologically defined subject, woman, with a universally identifiable social position continue to influence popular, anthropological, and particularly archaeological analyses. At the same time, anthropology, and anthropological archaeology in particular, makes a unique contribution to the study of embodiment and its relation to personhood, due to the wider range of societies that can be documented ethnographically and archaeologically than are known from text-based history. For both of these reasons, I argue that the contributions of contemporary feminist anthropology to discussions of embodiment are a particularly valuable perspective within the diversity of feminist approaches in anthropology. In the remainder of this chapter, I attempt to explore how concerns with embodiment examined from feminist perspectives have contributed to anthropological feminism, focusing on the area I know best, archaeological analysis.

Why All the Fuss About the Body?

Bodiliness has been the focus of extraordinarily rich intellectual attention across a wide range of disciplines that border anthropology. From the humanities, writers concerned with the ways that bodily differences have been conceptualized within the western European tradition have developed substantive analyses of gender difference that are critical for anyone doing historical analysis (Bynum 1991; Laqueur 1990). Feminist scholars critically engaging the work of Michel Foucault have explored ways bodily difference comes to be routinized through psychological and habitual experiences, including engagement with other materialities such as architecture or the products of bodily labor (Butler 1990, 1993, 1997b, 31–62; Grosz 1995, 83–137; McLaren 2002). Approaching the question of difference from a bodily perspective, Luce Irigaray, Hélène Cixous, and others based in the French feminist tradition have theorized that women's bodies are both experienced as a natural source of difference and socially construed as a source of signs of innate difference (Grosz 1994, 1995; Moi 1985, 102–49). But there is clearly a danger here of reducing difference to biology and equating women with the body, a danger which some have already called attention to in contemporary archaeology (Meskell 1996, 1998). Why, then, urge an engagement with embodiment, which, given the history of recent Western thought, surely risks reinstating an equation of the body with women? And what would be particularly feminist about such an engagement?

Henrietta Moore (1994, 33), summarizing lessons learned from ethnographic explorations of personhood and embodiment, draws the conclusion that contrary to unexamined assumptions, "the body is not always the source and locus of identity." She argues that anthropology inherits from Western philosophy an increasingly questionable premise that there is "an essence at the core of the person which exists prior to the person's insertion into a social matrix and which is fixed over time," such that in traditional anthropological writing "the most important characteristic of the person over time, and the one which constitutes its identity, is the fact of physical embodiment" (Moore 1994, 36). The anchoring of identity in embodiment is correlated with the fact that "the person and the self are not considered as gender neutral" in Western philosophy and the anthropological understandings based on it, so that an "elision between gender identity and physical embodiment accounts for the extraordinary emphasis in western discourse on the sexually differentiated nature of the human body," which is taken as "self-evident because there are two clearly differentiated and natural categories of the body" (Moore 1994, 37). One critical task anthropological engagement with embodiment has thus already accomplished is to denaturalize the two-sex, two-gender model.

Anthropologists and historians alike have long ago demonstrated that the body is not a universal precultural ground for a system of two dichotomous sexes, even in western European societies. Anne Fausto-Sterling (1985, 2000) has demonstrated how contemporary scientific descriptions of biology take for granted a natural two-sex system, and how medical practitioners reimpose it when necessary through surgical intervention. Ground-breaking work by historical archaeologist Roberta Gilchrist (1994, 1997, 2000b), paralleling historical studies like those of Caroline Walker Bynum (1991), examined the complexity of gender, sexuality, and material practices through which embodied sexuality was produced in the medieval European tradition. Nonetheless, there remain relatively few archaeological studies that examine the historically situated material practices through which other societies in other times produced gender systems either distinct from or even similar to that of modern Europe (see Hollimon 2000; Joyce 2000a, b; Meskell and Joyce 2003; Prine 2000; Schmidt 2000). What has become clear through the work of anthropologists, archaeologists, and historians is that explorations of the experience of embodiment necessarily engage analysts with considerations of personhood and subjectivity. Here again, feminist intervention is required to ensure that subjectivity and personhood are conceptualized in ways that take into account contemporary arguments about gender difference and do not reinscribe either the assumed natural two-sex model or an unexamined reliance on an ungendered, inherently masculine, universal body.

Bodies and Persons

The Western tradition has privileged the mind, rather than the body, as the site of identity since at least the rise of Enlightenment philosophy (Grosz 1994, 3–10; Turner 1984, 30–59). In this tradition, the body is seen as an object separable from the thinking subject's mind. The body's needs or desires stood in the way of the realization of full subjectivity and had to be subordinated to the ends of society (Turner 1984, 10–22; see also Turner 1991). Phenomenological approaches to experience, such as those of Maurice Merleau-Ponty (1962), challenged such mind-body dualism and the hierarchy of mind over body that they assume (Csordas 1994). But it can be argued that phenomenology assumed a single subject position, which, while never explicitly gendered, can clearly be demonstrated to be masculine, offered as a universal standpoint (Grosz 1994, 86–111).

Against this assumption of a universal gender-neutral position, many feminists have struggled to find a perspective on embodied experience that avoids essentialism while capturing a sense of what Moore (1994, 17) identifies as a universalizing particularity, or (citing Braidotti 1991) "collective singularity," ultimately always related to embodiment. Moore traces how Braidotti's arguments—at first glance a return to a biological essentialism that neither she, nor I, would espouse—in fact are something potentially quite different. "Braidotti argues that what is truly revolutionary about a return to the female body is the notion of speaking from the body, with all this implies both about the specificity of positionality and the embodied, material nature of one's relation with the world" (Moore 1994, 18).

As a counterpoint to universalizing theories that assume a disembodied (male) subjectivity, Elizabeth Grosz (1994, 189) provided an avowedly feminist exploration of "the question of the sexual specificity of bodies." She argued that subjectivity must be examined in relation to diverse bodily experiences, some of them only possible for those who possess particularly biological characteristics. She insists that engagement with sexual difference requires acknowledging the differential potentials of distinct biologies for experience, symbolization, and embodiment. Drawing on psychological theory, she notes that fragments shed from the body, such as saliva, hair, or nail clippings, mark the body as existing in a borderline state, open to being perceived as dangerous or vulnerable (Grosz 1994, 187–210). Body openings may be seen as "libidinal zones . . . continually in the process of being produced, renewed, transformed, through experimentation, practices, innovations" (Grosz 1995, 199).

Grosz (1995, 36) noted that Western psychoanalytic theory assumes that bodily sex differences affect the body image of human subjects, in particular, associating the presence or absence of specific body parts (markedly, the male genitalia) with a psychological experience of sexual hierarchy, always privileging masculinity. She suggests that the female body in particular may be seen as subject to leakage across insecure margins (Grosz 1994). Yet, as she wrote, in actuality "bodies are not fixed, inert, purely genetically or biologically programmed entities that function in their particular ways and in their determinate forms independent of their cultural milieu and value. Differences between bodies, not only at the level of experience and subjectivity but also at the level of practical and physical capacities, enjoy considerable social and historical variation" (Grosz 1994, 190). Anthropology and archaeology have critical roles to play in giving substance and specificity to this and related claims of variation in embodied experience.

Anthropological accounts of alternative ways of conceptualizing embodiment (A. Strathern 1996) and personhood (M. Strathern 1988) have already contributed centrally to the projects of reframing mind-body relations, subjectivity, and personhood. Embodiment has been a concern of anthropologists for decades. In an essay written in 1934, Marcel Mauss (1992, 455) wrote about "techniques of the body," which he defined as "the ways in which, from society to society, men know how to use their bodies." His specific examples, tied in each instance to a cultural and historical context, included swimming, digging, marching, and walking. He implicated education and imitation as the social modes through which these distinctive body techniques were reproduced, an analysis that prefigures those of later social theorists who emphasize bodily discipline (notably Foucault) and iteration of body practices (e.g., Butler 1990, 1993). For Mauss (1992, 461) "the body is man's first and most natural instrument. Or more accurately . . . man's first and most natural technical object, and at the same time his first technical means." Commenting briefly on distinctions he observed between men and women within specific societies, Mauss called for attention to the interplay between learning and nature to account for gender differences in body techniques.

Sixty years later, Thomas Csordas (1994, 1) could argue that the body was "a lively presence on the anthropological scene." Csordas (4–5) sketched an anthropological history of examination of the body in which the object of study shifted from an "analytic body" to a "topical body" to what he called the "multiple body." Against a history of taking the body for granted as an object of study, he suggested the need for an anthropological turn toward concern with embodiment. He advocated that anthropological approaches to embodiment emphasize "lived experience" or "being-in-the-world" in place of either viewing the body as a surface for "inscription" or an object of representation (10–11).

Building on the demonstration that biology is everywhere subject to cultural construal, anthropologists have further critiqued the Anglo-European "correspondence model of gender/sexuality that assigns anatomical sex a constant gender and a prescribed object of sexual desire" (Weston 1993, 348). Most radically, anthropologists have challenged the assumption of a natural correspondence between a body and an individual person, historicizing and contextualizing both (Lambek

and Strathern 1998; Mauss 1985; M. Strathern 1988). Feminist anthropologists, and feminist archaeologists, can provide unique demon-
strations of the productive implications of critiques of the Western
"correspondence model" of sex, gender, and sexuality, and its assumed
basis in "natural" biological facts, by exploring how embodied subjectivity is shaped under diverse historical, cultural, and material conditions.

Bodies That Matter

Archaeology has begun, slowly, to draw on the currents of social thought
concerning embodiment briefly reviewed earlier, and to contribute to
them specific analyses not otherwise possible (see Hamilakis, Pluciennik, and Tarlow 2002b; Meskell and Joyce 2003; Rautman 2000). Bodies,
of course, have long occupied a central place in archaeological analyses.
Recent approaches to personhood, including gendered personhood,
have increasingly troubled older assumptions of easy equations of biological sex and cultural sense (Arnold and Wicker 2001b; Hamilakis,
Pluciennik, and Tarlow 2002a, 4; Rautman and Talalay 2000). Human
remains may now be seen as sedimentations of the habitual actions of
the living person in the body, taken either as primarily informative
about the lived experience of the person, or of one or another category
to which that person belonged.

The recognition of physical traces as the result of repetitive action allows archaeologists to present descriptions of embodied existence in
past societies that foreground assumed models of embodiment and being. Inspired explicitly by theories of multiple genders, Sandra Hollimon (2001, 179) reconsiders her own previous work, writing that "I
may have appeared to subscribe to the notion that Arikara women cow-
ered in their doorways or cornfields during raids upon their villages and
gardens." She goes on to suggest that the traumas she observes in both
young men and women need to be considered as possible evidence of
participation as warriors, not (as she previously assumed) as male warriors and female victims. John Robb (2002) builds on the concept of
"osteobiography" to argue for an anthropologically informed narrativiza-
tion of archaeologically recovered human remains as testimony of the
incorporation in the body of physical traces of life experience, enduring
testimony to Mauss's "techniques of the body."

Other archaeological work on embodiment has been based on phenomenological theories, and has notably emphasized attempts to capture the embodied experience of monumental landscapes from periods
before the use of writing (J. Thomas 1990, 1993; Tilley 1994). Early phenomenological approaches in archaeology have been critiqued for privileging the visual over other sensory capacities, and for insufficient

examination of the effects of different subject positions on the ability to assume a universal phenomenological grounding (Hamilakis, Pluciennik, and Tarlow 2002a, 8–10). Notably absent from most early archaeological work in this tradition was engagement with issues of bodily difference, including gender. More recent phenomenological approaches in archaeology have explicitly built on feminist analyses of bodily difference to shift from the assumption of a universal subject experiencing a fixed landscape to a landscape differentially shaping different kinds of bodies and persons (Fowler 2002, 59, 64).

Perhaps most distinctive of recent archaeological work on gender, sexuality, and embodiment has been reliance on Judith Butler's (1990, 1993) discussions of gender performance. Butler's focus on the social mechanisms through which gender is produced, performed, and regulated shifts attention from presumptions of innate biological identity toward an emphasis on the fluidity of gender difference. For archaeology, a materialist discipline that treats residues of human behavior as the basis for representations of cultural identities, the confrontation with issues concerning the stability of identity and its relationships to materiality that Butler's work requires is critical (Perry and Joyce 2001). Without such a critique, archaeological materialism can represent biological residues as prior and natural bases for the social categories of gender.

At the same time, archaeology contributes a unique perspective on the proposals Butler makes concerning the relationship between the materiality of the body and its cultural intelligibility. The strongest critique of Butler's (1990) original proposal has been stated succinctly by Henrietta Moore (1994, 18), who argued that Butler risked "positing the body as a blank surface on which the social becomes inscribed, thus suggesting in some sense that the body is pre-social." Ironically, this is precisely the issue on which Butler critiques Foucault (McLaren 2002, 99–106). What appears to be passed over lightly in both Foucault and Butler is the materiality of discourse, and that is precisely where archaeology, with its necessary focus on the material, provides a critical intervention.

Butler (1993) insists that she was not suggesting a theatrical model of gender performance as something open to casual adoption and shifting, but one based on the repetition of socially evaluated action. In *Gender Trouble*, performance had been concisely defined as "an identity tenuously constituted in time, instituted in an exterior space through a *stylized repetition of acts*" (Butler 1990, 140; emphasis in original). A process unfolding over time in an exterior space, shaped through iteration of the bodies and representations circulating in the cultural milieu, gender performativity is ideally situated as an archaeological model (Bachand, Joyce, and Hendon 2003; Joyce 1998; Perry and Joyce 2001). An approach to embodied subjectivity that takes as central the differential positions of power of embodied actors and others in society (Butler 1997b), this analysis can help maintain a focus on one of the defining features of feminist analysis, an emancipatory understanding of how power differentials within society are naturalized (Butler 1997a, 141–56).

Butler (1990, 24–25, 112, 134–41) criticized the presumption of the priority of the body, and the dichotomy between nature (sex) and culture (gender), implicit in analyses that begin by defining gender as ways of culturally interpreting the sexed body. As Butler put it, the "production of sex as the prediscursive ought to be understood as the effect of the apparatus of cultural construction designated by *gender*" (1990, 7; emphasis in original). The sense that the body is "natural" is itself a byproduct of discourse *about* bodily materiality (Butler 1993, 1–16, 101–19). *Materiality* is consequently critical for the production and reproduction of sex, and of other aspects of subjectivity. Bodily materiality is best considered as the repeated *citation* of a disciplinary norm, a largely or normally nondiscursive (*not* prediscursive) enactment of a mode of being that is shaped by culturally situated precedents, and in turn shapes new cultural performances (Butler 1993, 12–16).

Gender performance involves public, repetitive actions of movement, gesture, posture, dress, labor, production, interaction with objects, and the manipulation of space (Butler 1990). As a result, archaeologists are in a good position to document gender performance through exploration of such material media. Since gender performance is by definition a repetition or citation of a precedent (Butler 1993), the kinds of material regularities that archaeologists document in the media of performance can profitably be viewed as potential mechanisms for the constitution, regulation, and contestation of gender.

Gender Trouble

The most sustained archaeological analyses inspired by Butler's work focus on the regulatory modes through which gender was produced and reproduced, finding in citationality a concept amenable to archaeological interpretation (Perry and Joyce 2001; Thomas 2002; see Joyce 2004). Archaeologists have always been successful in documenting the material dimensions of gender performance, even when they begin their analyses with the assumption of a two-sex, two-gender system. But when the focus is changed from the reflection of a system of classification and hierarchy grounded in the facts of biology, to the active reproduction of a culturally specific way of gendering persons, the same archaeological data may be transformed, "troubling" the easy assumptions of natural gender categories and inevitable histories of gender hierarchy that are still too typical of archaeological interpretation.

Alberti draws on Butler to make the argument that "there is no atem-poral, fixed 'core' to a person's identity . . . outside the acts and gestures that constitute it" (2001, 190). He thus interprets the reproduction of categorical relations of similarity among figurines produced in Knossos as the result of citation of prior practices of materializing gender, rather than as the representation of predetermined universals of sex (Alberti 2001, 194). Alberti (200) suggests that "breasts are an integral part of the costume of the figurines" that helps to produce a legible gender representation through citation of embodied sexed subjectivities.

A similar concern with the implications of Butler's analysis for the in-terpretive "legibility" of embodied performances, attained through an examination of representations, motivates other archaeological analyses. Often this is explicitly tied to the emancipatory implication Butler (1993, 231) draws from her own analysis of gender performativity, arguing that

the practice by which gendering occurs, the embodying of norms, is a compul-sory practice, a forcible production, but not for that reason fully determining. To the extent that gender is an assignment, it is an assignment which is never quite carried out according to expectation, whose addressee never quite inhab-its the ideal s/he is compelled to approximate. Moreover, this embodying is a re-peated process. And one might construe repetition as precisely that which undermines the conceit of voluntarist mastery.

Thus, in a discussion of "humanoid" masked images from Scandinavia, Danielsson (2002, 182) suggests that the images, and the embodied practice of masking that they suggest, may be archaeological traces of the "enduring incongruity of bodies in practice, and the way in which bodies go beyond the normative." She demonstrates that previous analy-ses of the same objects, using the two-sex model, left unclassified and outside the analysis images that did not conform to the binary clothing code being used to classify sexes (Danielsson 2002, 187). As Butler's analysis would suggest, it is in these moments of illegibility that we can see the possibility for disruption of imposed norms. Danielsson (188) argues that these images were literally transgressive, dangerous repre-sentations of "impossible" bodies in liminal states. Attending to their materiality, we might alternatively suggest that the existence of repre-sentations of these nonbinary bodily forms, executed in a precious ma-terial (gold), might imply a more varied gender performativity than we today assume from our standpoint in a two-sex system.

In my own work on Central American gendering and embodiment, I have emphasized the material richness of citational precedents, in the form of the iconic, idealized representations of bodily postures that abounded in these sites, and used these to suggest that living gendered performances were understood to be inherently unstable and in need of repeated disciplining (Bachand, Joyce, and Hendon 2003; Joyce 2001a, b, 2002). Drawing attention to the visual emphasis on representation of the bodies of young males in Classic Maya art, often shown actively engaged in dance or sports, I proposed that we understand the bodily incorporation of citational precedents itself as a pleasurable exercise of agency rather than simply as a disciplinary imposition of power on an unwilling subject (Joyce 2000b, 272–73).

I later (Joyce 2001c) extended this line of argument through consideration of Butler's (1997b, 10–13) analysis of the paradoxical nature of subjectivation: the simultaneous creation of a subject (an "I" who could exercise agency) through relations of subjection (as the "I" recognizes itself in the exercise of power over itself, and takes shape in relationship to that exercise of power). Butler (1997b, 31–53) offers an analysis of Hegel's discussion of "Lordship and Bondage" in light of this double move: "the bondsman in Hegel throws off the apparently external 'Lord' only to find himself in an ethical world, subjected to various norms and ideals" (32). The Lord and the Bondsman are differentiated by embodiment: "the bondsman appears as the instrumental body whose labor provides for the material conditions of the lord's existence . . . the lord postures as a disembodied desire for self reflection . . . who requires in effect that the bondsman be the lord's body, but be it in such a way that the lord forgets or disavows his own activity in producing the bondsman" (Butler 1997b, 35). Despite being the case example of the strongest possible exercise of power over the body of another, Butler (36) demonstrates that the subjective self-awareness of the bondsman cannot be erased, a self-awareness achieved precisely through the *materiality* of the body *and its extension* through its *material* products:

As the bondsman slaves away and becomes aware of his own signature on the things that he makes, he recognizes in the form of the artifact that he crafts the markings of his own labor, markings that are formative of the object itself. His labor produces a visible and legible set of marks in which the bondsman reads back from the object a confirmation of his own formative activity. This labor, this activity, which belongs from the start to the lord, is nevertheless reflected back to the bondsman as his own labor, a labor that emanates from him, even if it appears to emanate from the lord.

The autonomy of the *objects* created through the bondsman's labor provide a site for "contestation" of ownership: "this object with his mark on it implies for him that he is a being who marks things, whose activity produces a singular effect, a signature, which is irreducibly his" (Butler 1997b, 38).

Drawing on this work, I argued that conventional analyses in Maya archaeology have assumed the standpoint of the lord in relation to women's labor (Joyce 2001c). Feminist archaeologists have now argued for over a decade that the labor of women in textile production was a locus of an exercise of agency in which various forms of power were contested (Hendon 1991, 1997, 1999, 2002; Joyce 1992, 1993, 1996, 2001a, b). I suggested that textiles would have offered traces that could be read as signs of the laboring self by individual agents, the women whose labor dominant, antifeminist analyses of Maya archaeology dismiss.

Henrietta Moore (2000, 261) prefigures precisely why analyses like these, facilitated by feminist theory of embodiment, matter:

We could not live with ourselves if our archaeology produced accounts of individuals, cultures, and societies that left no space for individuality, freedom of choice, will, self-determination, creativity, innovation, and resistance. No archaeologist could live with such a view because humans would then have no role, or very little, in the making of their own history. What then would be the point of being human?

When the topic at issue is something like gender, which is so thoroughly biologized in contemporary Western thought, the danger of assuming that observed material simply reflects natural, adaptive, or otherwise inescapable characteristics of being is high. This would be an especially unfortunate outcome for archaeology, the discipline that seeks to capture the differences of human subjectivity in societies not documented in textual sources. Feminist theories of embodiment should help ensure that archaeology makes the kind of contribution to broader feminist and anthropological theory of which it is uniquely capable.

Parts of the present chapter are based on previously published work including a paper coauthored with Elizabeth Perry (Joyce 2004; Perry and Joyce 2001). I would like to thank the editors of the volumes in which these works appeared, Margaret Breen and Warren Blumenfeld, and Lynn Meskell and Robert Preucel, for their encouragement in pursuing these arguments, and Elizabeth Perry for inviting me to collaborate with her. Julia Hendon generously commented on an earlier version of this chapter. Of course, none of these individuals is responsible for, nor necessarily in agreement with, the views expressed here. Perceptive readers will have noticed the echoes of other writers in my section headings; these inscribe my acknowledgement of the places where others have led and I am merely following.

Chapter 3
Gender, Genes, and the Evolution of Human Birth

Dana Walrath

The feminist critique of science has led some biological anthropologists to consider their subdiscipline wholly removed from the theories and methods of feminist anthropology. Indeed, feminist critiques of scientific investigation (Lowe and Hubbard 1983; Bleier 1984; Keller 1985; Fausto-Sterling 1985; Martin 2001) contributed to the secession of several programs in biological anthropology from departments retaining feminist influenced sociocultural emphases due to mutual objection to the methods and theories of the other subspecialty. Despite these rifts, feminist approaches have played a crucial role in biological anthropology over the past thirty years. It has provided a toolkit for biological anthropologists to use as they investigate the human body, and has contributed to paradigm shifts in paleoanthropology and primatology (Slocum 1975; Zihlman 1978, 1981, 1987; Zihlman and Tanner 1978; Tanner 1981; Dahlberg 1981; Hrdy 1981; Fedigan 1982, 1986; Small 1984; Strum and Fedigan 1997; Hager 1997) as it has in archaeology (Gero 1985, 1993; Gero and Conkey 1991). Paleoanthropological discourse on the reproductive body benefits particularly from feminist theories and methods (Hager 1997; Sperling and Beyene 1997). Paleoanthropological reconstructions of the evolution of human reproductive biology and behavior are replete with contemporary notions of gender. Further, the feminist tenet that scientific knowledge is constructed, like stories, is particularly true in paleoanthropology. Evolutionary theories depend upon a combination of empirical evidence (often in the form of fragmentary fossil remains), data gathered from extant species, and storytelling. These disparate bodies of knowledge are joined together to form a coherent narrative in which the biological process of evolution accounts for specific states in the present, a creation myth or story told in the language of science (Isaac 1983; Landau 1984, 1991; Zihlman 1997). A feminist approach reveals that in addition to accounting for present biological states or facts, these stories frequently also account for social facts embedded in culture. The narrative aspect of evolutionary discourse confers upon it a powerful ability to naturalize social facts.

While scientific truths are generally refined and challenged through scientific methods such as hypothesis testing and quantitative analyses, narrative is best challenged through words. In this regard, feminist theories and methods have much to contribute to refining paleoanthropological discourse, particularly when its focus is the reproductive behavior and biology of humans. The present work combines feminist approaches with paleoanthropological inquiry in several ways. First, it takes the light shined by Martin on the gender stereotypes that she described as "sleeping metaphors" hidden in scientific descriptions of reproductive biology and focuses it on evolutionary discourse about childbirth and differences between the sexes. "Waking up" these sleeping metaphors Martin says, "is one way of robbing them of their power to naturalize our social conventions about gender" (Martin 1991, 498). The paleoanthropological notion of inevitable difficulty of human childbirth and related theories about biological differences between the sexes serve to naturalize Euro-American gender norms and the related cultural practices surrounding childbirth.

A basic tenet from feminist anthropology is that all forms of knowledge, including scientific knowledge, need to be contextualized culturally and historically. This tenet stands in opposition to evolutionary studies engaged with a search for universal biobehavioral truths that apply to all humans. As Ginsburg and Rapp stated after twenty years of feminism had already influenced academic discourse on reproductive biology, "No aspect of reproductive biology can be considered apart from the larger social context that frames it" (1992, 330). In the case of paleoanthropological discourse about human childbirth and sex differences, this means a thorough examination of the historical development of theories about the evolution of human reproductive biology and related childbirth practices. Ultimately, such analyses allow for the practice of a feminist science.

As part of building a feminist biological anthropology of the future, I will propose a potential genetic mechanism for successful human adaptation to the childbirth process. Comparative analysis of the androgen receptor gene suggests an alternative narrative for the evolution of the human pattern of sex differences that may underlie successful adaptation to childbirth. This hypothesis confers agency upon the human female at the level of biologically and symbolically powerful genes. Like other paleoanthropological models, this hypothesis also combines data with narrative. However, it differs by suggesting an active biological role for females that parallels the contemporary social roles achieved through feminism.

Gender and the Human Birth Narrative

In paleoanthropology, human evolution is conceived of as a process in which culture change gradually replaces biological change as our species' primary means of adaptation. Landau suggested that this paleoanthropological story takes the heroic epic narrative form in which the evolving hominid faces natural challenges and tests which he is culturally, but not biologically, equipped to endure (1984, 1991). I use "he" rather than he/she very deliberately to describe this evolutionary narrative because the story of the biological evolution of males and females tends to differ. As feminist scholars have noted, paleoanthropological hypotheses accounting for the human pattern of sex differences and the evolution of sex-specific biological tasks are infused with notions of male action and competence and female passivity, inadequacy, and even distress (Tanner and Zihlman 1976; Zihlman 1978; Dahlberg 1981; Gero 1985; Gero and Conkey 1991; Hager 1997). The story of the evolution of human childbirth epitomized the paleoanthropological depiction of a distressed female body. In this regard, the evolutionary story of human birth provides another component of heroic epics: a gendered "damsel in distress" in need of rescue. Though numerous feminist scholars have challenged the ways gender norms have shaped childbirth practices in the present (Kitzinger 1972; Jordan 1993 [1978]; Oakley 1984; Rothman 1982; Scully 1980; Shaw 1974; Martin 1987; Davis-Floyd 1992; Ginsberg and Rapp 1991; Davis-Floyd and Sargent 1996), the story of the evolution of human birth was not challenged until recently.

Reconstruction of the birth process in human evolutionary studies is a tale of compromise. In this narrative, females are beset by inevitable difficulty during childbirth due to the opposing biological requirements of bipedal locomotion and large brain size. This story emerged as part of the "new physical anthropology," a paradigm that developed in the middle of the twentieth century in response to the evolutionary synthesis—the combination of population genetics, advances in molecular genetics, and the Darwinian evolutionary theory (Washburn 1951). In the new physical anthropology, researchers focused their attention on explaining biobehavioral traits in terms of their contribution to human adaptation. Paleoanthropologists began to turn their attention to differences between the sexes infusing their discussions of biological difference with culturally established gender norms. A feedback loop established between tool use and increasing brain size was said to confer intellectual advantages to males and birthing difficulties to females. In a classic paper titled, "Tool Use and Human Evolution," Washburn stated, "Adaptation to bipedal locomotion decreased the size of the birth canal at the same time that the exigencies of tool use selected for larger brains" (1960). The competing demands of bipedalism and childbirth left humans with what Washburn termed the human "obstetrical dilemma" (1960, 74). In another *Scientific American* article from this same period, Krogman also defined human birthing difficulty as a "scar of evolution," stating, "There can be no doubt that many of the obstetrical problems of Mrs. H. Sapiens are due to the combination of a narrower pelvis and a bigger head in the species" (1951, 55).

Similarly, physical anthropologists of this period began to cite male pelvic morphology as representing the pure unfettered adaptation to bipedal locomotion. Napier, for example, measured the reduced biomechanical efficiency of the female stride as seen in the side-to-side displacement of the hips when walking (1967). Thus, the functional morphology of the female pelvis is interpreted as a strained compromise between the structural requirements of bipedalism and those of childbirth. This notion continues to be taught in many introductory texts and references.

For example, the *Cambridge Encyclopedia of Human Evolution* entry titled Posture and Childbirth states, "the anatomical differences between the human male and female pelvises that result from this conflict of functions, because of the childbirth needs of the female, led to less efficient bipedalism in the female—as shown today by the differences between male and female Olympic running and jumping records" (Jones, Martin, and Pilbeam 1992, 92). It continues, "bipedal females had the complication of having to give birth to a fetus with a large head" and "humans may have problems at childbirth." Delivery is described as "a maneuver calling for some effort on the part of the mother and which may need help from midwives and doctors." The paleoanthropological discourse on childbirth draws heavily upon contemporary "facts" such as Olympic records and medical complications of "Mrs. H. Sapiens" (i.e., a married woman giving birth in a hospital) to prove that the female pelvis is in distress. This occurs in part because very little empirical data from the fossil record exist to support the contention of human birthing difficulty as an evolutionary legacy (Walrath 1997, 2003). A handful of adult pelvic remains exist for the past five million or so years of human evolutionary history and no complete remains of neonates are preserved. The birth process itself, of course, does not fossilize.

Analyzing paleoanthropology's human birth narrative from a historical perspective opens a door to creating an alternative human birth narrative. Rather than positing that bipedalism and encephalization caused an inevitable obstetrical dilemma over millions of years, I suggest that the obstetrical dilemma was established through cultural processes over the last hundred or so years. These cultural processes can be documented in three phases of academic exchanges between paleoanthropology and biomedical obstetrics during the pre- and postfeminist twentieth century.

Constructing the Human Birth Narrative

The period between 1920 and 1950, when Euro-American birth moved from the home into the hospital (Kitzinger 1972; Jordan 1993 [1978]; Oakley 1984; Rothman 1982; Scully 1980; Shaw 1974; Martin 1987), marked the first phase of cooperation between obstetricians and biological anthropologists. With the medicalization of childbirth, X-ray techniques were developed to measure the adequacy of the maternal pelvis for childbirth (Ball 1938; Caldwell, Moloy, and D'Esopo 1934; Mengerts 1948; Moir 1946; Thoms 1941). Obstetricians designing these roentgenological methods relied heavily on osteological and anatomical knowledge provided by anthropologists. For example, Caldwell and Moloy, who provided the typological description of female pelvic anatomy (1933) that endures in most major obstetrical texts, worked extensively with Alex Hrdlička, the founder of the American Association of Physical Anthropology, and director of the U.S. National Museum at the time. The photographs of bony pelves in their original papers appear courtesy of Hrdlička (Caldwell and Moloy 1933; Caldwell, Moloy, and D'Esopo 1934).

The names of the pelvic types clinicians defined were obtained from the designations made by Turner in the nineteenth century: *Anthropoid*—as in the anthropoid primates because of a large antero-posterior diameter, which was contrasted with the flattened *platypelloid* pelvis, designated by these authors as "ultra human." The *gynecoid* pelvis or typical female pelvis contrasted with the *android* or male pelvis, though all types are found in women. These types came to be used in obstetrics to predict birthing difficulty. Though childbirth was not a concern of the discipline, physical anthropologists were the osteological experts who provided a morphological foundation for physicians interested in assessing obstetric risk.

The early twentieth-century emphasis in physical anthropology was on racial difference (Hooton 1926). Males and females were typically combined in skeletal collections and comparisons were typically made between so-called racial groups (Hoyme 1957). This anthropological emphasis on racial difference was incorporated into the developing biomedical approach to childbirth. Take for example, Turner's statement cited in the medical literature that the anthropoid pelvic type "was more frequently observed in the lower races of man and presented a 'degraded' or animalized arrangement" and that the gynecoid pelvic shape was "characteristic of the more civilized and advanced races of mankind" (Turner 1886 in Caldwell and Moloy 1933, 498). The racialized typological approach integral to early twentieth-century physical anthropology moved into biomedical obstetrics through the work of Caldwell and colleagues, and persists in contemporary obstetrical literature and practice (Cunningham et al. 2001; Scott et al. 1999). While one could argue that this racism was a part of society at large at that time, the specificity with which particular texts and ideas from some physical anthropologists were introduced within obstetrics documents an exchange of ideas among scholars. Further, some anthropologists (Boas 1905, for example) had already begun to challenge the notion of biological race by early in the century. Nevertheless, these notions of pelvic types were imported from physical anthropology into biomedicine, forming a fundamental part of the risk-oriented biomedical approach.

Phase two featured a transition from race to sex as the focus of anthropological inquiry. By the mid-twentieth century, hospital birth had become a standard cultural practice and anthropologists focused increasingly on sex differences. Schultz's 1949 paper "Sex Differences in the Pelves of Primates" perfectly captures this transition. Schulz compared the measurements of male and female pelvic bones of a variety of primate species to those seen in "two races of man." A series of drawings and diagrams compare only the adult female "Negro" to adult female apes and monkeys. Schulz goes on to propose that in species in which the fit between the newborn and pelvic size is tight, "any enlargement of the pelvic ring of the female may be a necessary requirement for the successful passage of the newborn and represent the result of natural selection" (1949, 412).

While Schulz maintained the notion of racial difference in the shape and size of bones in his paper, he also strove to interpret female pelvic anatomy through the lens of adaptation as part of the "new physical anthropology." As these scientific observations were meshed with the cultural practice of hospitalized birth, successful adaptation to the tight fit Schulz observed in "monkeys and man" through pelvic dimorphism changed to a notion of incomplete adaptation and an inevitable "obstetrical dilemma."

In this prefeminist paleoanthropology, the steady increase in brain size over the last two million years of human evolutionary history was thought to benefit males, while leaving females with birthing difficulties. Women evolved in positive directions only by what Fedigan has called the "coat tails" theory of evolution, pulled along to improved biological states only because of sharing genes with men (1986). This evolutionary narrative had practical consequences. By maintaining that the female pelvis is not fully equipped to bear large-brained young without assistance, the "obstetrical dilemma" of paleoanthropology effectively provided a scientific rationale for the medicalization of birth. Obstetric practice then appeared necessary for what evolutionary forces had left undone in the female body.

In the 1970s a number of very capable women entered the field of paleoanthropology, broadening evolutionary studies to include a focus on women in the past. Slocum's paper titled "Woman the Gatherer: Male Bias in Anthropology" (1975) was followed by a series of scholarly works elaborating on the importance of female activities for human evolution. This work forced a reexamination of existing "Man the Hunter" scenarios (Lee and Devore 1968) and recognized the importance of scavenging in early human evolution as well as female gathering and other activities (Zihlman 1978, 1981, 1987; Zihlman and Tanner 1978; Tanner 1981; Dahlberg 1981). Female paleoanthropologists began to document that women were not being "uplifted" as a consequence of their association with progressively evolving men. Rather, the human species evolved with each sex making its own important contribution to the process.

In response to these feminist influences, three interrelated biocultural solutions to the "obstetrical dilemma" were proposed by paleoanthropologists in the 1980s and 1990s: the evolution of secondary altriciality, a singular human birth mechanism, and obligate midwifery. Each of these solutions to the obstetrical dilemma drew heavily on the biomedical formulation of childbirth, and has become part of the evidence for the biological problem they ostensibly evolved to solve. This marked the third phase of cooperation between biomedicine and paleoanthropology. Because these solutions to the obstetrical dilemma were steeped in biomedical birth practices, gender norms were also embedded in these models.

Secondary altriciality, the relative immaturity of the human newborn was widely cited as a biological solution to obstetric constraint (Trinkaus 1984; Trevathan 1987, 1988; Martin and MacLarnon 1990; Rosenberg 1992; Ruff 1995; Rosenberg and Trevathan 1996). Secondary altriciality is considered unique to encephalized hominids and is said not to appear in human evolution until the genus *Homo*. In this model, the survival of the immature, helpless, immobile baby humans occurs because encephalization gives their parents, culture-bearing humans, enhanced caregiving skills (Lovejoy 1981; Trinkaus 1984; Trevathan 1987; Rosenberg 1992; Rosenberg and Trevathan 1996; Ruff 1995).

Still, birth is depicted as difficult, in part due to secondary altriciality itself. Nonhuman primate babies have been observed to use their hands to pull themselves out of the birth canal (Trevathan 1987), while human newborns are considered inert. However, I suggest that the depiction of the helpless human neonate stems from the biomedical formulation of birth in which infants are sedated via anesthesia delivered to their mothers because of cultural practices and beliefs about pain associated with labor. Without anesthesia, human newborns are remarkably alert and if left alone can find their way to their mother's breast and initiate suckling independently (Righard and Alade 1990).

The second solution, the evolution of the singular human birth mechanism, a series of orientations and turns taken by the fetus as it exits the birth canal, corresponds exactly to the biomedically defined "cardinal movements of labor." Contemporary biomedical practice does not allow labor to progress with mechanisms other than this singular normal (Cunningham et al. 2001; Gimovsky and Hennigan 1995; To and Li 2000). Concurrently, anthropologists came to interpret rotation and emergence with the newborn head facing away from the mother as evidence of the relative difficulty of human birth compared to that of the nonhuman primates (Trevathan 1987, 1988, 1996; Rosenberg 1992; Rosenberg and Trevathan 1996, 2001, 2002). By contrast, in the not so very distant past, a variety of fetal presentations were considered normal in biomedicine, as they are today outside of the biomedical context (Banks 1998; Cosminsky 1976; Davis-Floyd and Sargent 1997; Gaskin 1990; Kitzinger 1972, MacCormack 1994 [1982]; Rooks 1997).

Trevathan proposed the third solution to the obstetrical dilemma, "obligate midwifery," a requirement for assisted birth in humans. Though at times this theory emphasizes emotional support as the key ingredient of assistance, it cites rotation, face-down fetal emergence, and secondary altriciality as consequences of the anatomical changes of the pelvis associated with bipedalism. Trevathan states:

The anatomical change more important to my argument here requires that the human infant emerge from the birth canal facing *away* from the mother . . . With the origins of bipedalism the risks of mortality from unattended birth became greater. . . . With encephalization in the genus *Homo* (about two million years ago) the already tight fit became even tighter, although one of the compromises to the conflict between selection for large brains and narrow birth canals may have been to delay most brain growth to the postnatal period. (1996, 82)

Each of these paleoanthropological solutions to the obstetrical dilemma ultimately reinforces the notion of flawed female reproductive biology. Culture, in the form of birth attendants for vulnerable mothers and babies, steps in to rescue females and their young from the danger imposed by their biology. The scientific and obstetric literature continues to embrace a notion of the evolutionary basis of human birthing difficulty as seen in recent articles by paleoanthropologists in *Scientific American* (Rosenberg and Trevathan 2001) and *British Journal of Obstetrics and Gynecology* (Rosenberg and Trevathan 2002).

Because the notion of an inherent obstetrical dilemma derived more from the historical cooperation between paleoanthropology and biomedical obstetrics than empirical data, I have proposed its abandonment (1997, 2003). In its place paleoanthropologists can turn their attention to identification of biological mechanisms accounting for successful childbirth in our species that do not rely upon culture. Hager has proposed one such model by suggesting that sex differences of the pelvis evolved two million years ago as human brain size increased (1989). Other studies have documented successful female adaptation to childbirth through sex-specific patterns of pelvic growth (LaVelle 1995) and scaling between body size and dimensions of the birth canal (Walrath and Glantz 1996; Walrath 1997). Before exploring another potential biological mechanism for successful adaptation to childbirth, I would like to explore how feminist paleoanthropology has deconstructed another gendered story that is told in human evolutionary studies—the evolution of sex differences in body size or sexual dimorphism—because this story also impacts the human birth narrative.

Gender and Sexual Dimorphism

As stated above, the new physical anthropology of the middle of the twentieth century ushered in the study of sex differences. These studies concerned the shape and size of a variety of measurable body parts and proposed theories to explain these differences. This study of sexual dimorphism (two morphs or shapes) refers to differences in shape and size of biological features indirectly impacting reproductive behavior and biology. The study of sexual dimorphism tends to be gendered because the hypotheses proposed by physical anthropologists and their colleagues in evolutionary biology to account for sex differences include speculations about the behavioral implications of reproduction, the separate reproductive "strategies" for males and females (Fedigan 1986; Hager 1987; Zihlman 1987, 1997).

In these scenarios (e.g., Trivers 1972; Clutton-Brock 1985), larger male size is emphasized as it is said to serve males in their competition for access to mates. Male reproductive success is thought to be optimized through a strategy of "spreading seed," that is, by being sexually active with as many females as possible. Females, on the other hand, are considered gatekeepers who optimize their reproductive success through caring for individual offspring. According to these models, in species where male-male competition is high, males will be considerably larger than females. In monogamous species, males and females will be of similar sizes.

Invoking distinct behavioral strategies to account for sex differences dates back further than the "new physical anthropology." It began with Darwin's theory of sexual selection (1871). He proposed that the morphological specializations of males such as horns and vibrant plumage, and in the case of humans, intelligence and tools use, demonstrated selection acting upon the male to aid in the competition for mates.

In his book, *The Descent of Man and Selection in Relation to Sex,* Darwin stated, "Thus man has ultimately become superior to woman. It is indeed fortunate that the law of equal transmission of characters to both sexes prevails with mammals. Otherwise, it is probable that man would have become as superior in mental endowment to woman as the peacock is in ornamental plumage to the peahen" (Darwin 1871 in Fedigan 1986, 29).

Fedigan noted that this model of sexual selection incorporated the Victorian gender norms of Darwin's time: the passive female and active male. The updated versions of Darwin's theory of sexual selection still explain dimorphism and sex-specific behavior as a result of distinct reproductive strategies for each sex. They also consider male size the active variable in the cross-species analyses of dimorphism in body size. Large size is said to help males win this competition for access to mates. By contrast, animal groups that practice monogamy and where male-male competition is low, selective pressure for increased male body size is said to be low. Females remain passive in these models, with their size limited by the gendered relationship between food and female reproductive biology.

For example, during the same historical era in which paleoanthropologists were naming australopithecine specimens after rail-thin fashion models, this literature emphasized nutritional burdens borne by females. Evolutionary biologist Richard Dawkins characterized "female exploitation" as beginning with an egg saddled with the burden of providing nutrients to the growing embryo (1976, 153). Conversely, in adult life, the discourse on sexual dimorphism posits overall female body size as constrained by the extreme nutritional requirements of reproduction. The number of calories required to sustain a pregnancy was calculated at a shocking 80,000 and lactation at an extra 1,000 or so calories per day (Frisch 1988). While larger female size might serve well for childbirth, sexual selection models maintained that female size was constrained by the nutritional requirements of bearing young. This belief that females can't get bigger on account of nutritional constraints of reproduction contributes further to the notion of the human "obstetrical dilemma."

Sexual Dimorphism Across Human Evolutionary History

Interestingly, sex differences in body size appear to have decreased over the course of human evolutionary history. Paleoanthropological interpretations of this observation have also tended to reify the same gender norms. For example, in a highly cited paper, Owen Lovejoy proposed that the reduction of sexual dimorphism was related to a pattern of evolution toward monogamy (1981). Coopting the "Women the Gatherer" model while using the same framework of active males and passive females employed by Darwin (and criticized by feminist scholars), Lovejoy suggested that females evolved to stay around home bases tending their young while males provisioned them with foods obtained through hunting, scavenging, and even gathering expeditions. Though this "food for sex" hypothesis has been challenged on a number of fronts, it is "presented in introductory and upper division textbooks, described in popular articles and books, and even featured in special television productions" (Hager 1997, 8). However, primatologists documented the abilities of female primates to provision and protect themselves and numerous primate societies in which the relationship between male competition and sexual dimorphism does not hold, as well as demonstrated the lack of association between high male rank and the Darwinian currency of paternity (Hrdy 1981; Fedigan 1982; Small 1984; Goodall 1986). In addition, paleoanthropologists amassed data demonstrating other subsistence models in the past (Isaac 1983; Zihlman 1978; Zihlman and Tanner 1978). Paleoanthropologists have also demonstrated that sex differences in brain structures indicate the importance of females and their social capacities in the course of human evolution (Falk 1997). In the face of these data, the persistence of the notion that sexual dimorphism reduced as a function of evolution toward monogamy, like the obstetrical dilemma, persists only because of its ability to naturalize social conventions.

Genetics and Feminist Paleoanthropology

To the above critiques, I would like to suggest a feminist alternative: the reduction in difference in male and female body size across human evolutionary history stems from an increase in female size as part of a successful adaptation to childbirth. Comparative analysis of the androgen receptor gene suggests a possible genetic mechanism for successful childbirth through the reduction of size dimorphism in humans. Together these threads constitute an example of a feminist paleoanthropology of the future that does not abandon science but looks for new ways to use scientific investigation to understand human biology mindful of the influence of culture on the construction of scientific knowledge.

In the narrative of human evolution, human cranial capacity began to increase at a rapid rate some time after two million years ago at the same time that female size relative to male size also appears to have increased. How might this be regulated on a genetic level?

One way to study the genetic basis of the degree of sexual dimorphism is to perform cross-species comparisons of candidate genes known to be involved in sexual differentiation, in primate species with varying degrees of dimorphism. This method resembles cross-species comparisons in the shape and size of specific bones traditionally performed by biological anthropologists before such genetic analyses were technically possible. Today cross-species genetic comparisons are a standard part of biological anthropology but the questions asked using these methods can be shaped by feminist perspectives.

On a chromosomal level, male and female biology is determined by the presence of two X chromosomes in females and X and Y chromosomes in males. The Y chromosome contains genes controlling the differentiation of the testicles in males, which then start producing testosterone. Interestingly, however, the androgen hormone receptor through which testosterone exerts its effects is located on the X chromosome shared by both sexes. The role of the androgen receptor gene in sexual differentiation suggests it could be a good candidate for a modulator of dimorphism.

The androgen receptor gene's significance in clinical medicine further supports the notion of this gene as a candidate "molecular genetic regulator" of sexual dimorphism in primates. This gene constitutes the final common pathway for the effects of androgen hormones on primary and secondary sexual development of males. Mutations of this gene effectively cripple it, and the result is a genetically male XY individual who is by all outward phenotypic criteria female. Normally, androgen hormones cause the androgen receptor protein to regulate the transcription of androgen responsive genes. This gene contains a polymorphic trinucleotide (CAG) repeat segment that encodes for a polyglutamine tract in the protein affecting its function (Chamberlain, Driver, and Miesfeld 1994).

A genetic mechanism for the evolution of dimorphism must account for the continuous interspecific variation of dimorphism. For the AR gene, this possibility is best shown in accidents of nature wherein mutations of the gene result in partial defects of virilization. Normally, humans have around 17–33 CAG repeats in exon 1 of the androgen receptor gene. Males with a pathologic repeat expansion of the androgen receptor gene experience feminization, the development of breasts (gynecomastia), the atrophy of the testicles, along with a lethal degenerative disease of the nervous system called X-linked Spinal Bulbar Muscular Atrophy (La Spada et al. 1991). So far it is unknown whether variation within the normal range for this androgen receptor gene CAG repeat corresponds to varying degrees of virilization. But the diminished virilization seen in pathologic expansion of the repeat length fits with the possibility that variation in the length of this CAG repeat may exert an incremental effect on virilization in primates.

Considering that expansion of the tri-nucleotide CAG repeat in the androgen receptor gene might modulate dimorphism among primates, we set about sequencing the part of the gene that includes this CAG repeat sequence in different primate species (Walrath and Bingham 2003). The primates studied included chimps, gorillas, orangutans, gibbons, baboons, macaques, and humans. The repeat number found in the androgen receptor gene for each species was compared to the amount of dimorphism present in that species. We found a statistically significant correlation between repeat expansion and degree of body size dimorphism ($R^2 = 0.72$, $p = 0.004$) consistent with a role for the expansion of this simple sequence repeat in the evolution of primate sexual dimorphism. Species with high amounts of dimorphism have a low number of CAG repeats, while species with less dimorphism have a repeat expansion.

A couple of caveats pertain to interpreting these preliminary results. First, we have not done the molecular work to determine precisely how an expanded repeat could account for decreased virilization. We have simply used the observation of the feminization accompanying the increased repeat number and the observation that an increased repeat number leads to earlier onset and increased disease severity (Igarashi et al. 1992) to form a working hypothesis. Humans have the highest normal range in terms of numbers of CAG repeats in this part of the androgen receptor gene. Chimps and humans, species with similarly low degrees of sexual dimorphism, possess nearly identical mean CAG repeat numbers. Gorillas, the extremely dimorphic species to which humans and chimps are most closely related, possess repeat numbers like the very dimorphic old world monkeys in our sample. In humans, there is an upper limit on the number of CAG repeats in terms of viability, because above around thirty-five repeats a disease phenotype emerges.

Biologically, one of the attractive features of this hypothesis is that it provides a genetic mechanism underlying the observed continuous or stepwise variation in sexual dimorphism among species. Most importantly, because the androgen receptor gene is on the X chromosome it can affect the biology and behavior of both males and females. Reduction of sexual dimorphism in part through a concomitant increase in female size could be particularly advantageous to females as an adaptation to bearing large-brained young. The normal human range borders closely on what proves to be a pathological expansion of this repetitive sequence conferring an effective genetic liability to genetic disease at this locus in our species. Perhaps humans approach this edge because the benefits of the expanded repeat to successful childbirth outweigh the risk of disease.

While the precise mechanics of how the expanded repeat might modulate sexual dimorphism are unknown, this hypothesis contributes to the search for explanations that are less gender bound. As this and other feminist analyses have shown, scientists have tended to limit their thinking about the childbirth process and sexual dimorphism to models that fit with established gender norms. The naturalized social conventions embedded in those sleeping metaphors in science have far-reaching consequences.

Because differences in male and female size have always been theoretically cloaked in a gendered discourse of male competition and female constraint, scientific exploration of underlying mechanisms has been limited. The theory attributing the reduction of dimorphism to the evolution of monogamy and the corresponding reduction of male-male competition naturalized the prevailing social norms so well that exploration of other potential biological mechanisms seemed unnecessary. On the other hand, the androgen receptor hypothesis attributes a metaphorical biological agency to females, conferring power to a gene on the X chromosome to modulate size differences between males and females. Further, if larger female size relative to male size also permits successful childbirth in our species, this model also strikes at the core of gendered notions of female biological inadequacy as expressed in the "obstetrical dilemma."

The full biological plausibility of a relationship between the CAG repeat expansion of the androgen receptor gene and a reduction of sexual dimorphism can only be investigated if the hypothesis is opened for exploration. The connection between these two biological phenomena might be obscured more by prevailing social beliefs than by biological impossibility. Without a gendered belief that human females are destined to experience difficult childbirth due to their evolutionary history, scientists can search for biological mechanisms to account for successful adaptation to the birth process. Without a gendered belief that the reduction of sexual dimorphism is related to human evolution toward monogamy, scientists will start exploring other biological mechanisms to account for the reduction of dimorphism. Martin challenges feminists to continue to "wake up" "sleeping metaphors" in science because "making ourselves more aware of when we are projecting cultural imagery onto what we study will improve our ability to investigate and understand nature" (1991, 497).

Gendered Science and Reproductive Health

Waking up sleeping metaphors does even more than allow scientists to conduct better studies. It also impacts how scientific studies affect the lives of individuals. The "obstetrical dilemma," an idea developed through a partnership between evolutionary anthropology and biomedical obstetrics, directly affects birth practices. By perpetuating gendered notions of female incompetence, the obstetrical dilemma stirs up fears and strips individual women of the power to bear their young. Individuals taught that the combination of bipedalism and large brains leads to inevitable obstetric difficulty will undoubtedly approach the birth process with considerable trepidation. Fear slows the labor process and slowed labor leads to a variety of technological interventions, each with their own risks and costs (Rothman 1982; Rooks 1997; Davis-Floyd 1992; Jordan 1993 [1978]; Gaskin 1990; Goer 1995). Conversely, an evolutionary narrative emphasizing successful adaptation of humans to childbearing could lessen the fear surrounding childbirth and lead to easier deliveries in healthy women.

As pregnancy and childbirth became medicalized in industrialized nations, social and academic discourse on the dangers of pregnancy and childbirth provided justification for obstetrical practices. In particular, paleoanthropology provided a putative scientific basis for biomedicalization of reproduction by positing a specieswide "obstetrical dilemma" as an evolutionary legacy. This pseudoscientific story has been incorporated into biomedical knowledge and practice as "fact." The biomedical emphasis on obstetrical hazards has obscured the social, political, and economic origins of reproductive morbidity and mortality.

The medicalization of birth presents three barriers to women's reproductive rights. First, biomedical definitions of healthy parturition obfuscate the normal range of biological and cultural variation in birth. Second, technological formulations of pregnancy and childbirth effectively constrict women's range of reproductive choices. Third, emphasis on reactive, technological solutions to complications of pregnancy and birth may displace preventive efforts aimed at ultimate causes of reproductive hazards.

Women in the developing world and disenfranchised subpopulations in industrialized nations face relatively increased hazards in pregnancy and childbirth. High rates of morbidity and mortality related to the complications of pregnancy and childbirth reflect structural violence against women and the feminization of poverty, rather than a specieswide obstetrical dilemma. For example, fetal pelvic disproportion in a woman of short stature can be seen as a direct intergenerational effect of child-hood malnutrition (Martorell 1989; Rush 2000). Pregnancy and birthing complications associated with sexually transmitted diseases (Manderson 1999), rickets, and osteomalacia (Angel 1978; Bergstrom 1991; Sere-nius, Elidrissy, and Dandona 1984; Stuart-Macadam 1989) also demon-strate the complex interaction between reproductive biology and the cultural position of women. Excessive medical intervention, such as unnecessary cesarean section, signifies an iatrogenic form of structural violence against women.

Thus, bringing feminist perspectives into paleoanthropological and other scientific discourse is an issue that moves beyond the academy. As Wylie has said, "feminists have a prima facie interest in the sciences and in scientific methods as, in principle, a crucial source of just the kind of understanding we need to proceed effectively in the pursuit of our goals of creating a gender-equitable world" (1997b, 36). Movement away from the gendered obstetrical dilemma, a culture-bound notion of inade-quate female biology requiring cultural intervention to perform a dis-tinctly female biological task, will improve not only the quality of scientific investigation but also the lives of women. A greater emphasis on the social, historical, and political underpinnings of reproductive dif-ficulties will advance the development of policies to promote long-term reproductive health and rights.

Part II
Subverting Heteronormativity

Chapter 4

Marriage, Matrifocality, and "Missing" Men

EVELYN BLACKWOOD

Once viewed by anthropologists as the heart of kinship, marriage has been relegated to the status of a quaint custom relevant to particular societies rather than to universal truths. But not everyone outside (or inside) anthropology has heard the news. Bringing sociological and theological views into alliance, many religious conservatives in the United States believe heterosexual marriage is their last bastion of hope in a decaying world. The more lesbians and gay men demand the right to marry, the more conservatives enshrine marriage in glowing terms as a sacred bond between a man and a woman.

Such attitudes translate directly into the current alarm about an apparent increase in female-headed, or woman-headed, households (I prefer the second term, although both are problematic as universal categories of household). Especially since 1965, when Daniel Patrick Moynihan declared the woman-headed family structure of African Americans a self-perpetuating "tangle of pathology" (United States Department of Labor 1981, 47), policymakers have viewed such households with suspicion. Research on woman-headed households worldwide in the latter part of the twentieth century seems to suggest that this suspicion is well founded. A review of the literature found that "female-headed households are common in situations of urban poverty; in societies with a high level of men's labor migration; and in situations where general insecurity and vulnerability prevail" (Moore 1988, 63). Anxieties about this apparent trend have prompted a renewed exploration, primarily outside of anthropology, for the "causes" of and "solutions" to woman-headed households. But what are these households, and why are they the focus of so much concern? Is it the poverty of these households that is truly of concern, or is it the absence of heteronormative marriage that underlies the near hysteria about woman-headed households?

To address these issues, I explore anthropology's role in creating and sustaining heteronormative marriage and family. I use the term *heteronormative* here to refer to the normative status of a marital unit containing a dominant heterosexual man, a wife, and children. Other critics have made arguments similar to mine, but I emphasize the way anthropologists created the trope of the dominant heterosexual man, what I call the "Patriarchal Man," as an explanation for systems of marriage and family. I am not the first, nor will I be the last, to use this term, but by capitalizing it I want to draw attention to its status as a cultural representation. In classic kinship theory the Patriarchal Man was envisaged as activating and controlling marriage and family. It is his shadow that continues to trouble debates about kinship and marriage. I use this trope to demonstrate that the unmarked category "man" is always already dominant and heterosexual.

Debates about kinship and marriage are not new to anthropology.[1] Some anthropologists might even consider kinship itself to be a dead issue, a point with which I and many others in critical kinship studies would disagree. In fact, despite the long struggle to denaturalize and deconstruct kinship, not all anthropologists would cede the point that marriage is an anthropological relic. As one example, in his overview of kinship, Ladislav Holy (1996) expresses a determined fondness for the importance of marriage in creating kinship. Although admitting that Claude Lévi-Strauss's model of marriage as an exchange of women is no longer tenable, he declares that "[Lévi-Strauss's] more general view that kinship perpetuates itself only through specific forms of marriage is incisive" (Holy 1996, 37), thus reinforcing the centrality of marriage within kinship and culture. As John Borneman (1996) points out in his critical review of the institution, marriage still maintains paradigmatic status within ethnology and anthropology.

I offer a critique of marriage by revisiting the discourses and theoretical assumptions associated with so-called matrifocal societies, precisely those societies in which marriage and the heterosexual conjugal couple were said to be "weak."[2] Using gender as a tool of analysis to examine the anthropological construction of matrifocality, I argue that anthropologists have relied on the trope of the dominant heterosexual man to create and sustain concepts of "marriage" and "family." By examining the discourse on matrifocality in studies of Afro-Caribbean and Minangkabau households, I show how it is the "missing man," the dominant heterosexual man, who is the key to the construction and perpetuation of the matrifocal concept and, by extension, the motor of marriage, family, and kinship. I argue that, despite an ongoing critique of marriage and family, the concept of "marriage" continues to operate as a discourse to devalue, denormalize, and negate other forms of relatedness in which men are absent or ancillary.

The Missing Man in Matrifocality

In this chapter, I focus on two geographical areas in which the term *matrifocality* was used, the Afro-Caribbean region, which is neither culturally homogeneous nor unchanging but has served as the testing ground for early attempts to conceptualize matrifocality, and West Sumatra, Indonesia, an area that is known for its matrilineal practices. In the Afro-Caribbean context the term was coined generally to mark woman-headed households. The label "matrifocal" was applied to some matrilineal societies, particularly by Nancy Tanner (1974) in her efforts to make sense of a wide range of kinship practices in which women were focal.

In the years since it was first used by Raymond Smith in the Afro-Caribbean context, the term matrifocality spawned a whole new topical domain. Smith used the term matrifocal "to convey that it is women *in their role as mothers* who come to be the *focus* of relationships, rather than head of the household as such" (emphasis in original) (1996, 43).[3] Unlike Smith, Tanner defined matrifocality as a situation in which women, as mothers, have "economic and political power within the kin group" (1974, 132). The debates that raged over the definition of matrifocality subsided in the 1980s, allowing the concept to slink off the stage with certain issues unresolved. The failure to come to terms with some of the presumptions behind the concept have allowed it to be resurrected in the terms *female-headed*, or *woman-headed, households.* Woman-headed households have achieved renewed importance, albeit negatively, as a supposed source of poverty in the era of global capitalism.[4] Although matrifocal and woman-headed households are distinguished analytically in the literature, the first term readily slides conceptually into the second because both types include households in which men are supposedly missing. The term *woman-headed household* is usually reserved for households in which men, as husbands, are absent, not just marginal, as they are said to be in matrifocal households (see Geisler 1993). I do not distinguish between these two terms here because the same assumptions underlie both concepts.

Studies of working-class Afro-Caribbean families in the 1950s and 1960s attempted to classify the forms of households and kin groupings practiced there. Of primary concern in these studies was the form and durability of the conjugal unit. Equally important was the effort to ascertain why so many women were heads of households. A range of terms was concocted to identify the various forms of heterosexual relations found among Afro-Caribbean families. In his early work, Raymond Smith (1956) identified eleven forms. Other researchers devised additional terms, but the more common designations used, in addition to *married, single, widowed,* and *divorced,* were *common-law marriage, stable unions, visiting unions,* and *casual relationships,* each marking the permanence or impermanence of relationship between the woman designated as head and a man.[5] The relationships were also described as being unstable or in constant flux. Explanations for women's position as household head were attributed primarily to men's absence because of labor migration or poor and unstable economic conditions.[6] Relationships within matrifocal households were defined according to their genealogical connection to the putative head.

Feminist critiques pointed out how these representations of Afro-Caribbean households relied on an assumption of the universality of the (Western) nuclear family and the normality of middle-class marriage with a stable husband provider (see Barrow 1996; Olwig 1981). By attending to the diversity of households in Afro-Caribbean communities, they demonstrated the uselessness of labels such as "matrifocality" as a descriptor for one region, let alone all of the Afro-Caribbean region with its multiplicity of histories and cultures. Feminist researchers documented households shared by two adult kinswomen (sisters or mother and daughter) and their children (Barrow 1986), by consanguineal units of related kin (Gonzalez 1984), and by adult kinswomen with kinsmen and close women friends who were regularly present (see Bolles 1996; Monagan 1985). Carol Stack's (1974) work on urban African American households is also instructive in this regard. Stack was the first anthropologist to argue against the "pathology" label used by Moynihan (United States Department of Labor 1965) to describe U.S. households headed by African American women. She argued that, because Moynihan's data were based on census statistics, they failed to accurately reflect African American domestic organization. She illustrated the vitality and flexibility of extended kin relations in these households, which were typically three-generation units that shifted over time and included members who were not always physically present. These findings underscore the critical importance of networks of kinswomen, related men, and friends, within and across households, in the constitution and viability of families and households.

Given the debates about matrifocality and the demonstrated complexity of relationships found in supposedly matrifocal societies, what has happened to the term? According to the *Dictionary of Anthropology,* matrifocal households are "structured around the mother and . . . the father is absent or plays a relatively limited role" (Barfield 1997, 313). Drawing on Raymond Smith's work, Holy defines a matrifocal family as a "fleeting and tenuous relationship between a man and a woman and her children . . . in the Caribbean in which women and their children form the core of many households. A man may be attached to the woman only temporarily, usually as her lover but not necessarily as a 'father' to her children" (1996, 310). In one ethnographic study, *matrifocality* was used to signify broadly a temporary situation in which kinswomen and nearby women neighbors visit, share food, and work closely together while the men are away on a trade expedition (see Rasmussen 1996).[7] What continues to be either implicit or explicit in these definitions is the failed heterosexual couple with its missing man. These definitions suggest a longing for the one who should be the primary earner, the one in control and in charge, in fact, the Patriarchal Man.

Although ostensibly about women, the concept of "matrifocal households" is an ongoing conversation about the "missing" man. Matrifocal households were identified and designated as nonnormative forms of household because of the absence not just of a permanent married heterosexual couple but, more precisely, the absence of a *husband*. And, yet, much of the research in the 1980s and 1990s on working-class black and Afro-Caribbean families clearly showed that these families were groups of kin and close friends that included men but were not defined by the entry or exit of a man in a heterosexual relationship with a family member. According to Stack (1974), households changed because of births and deaths within the kin group. In fact, in Afro-Caribbean households married couples might be present as well as unmarried heterosexual couples.

So, if there were reproductive heterosexual couples, even of limited duration, and fathers who had ongoing contact with their children in these kin groupings, why the concern over these families? It was not only the loss of the normative heterosexual family of a coresiding man, woman, and children but also the absence of the dominant heterosexual man that led researchers to regard matrifocal families as nonnormative. Rather than recognizing and valuing the actual relationships in these households, this narrative of loss sought to explain only why men, as husbands, were not providers and heads of these households. In fact, even many feminist researchers, including Stack, evinced concern about the "weak" position of black men in matrifocal families. The hidden presumption was that men not only should be present but also dominant within the family. The concern for men's "weakness" or absence in matrifocal families, despite men's actual presence and active heterosexual relationships, derives explicitly from classic kinship theory's expectation that men should have control of women and children. The concept of "matrifocality" created a type of household and kin relationship that foreclosed other possibilities by continually turning attention to the missing Patriarchal Man.

In fact, what actually turns up missing because of the trope of the Patriarchal Man is men in forms of relatedness other than that of heterosexual dominance. As the Afro-Caribbean literature from the 1970s on indicates, men were always present in these families, as adult sons, boyfriends, brothers, fathers, stepfathers, uncles, and friends. The concept of the "black extended family" (Shimkin, Shimkin, and Frate 1978) or the "kin-based household grouping" (Stack 1974), which included kinsmen and friends, was clearly articulated by researchers but failed to dislodge the centrality of the heteronormative family.[8] Men in these kin networks cooperated with and assisted in the economic and social lives of their kin, but they were neither dominant nor decision makers. Few stories have been told about these men's lives because they have been viewed as failures, as men who did not attain the patriarchal norm. Consequently, anthropology's study of men and masculinity has yet to attend to the diversity of men's gender relations.[9]

Not surprisingly, when women's sexuality "strayed" from the heterosexual, it was also attributed to the missing man. Studies of the Afro-Caribbean region from the 1950s and 1960s drew on the legacy of classic kinship theory's presumptive masculine heterosexuality to marginalize relationships between women. M. G. Smith mentions only in passing that lesbianism is "partially institutionalized" in Carriacou, where "women who practice such homosexual relations are referred to in the French patois as madivines or zami" (1962, 199, 200). His informants told him that *madivines* could be married or unmarried, generally had heterosexual relations, as well, and were often mothers. Smith comments that women were likely to establish relations with other women "during their husband's absence overseas" (1962, 199). Smith's assumptions echo Yehudi Cohen's (1953) earlier analysis of Jamaican women's interpersonal relationships. Cohen claimed that, according to informants, once heterosexual opportunities appear, the homosexual partners are discarded. Relying on a heterosexual deprivation theory, both Smith and Cohen assumed that same-sex practices would occur only in instances of deprivation of the other sex.[10]

The presence of women in same-sex relationships in Afro-Caribbean extended kin networks and families continues to be misrecognized as outside of normative kin groupings. Part of the reason for the marginalization of these relationships can be attributed to discriminatory attitudes within the research context that make inclusion of such data difficult for anthropologists. Most accounts of women in same-sex relationships indicate that these women also had boyfriends. But so persuasive is the trope of the dominant heterosexual man that researchers tend to treat same-sex relationships as less consequential even than those with temporary boyfriends. Stories by Afro-Caribbean and African American writers provide ample evidence not only of lesbian relationships in the Caribbean islands but also of women partners who help raise children and are considered part of the extended kin group long after the children are adults.[11]

Gloria Wekker's (1999; 2006, 105) work focuses specifically on the *mati* work of Afro-Surinamese working-class women in the city of Paramaribo, Suriname. Mati are women who have sexual relationships with men and with women. Although some mati, especially older women, do not have sex with men anymore, younger mati have a variety of arrangements with men, such as common-law marriage or visiting relationships. Mati relationships between women mostly take the form of visiting relationships, although some women couples and their children live together (Wekker 1999). According to Wekker, the mati relationship "is embedded in a rich flow of reciprocal obligations, which include the sharing of everyday concerns, the raising of children, nurturing, emotional support, and sexual pleasure" (1999, 127). Crucially, whether "visiting" or not, mati relationships constitute and are constitutive of extended kin networks, participating in the same flow of sociality and intimacy found in non-mati households.

The discourse of matrifocality (and woman-headed households) in the Afro-Caribbean context recalls classic kinship theory's assumptions about the centrality not only of marriage and family but also of the Patriarchal Man. The expectation lingers that households and extended kin groups should include a heterosexual couple in which a man is dominant. Because matrifocal Afro-Caribbean households are generally not organized around a heterosexual man and, despite the fact that they may include heterosexual couples who are present for varying lengths of time, they are viewed as problematic departures from the heteronormative family, rather than as viable forms of household constituted through women. Likewise, the headship women are accorded in woman-headed households is rendered meaningful only in conjunction with men's absence. This myopic view works to obscure other relations present within and beyond households, whether of kinswomen, kinsmen, close friends, or same-sex couples.

The "Problem" with Marriage in West Sumatra

The discourse on matrifocal societies in the Afro-Caribbean context shares certain strong similarities with the discourse on matrilineal societies, such as the Minangkabau in West Sumatra, Indonesia, who have been called "matrifocal" because of the large number of so-called woman-headed households in rural villages.[12] In the Minangkabau case, studies of village life sought to explain and debate the focal position of women in social, economic, and kin relations.[13] Examining the discourse about Minangkabau matriliny, then, offers another avenue to think about the centrality of heteronormative marriage and family in anthropology. As with Afro-Caribbean extended kin groups, I show how it is the "missing man," the dominant heterosexual man, who is the key to the construction and perpetuation of the "puzzle" of matriliny.

As were other so-called matrifocal societies, the Minangkabau were said to have weak marriages because of the problematic position of the husband. A Minangkabau man at marriage generally moves into his wife's natal household. Assumptions about men's proper place as husbands have led many an anthropologist to focus on the "plight" of the husband in matrilineal societies. Since colonial times, men of West Sumatra and Negeri Sembilan (in Malaysia, an area with ancestral ties to the Minangkabau) have come under scrutiny, if not outright ridicule, for living in their wives' houses and "letting" their mothers-in-law "call the shots." Across Malaysia, the practice of husbands living in their wives' extended kin household is jokingly referred to as "queen control" (Peletz 1994; Stivens 1996). Kinship theorists considered the conjugal bond in matrilineal societies to be "weak" for several reasons: the assumed tension and struggle for power between the husband and the mother's brother, the "interference" of the mother-in-law, and the demands of the husband's own natal lineage.

Attempts to resolve the "problem" of women's control of houses and land were directed, as in other matrifocal cases, at the husband's position within the household. Minangkabau men are well known for leaving their home villages in search of fortune (see Kahn 1980; Kato 1982; Naim 1985). Several anthropologists have proposed that Minangkabau men's migration (*merantau*) is in part responsible for Minangkabau women's position of power within households and lineages. Cecilia Ng suggested that the relative absence of men due to migration "enhances women's position" (1987, 70). Mochtar Naim argued that migration left too few men to work in the fields so that "women are *forced* to make decisions without consulting the men" (1985, 116, emphasis added). Here the absence of the husband, the missing man, is presented as the reason for women's control.

The story that men are often away in search of economic fortune prompted a discourse of moral economy by Minangkabau men that associated women's land rights with men's (brothers') altruism. In this scenario, women "are given" land because their husbands are unreliable or absent and their brothers have other forms of income available to them. This refrain is voiced by men in West Sumatra and Negeri Sembilan. Michael Peletz notes that, in Negeri Sembilan, "women are believed to require greater subsistence guarantees than men partly because they are held to be less flexible, resourceful, and adaptive than men" (1994,

23). Women must have resources to fall back on, so he was told, because they may not be able to depend on their husbands.

Some Minangkabau men point to Islamic precepts that enjoin men to protect women. The Minangkabau are devoutly Islamic with a long history of resistance and accommodation to different Islamic schools of thought. In his *adat* writings, the Minangkabau scholar and Islamic cleric Dt. Rajo Penghulu asserted that women have use (benefit) of resources, which is justified by invoking a gender hierarchy of control attributed to Islamic law (see Blackwood 2001).[14] In this case, it is Islam that is said to enjoin brothers to step in and ensure that women are taken care of by "giving" them the land and houses.

The discourse about women's rights to property in matrilineal societies has usually been taken at face value by anthropologists. These claims, however, draw on assumptions about marriage and dominant masculine heterosexuality that are then used to explain women's control in the absence of the Patriarchal Man. Rather than reflecting a moral economy in which brothers give up rights to protect their sisters, these claims reflect the tensions between Islamic and state discourses of masculinity and marriage, which ridicule husbands for being under "queen control" and men's own matrilineal practices of cooperation with their natal kin. In effect, the claim that women need protection allows men (who are not dominant in their conjugal relationships) to secure their own masculinity by asserting their agency and control over women who are their sisters. I am not suggesting that all men make this claim but that the discourse is available as a justification for and continuation of matrilineal practices that are not in line with state and Islamic ideologies. Thus, men's claim of altruism can be understood within a larger context of state and Islamic discourses that encourage and, in fact, demand such explanations to preserve masculinist practices.

The assumed connection between migration and women's control of houses and land is another misreading of kin relationships. The rural village that was the site of my study has a strong economy based on rice farming; it has not suffered from heavy out-migration.[15] According to my research, migration from one hamlet in the village in 1990 averaged 21 percent of men and 17 percent of women. The ratio of adult women to adult men in the hamlet is 55 percent to 45 percent.[16] Crucially, during the main child-rearing years (ages twenty-six to forty), the numbers of men and women in the village are equal. Household composition figures also show that most households (85 percent) have resident, working men, usually husbands, who contribute to household resources, but married brothers and unmarried sons living at home also help their mothers and sisters financially or with their labor. As the numbers demonstrate, this village has not experienced a massive out-migration of men. Minangkabau women in this village are not left behind to manage as best they can without men. In fact, men's ability to leave is often dependent on the willingness of their kinswomen to support them in their ventures. The discourse of missing men in this instance functions to foreground and normalize the conjugal unit and the importance of the husband's position while diverting attention from and obscuring the relations among consanguineal kin, particularly mothers and daughters but also brothers and sons.

Kin Relations in Matrihouses

Assumptions about marriage and conjugal couples prompted a discourse about matrilineal kin groups that secured the validity and importance of the husband and the conjugal couple even in their subordinate positions. Rural Minangkabau kin groups constitute a form of relatedness primarily on the basis of the mother-daughter line and its extended kin, both women and men, and only secondarily on the basis of marriage and conjugal ties. This statement does not deny that the Minangkabau consider marriage essential for creating affinal ties and producing lineal heirs. Full adulthood is achieved only through marriage and childbearing, a view supported by Islamic beliefs. A better view of marriage, however, comes from examining Minangkabau kin groups and the intertwining of men's positions as husbands and sons.[17]

In rural Minangkabau households one can find multiple forms of kin groupings, including nuclear households and extended households.[18] Nuclear households are composed of wife, husband, and children, whereas those kin groups associated with extended households of three to four generations are centered on a core group of kinswomen.[19] In extended households, a son moves out at marriage to live with his wife; a daughter remains in her mother's household after marriage and shares the house, the land, and the food produced. I use the term *matrihouse* to refer to the extended kin group living in one house. The resident group in such households is usually composed of a senior woman, her husband, her married and unmarried daughters, and her daughters' husbands and children. In 1990 there were twenty-eight matrihouses in which a senior woman and at least one married daughter were present. Husbands were present in 86 percent of these matrihouses, a figure consistent with the overall numbers of husbands in households in this village.

In matrihouses, the conjugal couple, the husband in particular, occupies an important but subsidiary position. They can consider only one room in the house, their bedroom, as theirs alone. As an in-married man, a husband is considered a permanent guest in his wife's house. He does not become incorporated into his wife's group" (Reenen 1996, 29; see also Tanner 1971). In the earlier part of the last century, a husband visited his wife's house only at night, but the effects of state, colonial, and Islamic ideologies have led to the full-time presence of husbands in their wives' houses, when not working elsewhere. Husbands' financial contributions to their wives' households go toward their children's needs and schooling costs. Husbands assist financially in ceremonial events for their wives' matrilineages, especially if those events involve their children. They also participate in the care and nurturance of their children.

In addition to his marital obligations, a Minangkabau man retains membership, responsibilities, and duties to his own natal household and kin group. As a son, he maintains close ties with his natal family throughout his life and can expect to return to his mother's house if he is divorced. Not only is he expected to provide assistance to his mother's household, but he is also an important part of all family deliberations, returning home, if possible, to participate in kin-group meetings.

Because he does not belong to his wife's sublineage, a husband is marginal to the affairs of the kin group centered in his wife's house. He cannot make decisions concerning his wife's lineage affairs, although he may be asked his opinion, especially when it concerns his children. As Sanday (2002) notes, fathers do not have authority over their children, although they typically maintain close emotional relationships with them. For her part, a woman is centrally involved with the politics of maintaining and improving the status of her household and kin group, through hosting ceremonies and ensuring good marriages for her children, among other things (see also Sanday 2002; Whalley 1998). These are concerns that her husband shares somewhat peripherally because of his interests in and responsibilities to his own lineage. Yet, even if men are divorced, as fathers they remain connected with their children and participate along with their kinswomen in ceremonies involving their offspring.

With the significant household relations moving through and managed by women, the husband and conjugal couple in the Minangkabau matrihouse unequivocally take a backseat. Households are identified with the members of the matriline occupying it, not with the conjugal unit of husband and wife. As a pair, they provide very little in the way of household resources. In the large majority of matrihouses, each member of a conjugal pair controls his or her own resources and makes separate contributions to the household, whether in cash income, land, or labor on that land. Their primary task as a couple is to provide heirs to the matriline. Even that reproductive role is somewhat limited, however, because child rearing is also carried out with the help of other kin, both women and men.

Concern with the missing man, the absent or subordinate husband, has led to the misrepresentation of kin relations in Minangkabau households. Men are present in these households and kin groups as husbands, but it is the mother-daughter and consanguineal ties that are central. My research demonstrates that men as brothers are integral to and cooperate in Minangkabau kin group relations but as husbands, they are subordinate in their wives' matrilineages. As Sanday (2002) also notes, men are proud of their roles as brothers and uncles and value the respect and security they have within their natal households.

Nuclear Households

As noted earlier, matrihouses are not the only form of household in rural Minangkabau villages. In the rural village that was the site of my study, a number of households ($n = 62$) are one- and two-generation households, the majority of which are nuclear households composed of a wife and husband with children. Because there is no senior woman explicitly present in a nuclear household to exert control over her daughter's husband, such households provide an opportunity to examine the husband-wife dynamic in a different context. Does the Patriarchal Man show up? By examining the conjugal unit in nuclear households, I show that even in this context, assumptions about marriage and men's centrality do not hold up in rural Minangkabau villages.

As in matrihouses, both husbands and wives in nuclear households engage in a variety of income-producing activities, some of which they carry out together and some separately. By averaging data on land ownership or access across all nuclear households, I found that the husband, on average, provides 23 percent and the wife 64 percent of land that is available to the household; the remainder is land that the couple has obtained jointly. Women's greater control of land through matrilineal inheritance means that nuclear households are organized around and dependent primarily on the wife's land.[20] A husband's contributions to the household are important, but the bulk of land and resources flow through and are controlled by the wife. In these nuclear households, then, property and inheritance do not flow from parents as a unit to children, but primarily from mothers to daughters. Fathers may pass on some of their earned income to children, a practice that has become more common because of Dutch and Islamic influences, but ancestral land and houses remain with their sisters. Contrary to assumptions about men's agency and authority, husbands in Minangkabau nuclear households cooperate with, rather than control, their wives because wives usually have greater control of household land and production.

Some nuclear households in my study seem to reflect heteronormative assumptions about nuclear families because women in these households are housewives, that is, "nonworking" wives. When farm households achieve a certain level of income, some, but not all, women cease working in the fields. Rather than retiring to the house, however, these women become overseers of the agricultural operation on their lands. Although often pegged as housewives in state surveys, these women are economically active managers and landowners with their own sources of income. Almost all the "dependent" wives in the village are young women with very small children. Most of these young mothers, however, live in matrihouses, in which the number of income producers allows the women to concentrate on the care of their small children. As wives, only a tiny percentage of women in the village fit the model of the at-home housewife dependent on her husband's earnings and good will. These household arrangements suggest that what might be labeled simply a "nuclear" household may not reflect normative assumptions, thus raising questions about the reliability of cross-cultural comparisons on the basis of household composition.

The status of new houses built by husbands for their wives and children has raised questions about the possibility of husbands gaining greater control in such situations. Husbands are expected to build houses for their wives as a sign of their own prosperity, but these houses are considered the property of the women and after them, their daughters. Peletz (1994) calls this practice "patrifiliation," the creation and transmission of property rights by men to women. Although this designation recognizes the husband's agency in building the house, that recognition needs to be balanced with a consideration of the rights of the matrilineage in the husband. To understand this relationship, one needs to examine the exchange of men in marriage.[21] On the day of a wedding ceremony, the groom is picked up by the bride's kin and brought to her house. During the formal speeches by men elders, the groom is led to the wedding seat to sit beside the bride, signifying his transfer from his own kin to the bride's kin group. This move also signifies the transfer of rights over his offspring to his wife's kin.[22] That no one questions why women get houses that men build indicates that rights to the products of a husband's labor, other than earned income, also transfer to his wife at marriage. These rights are continually reconstituted as properly belonging to women, despite the hegemonic discourses of the state and Islam, which identify men as heads and owners of households (see Blackwood 1999).

In sum, in studies of so-called matrifocal societies such as the Minangk-abau, many of the questions asked and conclusions reached by re-searchers were the result of assumptions about the dominant heterosexual man, the Patriarchal Man. These assumptions divert attention from the constitutive relations in Minangkabau households and kin groups, lead-ing to a focus on absent or marginal men as the probable cause for women's control of land and lineal affairs. In my research, I found that the normative model of conjugal relations is absent. In this particular case, intergenerational ties through women, rather than heterosexual conjugal bonds, are constitutive of households and kin groups. Minangk-abau women, their daughters, and kin, both women and men, constitute the principal links and dominant figures in rural Minangkabau house-holds and kin groups, whether situated in nuclear households or matri-houses, whereas men, as sons, become important links to other lineages and serve as elders in their own lineages. Men, as husbands and fathers, are present and involved with child rearing and other activities of the household, but their presence alone does not imply anything about the relationships in the household. Kin relations oriented toward and con-trolled by kinswomen, in particular the mother-daughter unit, are both the normative and empirical form of household for rural Minangkabau.

Conclusion

The trope of the Patriarchal Man continues to cast a long shadow over theories of marriage and family. Feminist challenges to kinship theory have been successful in denaturalizing kinship and gender, underscor-ing the social constructedness of forms of relatedness. Nevertheless, the dominant heterosexual man has remained at the heart of marriage and family. This fixity on the trope of the Patriarchal Man has led anthropol-ogists to misrecognize other forms of relatedness as less than or weaker than heteronormative marriage.

The debates about matrifocality reveal the assumptions that create and then perpetuate matrifocality as a nonnormative form of kinship. In studies of both Afro-Caribbean and Minangkabau households, the key to the construction and perpetuation of the concept of "matrifocality" lay with the absent or weak husband. In the Afro-Caribbean context, the dizzying proliferation of household types defined not only by the pres-ence or absence of a (dominant, heterosexual) man but also by the du-ration of his visits reinforced the heteronormative ideal of family. The discourse of masculine rescue deployed in West Sumatra works in the same way to reinforce women's lack of agency and need for a dominant heterosexual man. Senior Minangkabau women have control in all ways typically attributed by researchers to men in households, through seniority, control of land, and access to rank, but the trope of the Patriarchal Man continues to make this assessment problematic.

Comparison to patrilineal societies is instructive. The subordination of the conjugal couple to agnatic relations (between fathers and sons or between brothers) is well accepted in studies of patrilineal households. For instance, in his rich rendition of Nepalese Silwal joint households, John Gray (1995) casts the patriline as the constitutive unit of the household. Men of the patriline, who share rights to land, are expected to stay in the same household, making the brother-brother tie an extremely important one. The conjugal couple, although important in producing heirs, is viewed as secondary; it is also said to conflict with agnatic relations (Gray 1995). Further, entry and exit of women, as wives, does not change the way the household and kin group see themselves because they are defined by the patriline of father and sons. In this case, the centrality and dominance of reproductive patrilineal kinsmen allow Gray to put marriage and the conjugal unit in its place.

As my discussion of so-called matrifocal societies demonstrates, there is ample evidence of kin practices and intimate relations without marriage or lacking marriage in the normative model of a dominant heterosexual man, a wife, and children, yet these cases have been and continue to be reconfigured to reflect heteronormative assumptions about marriage and masculinity.[23] The debates about matrifocal practices expose the way men, even when they are "missing," are foregrounded in couples as primary, whereas women without men are thought to be incomplete halves.[24] Fueled by the trope of the Patriarchal Man, the missing man narrative fails to take into account men's multiple positionalities. According to this narrative, the only acceptable condition of manhood is dominance and heterosexuality. The real missing men turn out to be those men positioned within families, extended kin networks, and other forms of sociality or intimacy, who do not stand in a relationship of heterosexual dominance or control over others.

Current concerns about woman-headed households and single moms in the United States and elsewhere employ readily available normative models of family to problematize the woman "alone." These categories of household demand recognition that something is missing despite the presence of other relationships. I am not suggesting that we ignore the material conditions of women's lives or that we ignore marriage where it is socially relevant, but that, as anthropologists, we work to question categories that depend on heteronormative assumptions about men and heterosexual couples for their meaning.

I would like to thank Deborah Elliston, who tackled more than one incarnation of this chapter, for providing excellent advice and much needed encouragement; Gloria Wekker, Saskia Wieringa, and Michael Peletz for their generous and thoughtful comments; Lynn Bolles, Mary Weismantel, Joel Kahn, and Jeffrey Dickemann for helpful pointers. This chapter is a shorter version of an article that appeared as "Wedding Bell Blues: Marriage, Missing Men, and Matrifocal Follies," *American Ethnologist* 32, 1 (2005): 3–19, copyright © 2005, reprinted by permission of the American Anthropological Association.

Chapter 5

Archaeologists, Feminists, and Queers: Sexual Politics in the Construction of the Past

Thomas A. Dowson

As a queer archaeologist I feel that I occupy, and am often placed in, an ambiguous position. Although I am no stranger to ambiguity (after all I have been called queer for as long as I can remember), producing this chapter in which I contribute to thinking about past impacts and future directions of feminism in archaeology has brought to the fore certain tensions that until now I have acknowledged but failed to grapple with in a sustained manner. The tensions I speak of derive from my emotional, intellectual, and political relationship to feminist archaeology. The ambiguity I negotiate is the relationship between queer theory and feminist theory as used to inform and subvert heteronormative and androcentric archaeological practice.

My attempts to queer archaeology (Dowson 1998, 2000a, b, 2001) do not fit unproblematically into discussions on the past and future impact of feminist theories within archaeological practice and discourse as they might at first appear to do. I am immediately reminded of an often overlooked point Elizabeth Weed makes in her introduction to *Feminism Meets Queer Theory* (Weed and Schor 1997); for Weed, that "feminism and queer theory share commonalities and affiliations is not to say they are easily commensurable" (1997, vii). I have no problem with acknowledging an intellectual and personal debt to feminism. For instance, in attempting to negotiate issues of standpoint epistemologies in the context of queer theory I have benefited greatly from recent feminist discussions of epistemology and objectivity (particularly Bar On 1993; Harding 1993; Longino 1998; Haraway 1999). And, I am certain I would not be exploring the implications of queer theory for archaeology, and publishing such thoughts, were it not for the political inroads made by feminist archaeologists. But my turn to queer theory in the mid-1990s, and my receptiveness toward the ideas and politics it embraces, was the result then of a growing sense of frustration with both feminism in archaeology and the practice of feminists in the discipline.

I do not perceive queer theory to be a natural progression of ideas that simply developed out of "second wave" feminism. But at the same time I do not use queer theory to challenge and ultimately dismiss feminism. In this chapter, from an explicitly queer standpoint, I contribute to discussions about the role of feminism in archaeology by exploring how it is I come to queer theory in my practice as an archaeologist, and how I believe queer archaeologies fulfill certain political and intellectual commitments; commitments that need to be explicitly recognized as such. I begin with a personal account of how I became actively engaged with the sexual politics of archaeology. Then, by examining the way in which "the family" is constructed as a timeless entity I outline certain silences in feminist archaeology; silences that are disrupted by queer theory. But, I am more interested to know why those silences persist. And so I demonstrate, with the help of recent research and comment on imagery found in a fifth-dynasty tomb in Egypt, how and why the silences remain. The potential of queer critiques in archaeology spurred me on to reflect on my own lived experiences. I conclude this chapter with a self-reflective discussion of how and why I believe my sexuality informs my practice as an archaeologist. My own marginalized experiences do not provide answers, but they are necessary to asking better questions.

Encountering Feminist Archaeology

S was the first committed and active feminist I encountered. We were both archaeology students at the University of the Witwatersrand, Johannesburg, South Africa, in the early 1980s. S was an extremely intelligent young woman; she also had a striking beauty. Not surprisingly, S attracted a lot of attention from our fellow male students (and lecturers). Besides the usual comments about a beautiful young woman, they regularly commented on her "lefty" views and appearance. But the real issue was that S ran rings around the testosterone-charged Indiana wannabes. I remember some of those discussions, often quite heated, as if they were yesterday. Hearing S on feminism scared me, no, she frightened the life out me. I agreed with much of what S was saying. But I did so quietly, often only when she and I were talking alone. Not out of choice, out of self-preservation. I did not want to be discovered.

Since the time I could appreciate what feminism was about I was sympathetic to its cause. Certainly, long before this appreciation I realized I was not the son my parents, my family, or the community in which I lived expected me to be. I was different. At times when I could not successfully hide that difference I was a "sissy," I was "queer." One way to challenge such bigotry was to hide that difference, to be more masculine. For decades I felt isolated. I did not know anyone else who was like

me. Of course I knew I was not the only person society defined as homosexual. The media often had stories of gay men and the depraved lives
they were said to lead. For instance, I remember a story of a woman who
returned home one day to find her husband in bed with another lover.
The story would have been nothing were it not for the fact that the lover
was a younger man. She shot her husband while he and his lover were
making love. There were also endless stories about Cliff Richard. Everyone seemed to know about the Village People.[1] And school kids gos-
siped maliciously about certain teachers. But I never knew anyone who
was gay, definitely not anyone I could talk to. By the time I first encountered feminism then, and I do not remember when this was, I was
acutely aware from firsthand experience that white, heterosexual
women were not the only targets of a masculist hegemony.

I grew up in South Africa where so-called sexual deviancy was on a par
with interracial relationships of any sort. But, by the beginning of
the 1990s, even in South Africa, gay and lesbian politics were very
prominent—not least because of the AIDS crisis (see Gevisser and
Cameron 1994). I read numerous personal accounts, both at home and
abroad, of prominent men and women "coming out." The message I repeatedly received from these often harrowing life stories was that it was
futile for me to think I could change. I had to accept what I had been
fighting for so long. And so after a few agonizing and desperately lonely
years, I decided in March 1994 to come out.

By now I was a professional archaeologist with a post in what was then
the Rock Art Research Unit at the University of the Witwatersrand. Having made what seemed to be an entirely personal choice, I believed at
once I was confronted with a professional choice. The first thoughts
I had about the relationship between my sexuality and my practice as an
archaeologist did not develop in any logical, step-by-step manner. Nor
did I think there existed any rules that precluded gay men from being
archaeologists. Subconsciously, I suppose, I believed that the disciplinary culture of archaeology would not tolerate my sexuality. There
seemed no doubt in my mind: I would have to give up my career in archaeology. I mentioned this to an archaeologist I decided to confide in.
Although that person never challenged, not even slightly, the assumptions I was making about my being openly gay and being able to continue my work in archaeology, it was suggested I might find it easier if
I got a job elsewhere. On the one hand my views about the disciplinary
culture of archaeology were reinforced, on the other there did at least
appear to be some hope. Some months later I was given the opportunity
of taking up a new post in the Department of Archaeology at the University of Southampton.

Moving to Southampton lived up to my expectations, it was both personally and intellectually liberating. In many ways I identified with the

much-written-about gay man who leaves the small rural town for a better life in a big city. The difference being I left a big city for a smaller one, and those who came to know me knew me as gay from the start. To be able to go into a bookshop that has a substantial and significant gay and lesbian section, and to be able to browse through those books without constantly looking over my shoulders is one of those seemingly insignificant aspects of daily life I now take for granted. Back in October 1994 such insignificant acts were part of a personal freedom I had never experienced before.

I joined the department at a time when there was a stimulating mix of staff and postgraduate students exploring a variety of issues in gender archaeology. A gender reading group was suggested, and, despite my new sense of freedom, it was with a feeling of ambivalence I decided to join in. I was torn between a desire to become intellectually engaged with issues of gender in archaeology and a realization early on that not everyone was comfortable about having a gay colleague in their midst.

One of the papers we considered at our seminars was Moira Gatens's "Power, Bodies and Difference" (1992). This paper was considered by the majority of the group as a key paper for the development of feminist thinking in archaeology (note Gatens's influence in, for example, Baker 1997; J. Thomas 2000; Alberti 2001). While I agreed with and was unequivocally sympathetic toward the intellectual and political position of that paper, not least because of the direction it proposed, for me neither the paper nor my colleagues' reception of it went far enough. Although Gatens offered a conception of sexual difference that entertains a multiplicity of differences, not a dualistic notion of sexual difference, I remained struck and disturbed by the manner in which "the male" was treated as a monolithic, homogenous entity here and in much of feminist-inspired archaeology. While I agreed that dominant theories of social and political life, past and present, "harbour fundamental, not superficial, biases against women" (Gatens 1992, 121), from my own experiences in life it was abundantly clear to me women were not the only people disadvantaged by a society that privileges "male" interests and values at the expense of all others.

Roger Horrocks provided a telling example of the way in which a feminist critique of the inner-city riots in Britain during the 1980s somewhat naively posits a lawless masculinity against its own community. The feminist writer Beatrix Campbell suggested "crime and coercion are sustained by men. Solidarity and self-help are sustained by women. It is as stark as that" (1993, 319). But, as Horrocks (1995, 9) pointed out,

Campbell ignores . . . the contemporary epidemic of suicides among young men. If we take this along with alcoholism and drug addiction—also much commoner among men—we get some insight into the profound despair among men in Britain's wastelands. So far from revealing an eternal savage masculinity, concerned above all to keep women down, these social indices present a picture of men in despair, broken, without meaning.

Masculinity myths are concerned with the assertion of toughness, stoicism, courage, rationality, and distinguishing this from "soft" femininity. And it is because of this, gay men, bisexual men, transgendered individuals, and so on have obviously also suffered, and continue to do so, as a result of a masculist hegemony—as have heterosexual men. To set men up as a monolithic class, all waging war against women is naively inaccurate. There have been times then when I have felt as marginalized by feminism as I had ever been by the disciplinary culture of archaeology.

The Family and Silence

Not only did I feel politically marginalized, but also I believed that feminist archaeologies did not go far enough. This is evident, I believe, in the way in which archaeological reconstructions and representations of 'the family' as a heterosexual unit have gone unchallenged. A series of dioramas, created for the Festival of Britain in 1951 and now in the Jewry Wall Museum (Leicester, England), demonstrates my point. Five dioramas were produced in total, each one a representation of a 'family' from one of five ages of British prehistory: the Mesolithic, the Neolithic, the Bronze Age, the Iron Age, and the Anglo-Saxon (Hawkes 1951). Each diorama has a pair of adults (a male and a female) and a varying number of children of various ages. In two cases even the family pet is included. The captions for these models concentrate on artefacts associated with each period. For example, the caption for the Bronze Age group reads:

The clothes worn by the figures are based on examples found in Danish bogs, even the mini skirt. Special conditions in bogs allow cloth to survive. The figures are richly equipped with a jet necklace, jet buttons, a bronze dagger and a bronze spearhead. Flint is still used for arrowheads.

Poststructuralist critiques of representations like these challenge the way in which a single image can be representative of an entire period. In British prehistory discussions of the representation of the past began with critiques of the Iron Age, or the Celts. It is understandable that the following caption now appears for the Iron Age group:

These figures from the Festival of Britain in 1951 give an impression of an Iron Age family, although the artefacts are of a too diverse age range to ever have been used at the same time.

The same could be said of all the dioramas. The artefacts used for each of the period-specific exhibits are brought together in one "family" when in fact these artefacts were spread too widely in time and space ever to have appeared as they do in the dioramas.

Feminist critiques of archaeological constructions challenge the androcentric bias inherent in those constructions of the past. The caption for the "Mesolithic Family" provides a good example from which to begin. It reads:

People at this time lived by fishing, hunting and gathering food. From this distant past few things survive. Those that do tend to be made of stone and flint but are only parts of complete tools. The wooden shaft of the harpoon and the fishing net would rot away.

Communities that archaeologists and anthropologists study, like the Mesolithic family, are very often characterized by the way in which food is obtained, and they become known as "hunter-gatherers" or "hunting societies." The dichotomous relationship between hunting and gathering is not a symmetrical one. It is asymmetrical: men and their activities are seen as superior to women and their activities. The caption, like most constructions of hunter-gatherers past and present, highlights male tools and male activities. And it is the representational prominence given to the artefact that has been the subject of the feminist critiques of these dioramas: "each male clutches his symbol of power of authority; each female watches anxiously over a small child" (Jones and Pay 1990, 162; see also Jones 1991). Consequently, in attempts to understand the development of humanity more generally, it is "man the hunter" models of human evolution that have cultural and social capital.

Detailed analyses of ethnographic studies, however, show that women's activities can account for as much as 70 percent of their community's dietary intake—women clearly did not only look after the children. Feminist anthropologists and archaeologists rightly point out that women's activities should not be seen as inferior to hunting activities. Some feminist writers then prefer to label these people as "gatherer-hunters," or more neutrally, foragers. And, also, "woman the gatherer" models of hominid evolution were proposed to challenge the androcentric models.

These feminist-informed studies expose the way in which anthropological evidence has been colored by androcentric bias. And in that sense, it is irrelevant whether "gatherer-hunter" is more appropriate, or "woman the gatherer" models are right or wrong (Okruhlik 1998). These critiques of androcentric studies invert and revalue the categories of a dominant, masculist sex/gender system (see Fedigan 1986), and in so doing they promulgate a reverse discourse. While many researchers are quick to point to androcentric biases, there is rarely an explicit recognition of heterosexist biases. Nowhere do we find sustained critiques of the heterosexual basis of the nuclear family unit in the past. In the Jewry wall dioramas, for example, the heterosexual family is presented as such from earliest times, the Mesolithic, to more recent historical periods, the Anglo-Saxon; the modern, conservative notion of the family appears as ancient as humanity itself. Also, the presence of relationships other than male-female heterosexual relationships are seldom considered (but, for example, see papers in Schmidt and Voss 2000a). Often where they are included they are so heavily colored by a Western, essentialist construction of homosexuality (cf. Whitehead 1981; on the Berdache, see also Roscoe 1996, 1998).[2]

When reconstructing prehistoric communities archaeologists impose modern, Western notions of the nuclear family unit; father, mother and children—and in some constructions even family pets are included. In the Jewry Wall dioramas, for example, the Iron Age father restrains the family dog, while the young Anglo-Saxon girl cuddles her cat. The possibility that prehistoric communities were made up of units other than the Western ideal are seldom explored, despite considerable ethnographic evidence to the contrary. The recent, Western concept of the family is presented as the norm, and as it is considered the norm in Western society the consumption of those constructions goes unchallenged. Archaeology presents this idealized notion of the family as being asocial and ahistorical; and in so doing it merely legitimizes conservative attitudes to and policies on modern family values. Archaeology provides the "tradition" in "traditional family values." These constructions then justify and legitimize phobias and prejudices in our society today. As archaeology underpins a heterosexual artifice of human history, archaeologists need to be mindful of their complicity in Western society's institutionalized homophobia. It is this presumption of heterosexuality in archaeological practice that queer theory seeks explicitly to disrupt.

Challenging the Silence of Heteronormativity

A number of archaeologists are committed to sociopolitical critique within the discipline, and they have paid attention to such issues as training and employment in archaeology. Explorations of these issues, "equity" critiques (Wylie 1997a, 82–83), include feminist analyses of the status of women within the discipline, but can also include analyses of the impact of class, race, and nationalism on archaeological practice. There have also been numerous "content" critiques (81–82) that have explored bias founded on sex, race, class, and nationality. But, as Wylie (83) pointed out, "sociopolitical critics in archaeology have tended to side-step explanatory questions about how the silences and stereotypes they delineate are produced or why they persist." Equity critiques have rarely been deployed to show how the content of archaeological knowledge is produced, and, vice versa, content critiques rarely make a connection between the content of archaeological knowledge and specific equity issues. Queer theory does enable us to reveal why and how those silences and stereotypes exist.

Queer theory identifies the epistemological privilege inherent in heteronormative characterizations of society and science (see, for example, Halperin 1995; Jagose 1996; Spargo 1999; Kirsch 2000; Hall 2003). In archaeology I recognize the impact of epistemological privilege in three interdependent stages of disciplinary culture. Briefly, to begin with, the game of archaeological discourse is set up by determining who has the authority to construct the past, to determine who are the players. Second, those authoritative voices require their own favorable terms and methods, the rules of the game, by which to act in an authoritative manner. And finally, those authoritative actions then promote the production of specific constructions of the past.

Questioning the place of the heterosexual family unit in archaeological constructions of the past is not simply a "content" critique. That analytical fiction is a direct consequence of the politics that shape the structure of the discipline. The values and activities of those at the top both organize and set limits on who gets to practice archaeology and how they do so. As the discipline was established and has long since been controlled and maintained by white, heterosexual men every interpretation of the past is always already heteronormative, in terms of both its content and its methodology. Chronocentricism is not simply the result of some objective, sex-neutral chosen way of approaching the past; it is a methodological manifestation of phallocentric values and ideals (Dowson 2001, 316–17). In the following discussion I give a specific example of how that heteronormativity is set up and persists in archaeology.

In 1964 a Fifth Dynasty tomb built for two men was discovered in Lower Egypt (see Basta 1979; Moussa and Altenmüller 1977; Baines 1985; Reeder 1993, 2000). In the bas reliefs of the tomb Niankhkhnum and Khnumhotep are often depicted in intimate postures. But nowhere are there any inscriptions that reveal the exact nature of their relationship. The "exaggerated affection" these two men display was not considered normal by archaeologists, and therefore required explanation. Various suggestions were proposed. For instance, they were thought to depict twin brothers, or perhaps two men who were on an equal footing with one another, sharing similar values and holding the same power. The representation of intimacy between the two men was thought to be symbolic of their closeness during their time together on earth. The questionable becomes acceptable—the unspeakable is neatly avoided.

Representations of intimacy between men and women also exist in other Fourth, Fifth, and Sixth Dynasty tombs. But these are acceptable and require no explanation. Obviously they represent males and females in marital relationships. Archaeologists then identify an iconographic canon and suggest it was deployed by dynastic artists to represent husbands and wives (see Cherpion 1995). But, by analyzing the iconography used to portray Niankhkhnum and Khnumhotep, rather than making judgmental observations, Greg Reeder (2000), an independent, gay writer (i.e., not a normatively trained archaeologist), has shown that the same canon was used to depict these two men as was used supposedly to represent husband and wife at the same time. But, the idea that Niankhkhnum and Khnumhotep might have been a same-sex couple has never been entertained until now, not even in very recent studies of homosexuality in Ancient Egypt (see Parkinson 1995). Given the overt display of their relationship in their tomb, and the lack of any other evidence that might have revealed the nature of their relationship, we can only speculate on the nature of that relationship.

Critiques such as Reeder's are often dismissed as being political correctness run riot. In referring to Reeder's research, Lynn Meskell (2002, 145) rather gratuitously asserted "there has been a tendency to push the ancient data in the service of contemporary sexual politics, irrespective of the evidence (e.g., Reeder 2000)." There is no reasoned critique of Reeder's analysis; such a critique is indeed unnecessary. Reeder and others are required to produce closely argued analyses for why a particular relationship should be seen as homosexual, whereas heterosexual identities are merely and credibly presumed. The rules of the game of archaeology, and who plays the game, are predetermined. It is enough to dismiss Reeder as gay, to belittle and ignore what he has to contribute.

Ironically, the point I would now make in response to Meskell's offhand dismissal of Reeder's critique is similar if not identical to a point Meskell herself has already made. In an earlier publication responding to critics of those authors whose research of ancient peoples was influenced by Foucault, Meskell (1999) wrote:

personal motivations have been called into question and fingers have been pointed at various groups in the gay, feminist and other radical social movements who have appropriated elements of Foucault's theory or historical research in order to advance their respective political struggles (Lamour et al. 1998a:2). Why such subjectivities should be singled out against other political positions surprises me, as if we can ever be objective in our interests or arguments, and at least in this case feminists and queer theorists have been up front in their politics. (92–93)

In her later publication Meskell (2002) does not offer the same support to Reeder; in fact, she becomes one of those pointing the fingers at a gay writer, accusing him of using archaeology to service contemporary sexual politics. There is no clue to the apparent change of heart. But, because the heterosexual authority of archaeology protects her, Meskell is not required to explain herself. The reason for the difference is that Reeder is not an archaeologist, and he does not play the game of archaeology as Meskell would. Contrary to what Meskell says about the paper, Reeder's analysis of the tomb is thorough in its attention to detail. It is also not riddled with references to fashionable French or cultural theorists in a vacuous attempt at intellectualism. Rather, Reeder presents us with a straightforward challenge to Egyptian archaeology.

Whether or not the representations of intimacy between Niankhkhnum and Khnumhotep are evidence for some form of same-sex desire or sexuality is unimportant. What Meskell and others fail to appreciate is that Reeder's study shows there exists an unequivocal heterosexist bias in archaeological interpretation of this particular tomb. Either, the two men did have an intimate, perhaps accepted, sexual relationship, in which case archaeologists would need to rethink the nature of marital relationships in Ancient Egypt at this time. Or, Niankhkhnum's and Khnumhotep's relationship was not sexual, in which case the accepted iconographic analysis that reveals a heterosexual, marital relationship is itself wide of the mark. Reeder does not provide the answer; he does not claim to do so. But he does draw attention to an obvious problem. As Sandra Harding (1993, 78, original emphasis) pointed out, experiences of "marginalized peoples are not the *answers* to questions arising either inside or outside those lives, though they are necessary to asking the best questions."

The discourse surrounding the archaeology of these tombs (one depicting intimate scenes between two men, and others depicting identical scenes between men and women) provides evidence for one of archaeology's overall strategies: to construct and maintain unquestioningly a heterosexual history of humanity. Western, masculist, and heterosexist judgments against homosexuality override an accepted methodology used to determine marital relationships. What Reeder has shown using an established methodology employed by Egyptologists is that there is more evidence to suggest an intimate, same-sex relationship between Niankhkhnum and Khnumhotep than there is to suggest they were brothers of some sort. It is because of the presumption of heterosexuality that these elaborate and unsubstantiated hypotheses of "twinship" or "metaphorical brothers" are permissible—more palatable is perhaps more accurate. And, it is the epistemological privilege in archaeology that enables Reeder's research to be simply dismissed as being in the service of contemporary sexual politics. The superficial dismissal of Reeder's work shows that the rules of the archaeological game are stacked in favor of maintaining that bias.

I have used the Reeder-Meskell interchange to highlight one way in which epistemological privilege is produced and recursively reproduced in archaeology. The heterosexist bias Reeder exposes, underwritten by all aspects of the disciplinary culture, is not specific to a few isolated examples; it is also present in feminist archaeology. Despite the presence of a heterosexist bias in some feminist archaeologies I do not propose queer theory as the latest in a series of successive theoretical frameworks, toppling feminist theory. Such a characterization of the development of science generally, and archaeology more specifically, is surely the kind of thinking both feminist and queer scholars want to move away from. But at the same time I do not want to gloss over differences between queer archaeologies and feminist archaeologies with the suggestion of a cosy relationship, sharing similar goals. There are fundamental points of difference, and certainly, in some instances, of outright disagreement—but these are I believe the result of the localized operation of political or interpretative principles rather than a struggle over details of political and intellectual commitment. More importantly, queer positions should not be seen as one of many manifestations of a "third wave" feminism. Such a reductive formulation is not only incorrect, but it merely serves to maintain a sense of impotence for those challenging masculist hegemony from the variety of standpoints encompassed by "queer" and "feminism." Queer standpoints expose established positions, and allow for a reordering of not just heterosexist characterizations of sex/gender, but also a reordering of forms of knowledge, regimes of logic, modes of self-constitution, and practices of community (Halperin 1995, 62). All of which are relevant to archaeological practice.

A Queer Position

On the evening of Thursday 8 October 1998 Matthew Shepard, a young gay student from the University of Wyoming in Laramie, USA, was lured out of a student bar. Two men, who led him to believe they were also gay, took him to a remote spot on a country road on the outskirts of town. As they drove him away they hit him on the head with a pistol. Matthew was then dragged from their truck, tied spread-eagle to a fence, beaten over the head with a baseball bat, burned and robbed, and finally left to die in near freezing temperatures. Some twenty hours later Matthew was found by passing cyclists, who at first mistook his body for a scarecrow. His face was caked in blood, except for streaks that had been washed clean by his tears. He arrived at hospital in a critical condition having sustained severe head injuries; his skull was so badly fractured doctors were unable to operate. He lay on a life support system in a coma while news of this brutal attack spread around the world. On Monday 12 October at 12:53 am Matthew died.

In her book *Losing Matt Shepard* (2000) Beth Loffreda outlines how the murder of a young man had a profound impact on life and politics in Laramie and beyond. When I heard this awful news various thoughts tumbled about in my mind: gay-bashing—fear—Laramie—archaeology. I suppose initially I thought, perhaps along with other gay men and women, "there but for the grace of god go I." Despite the rhetoric of liberal politi-cians, gay and straight, homophobia is as rife and as violent now as it has ever been; perhaps more so. And yes, there are times when I feel threat-ened and scared. I remember thinking of two archaeology students who had "come out" to me in confidence. I was reminded of their fears and anxieties, and the burden of ignorance they carried for their peers and family. I relived my attempts to alleviate their fears. But in the face of such a gruesome tragedy my words could never be reassuring; they rang hollow and meaningless in my own ears. My heart went out to them, and the many other people negotiating the minefield of coming out. I knew only to well how trapped and even desperate some of them must have been feeling. I thought also it was inconceivable that such a savage assault could have taken place in that town, a town that, up until then, had such pleas-ant memories for me. In 1992 and 1993 I visited Laramie a few times while on research leave from my post in the Rock Art Research Unit. I visited the Department of Anthropology at the University of Wyoming. In 1993 I gave the banquet address at the Wyoming Archaeological Society's annual conference. I met a number of friendly and interesting archaeolo-gists in Wyoming, and I was made to feel very welcome there. In October 1998 I wondered what they were thinking. To them and the world, I was sure, archaeology seemed so far removed from the events surrounding Matthew's death that no one could possibly imagine a connection. Slowly but surely I began to realize there was indeed a connection.

During October 1998 I was writing an article for a Catalan archaeo-logical journal, *Cota Zero*, in which I was exploring the relationship be-tween archaeology and homosexuality (Dowson 1998). Specifically though, I was reading David Halperin's *Saint Foucault: Towards a Gay Hagiography* (1995) when I heard the news of Matthew's death. It was, I believe, simultaneously hearing the news from the United States and reading Halperin's book that caused two aspects of my life to collide. At once, I was fearful of and angry at the homophobia that resulted specif-ically in Matthew's death and the homophobia we all confront regularly. But also I was reading of Halperin's account of his experiences as a "gay" academic. It was then that I started to question my responsibilities as an archaeologist in the light of my sexuality. Something I had not al-lowed myself to do in any way previously.

In fact, for some time after "coming out" I emphatically believed my sexuality had absolutely nothing to do with my being an archaeologist. And with the growing interest in gender studies in archaeology then, I was determined not to get too actively involved. I know a number of les-bian, gay, and bisexual colleagues, in various disciplines, who have had, and still have, similar reactions. This sort of reaction does not result from being unsympathetic toward issues of gender. Rather, it derives from an unspoken social rule whereby academic men and women are forced to maintain an authority to act by denying or downplaying their sexuality. Although writing specifically of himself and his intellectual and political relationship to Foucault, but acknowledging a much wider social relevance, Halperin explicitly expresses the status quo many if not all of us gay, lesbian, and bisexual academics find ourselves in. We all share the problem of how to

Acquire and maintain the authority to speak, to be heard, and to be taken seriously without denying or bracketing [our] gayness. It's not just a matter of being publicly or visibly out; it's a matter of being able to devise and to preserve a positive, undemonised connection between [our] gayness and [our] scholarly or critical authority. That problem of authorization, to be sure, dramatizes the more general social and discursive predicament of lesbians and gay men in a world where a claimed homosexual identity operates as an instant disqualification, exposes you to accusations of pathology and partisanship . . . and grants everyone else an absolute epistemological privilege over you. (Halperin 1995, 8)

Here Halperin is drawing on Eve Kosofsky Sedgwick's analysis of the *Epistemology of the Closet* (1990).

Sedgwick explores the consequences of the binary distinction between heterosexuality and homosexuality that began to be the primary defining characteristic of men and women from the end of the nineteenth century onward. Sedgwick argues that the distinction resulted from a homophobic desire to devalue one of those oppositions. Consequently, homosexuality is not symmetrically related to heterosexuality— it is subordinate and marginal, but necessary to construct meaning and value in heterosexuality (Sedgwick 1990, 9–10). In her ground-breaking study Sedgwick argues this asymmetrical relationship between homosexuality and heterosexuality has been at the heart of every form of representation since the start of the twentieth century. And the disciplinary culture of archaeology is surely not invulnerable to such social forces.

My strategy to preserve a positive connection between my scholarly authority and my sexuality was to distance my academic research from dealing with issues of gender. I was under the impression that my explicit researching of gender relations in rock art would only serve to draw attention to my sexuality, and reinforce my colleagues' (misguided) sense of epistemological privilege. I was explicitly, and in some cases gently, told by some very liberal-minded archaeologists not to be too vocal about my sexuality. While I was prepared to "come out," it seemed obvious to me that I could only do so by downplaying my sexuality.

When homosexual men and women "come out" of the "closet" there is the widely held view they are emerging into a world of unfettered liberty. Sadly, as Sedgwick, Halperin, and many others have shown, this is not the case; "the closet" is not some personally perceived space, it is a product of complex power relations. And one cannot magically emerge from those power relations. "To come out is precisely to expose oneself to a different set of dangers and constraints" (Halperin 1995, 30). In archaeology those dangers and constraints manifest themselves in a powerfully and universally masculist disciplinary culture that is repeatedly negotiated in all aspects of professional archaeological practice as well as popular representations of the discipline. The same disciplinary culture that led me to believe one could not be an "out" gay man and a practicing archaeologist at once. I now appreciate I did not need to specifically address issues of gender to be dismissed—whatever I wrote or said was easily dismissed (even by feminists) because of an authority based on the superiority of heterosexuality. And again from Halperin (1995, 13),

As I discovered to my cost . . . if you are known to be lesbian or gay your very openness, far from pre-empting malicious gossip about your sexuality, simply exposes you to the possibility that, no matter what you actually do, people can say absolutely whatever they like about you in the well-grounded confidence that it will be credited. (And since there is very little you can do about it, you might as well not try and ingratiate yourself by means of "good behaviour".)

So, just as I was once no longer prepared to deny my sexuality, by the end of 1998 I was no longer prepared to compromise it either. I am now comfortable with my sexuality, and clear about how it influences my lifestyle as well as the way in which I think about and construct the past. I am proud of who I am and what I produce. But more importantly, because epistemological privilege in archaeology is unequivocally related to homophobia (see also She 2000; Claassen 2000), I now actively challenge the manner in which epistemological privilege is negotiated in archaeology. Not just as it affects me, or other deviant archaeologists, but also the way in which the very practice of archaeology authorizes an entirely heterosexual history of humanity. It is that heterosexual history of humanity that, I argue, legitimizes the mindless acts of homophobia we continue to witness today.

First, my thanks to Pamela Geller and Miranda Stockett for inviting me to participate in the American Association of Anthropologists session on which this edited volume is based. I am also grateful to them, Alison Wylie—the session discussant, and the reviewer of the volume proposal for their helpful comments on an earlier draft of this chapter. The ideas in this chapter have developed over a number of years with the encouragement of a number of friends and colleagues. They are too numerous to list all by name, but that in no way devalues the acknowledgment of my gratitude to them. I must, however, single out two people, Mary Baker and Sue Pitt; they have inspired and encouraged me greatly.

Part III
Metaphor, Performance, and Materiality

Chapter 6
In the Midst of the Moving Waters: Material, Metaphor, and Feminist Archaeology

Susan Kus

When used in the fashion of first and traditional peoples, metaphors are incentives to imagination and edification (e.g., Fernandez 1986). However, as Lakoff and Johnson (1980) have suggested, metaphors can be blinding and they come with entailments. As anthropologists it is hoped, however, that we will continue to find ourselves in a position to be more edified than to be blinded and bound by entailments. Indeed, if "metaphor is a part of all thought" (Jackson 1989, 145) then anthropologists are in a privileged position since we have abundant opportunity to learn how to wield metaphor from its mistresses and to learn much from "masters of iconic thought" (Fernandez 1986, 186).

The Malagasy term "riaka" can be translated as wave(s). One early nineteenth-century Malagasy sovereign, Radama, declared his sovereignty over the island of Madagascar by assuming the title of "Mpanjaka anivon'ny riaka" or "Ruler of [the land] in the midst of the moving waters [waves of the ocean]." I was certainly struck by his pretension, but I was also struck by the poetry of that image: Madagascar, the fourth largest island in the world, surrounded and buffeted by waves. For off-islanders Madagascar was often referred to as "The Island at the End of the World." Indeed, Madagascar's late occupancy (less than 2000 years) testifies to it lying at the edge of some peoples' worlds as conceived and as experienced. This island still often lies at the intellectual edge of academic worlds that sees it betwixt and between Africa and Southeast Asia and at the edge of prehistory and ethnohistory.

Madagascar was indeed buffeted by numerous waves of populations and cultural beliefs and practices, and in some sense everyone and everything cultural in Madagascar is from somewhere else. Yet Madagascar was and is not at the end of the world for some. For the Malagasy, Madagascar is at the center of the world. Practices and practitioners of "high traditions" from Persia, Indonesia, Asia, and Azania, once on this "island at the end of the world" were removed from direct or sustained contact with the centers of their "high traditions." Such practices and practitioners had to be adapted to local ecology, ongoing political affairs, and preexisting symbolic constructs. Other material items and behavioral practices that came to the island as flotsam and jetsam—bits and pieces of technology, customs, and belief brought by sailors and traders and passed by numerous mouths, hands, and routes across the island—were not constrained to roles of predetermined and delimited cultural application for they too had to be fitted into cultural logics and structures already in place.[1]

I find edification in the image of the "land in the midst of moving waters" that receives the buffeting of many waves yet creates its own integrated cultural collage—which creates its own centering—because that is what one must do to act effectively in a world in the midst of moving waters.

Riding the Crests of Waves

Not only is my site of fieldwork, Madagascar, at the end of the world for many academics, but so too is my professional job location, a little liberal arts college, at the edge of the academic world. I have only the occasional colleague from another academic department to discuss research interests that overlap. I do not have graduate students to help me survey the ever-growing swell of literature on archeological concerns; no graduate students to engender seminars on classic or trendy topics in the field. I have had to rely on feminism's breakers to buffet my own shores, and to use them to forge a centering of my own understanding of feminist theory and practice.

However, I want to begin my reflections from a time when I was more at the center of the world; when I was a graduate student at the University of Michigan during the 1970s.

The "New Archaeology" was such an intellectual excitement! It ushered in, for the archaeologist in North America, billowing aspirations of participating in the production of high theory in anthropology. But it also brought in a significant challenge to the archaeologist's ability to interpret archaeological materials. It brought in the challenge of "middle-range" research and theory. I still believe the challenge of middle-level research and theory to be the strength of archaeology and the source of its important and necessary contribution to the larger discipline of anthropology. From my archaeological perspective, middle-range theory in archaeology can offer anthropology a finely hewn appreciation of the materiality of our cultural being. From my feminist perspective, this appreciation is needed as underpinning for a sophisticated understanding of how the behaviorally quotidian and the materially mundane become the meaningful matters of our poetries and philosophies. My understanding of this strength and my formulation of this contribution of archaeology to anthropology are not just lashed to the aspirations of feminist high theory, but more significantly, they are anchored in the achievements of low-range research of feminist archaeologists.

Returning to the 1970s, the "empirical responsibility"[2] and challenge of middle-range research, unfortunately, were too easily confounded with the high theory of restricted forms of material determinism (technological, ecological, demographic, economic, etc.). This was due in part to the fact that such theories privilege the areas "of human existence that leave relatively clear-cut evidence in the archaeological record" (D. Thomas 1999, 51). For many archaeologists, like me, who were then (and still are now) interested in "ideas," ideology, and the like, the lacunae of a such materialist stances not only offered no "insight," but further relegated such interests to the domain of methodological impossibility and theoretical emasculation (declaring such interests to be features of the social/cultural superstructure.) Postprocessualism gave voice to our railing against the "epiphenominalization" of meaning and symbol (among other things) within impoverished, but robust, materialist stances. Postprocessualism brought the full force of the "arbitrariness" of the symbolic to bear in its challenge. This force of the symbolic came from the high-range of theories of semiotics, structuralism, deconstructionism, and so on, but it also reverberated down into low-level archaeological theory, forcing us to recognize that even our most intimate and direct confrontation with our "data" is perspectival and incomplete.

The free-floating meaning of the postmodernist variety, however, often set one adrift in the doldrums of the absurdly trivial[3] or left one trapped within a maelstrom of overly dramatic political claims and political accusations. I would argue that the first waves of feminism in archaeology, with reference to grounded and gendered "being in the world" that comes with the entailments of body and emotion, provided and continues to provide a more effective mooring for a discussion and appreciation of "meaning" in archaeology than much of high postprocessualist theory. The headiness of work in high theory can lead one to believe in the primacy of the abstract sign and the unbounded power of the symbol. However, the philosopher Pierce brought our attention to three kinds of signs: the symbol, the icon, and the index. While the symbol grabs our attention for its power to distinguish us from other sentient creatures, the iconic (patterned physical resemblance) and the indexical (sensorial correlation) with corporeal entailments offer us mind and body bound into a whole. Feminist low-level and middle-level theory has continually sought to address the "sensuous" and the sentient in human practices by focusing on body, agency, performance, gendered being, the gendering of nonsexed objects and phenomena, and so on. Consequently, the indexical and the iconic forcefully accompany the symbolic in feminist discussions in archaeology.

Archaeology by Women, About Prehistoric Women, and for Everyone!

Early waves of feminism focused attention on "archaeology by women" and emboldened many to speak out about inequitable practices and missing histories of early women within the discipline and I am grateful for this.

Early waves of feminism "about prehistoric women" were also confronted by the challenge of low-level research to "find women" in the archaeological record. Certainly, it is clear to us all after endless recitation of the argument, that it is not exclusively about finding women at the low level of research, it is about (en)gendering middle-range and high-level theory. Nevertheless, in the first assault, waves of feminist archeologists took up the challenge of low- and middle-level research to bring women and gender into the material archaeological record and they have done so with such cleverness, such insightfulness, and with such force that their point is being made in (and by) spades. Women have been found in the household (e.g., Tringham 1991) and outside the household (e.g., Nelson 2003) as social agents. Gender has been found to inform domains of subsistence (e.g., Watson and Kennedy 1991), technology (e.g., Spector 1993; Gero 1991; Dobres 1995; Hurcombe 2000), economics (e.g., Gero and Scattolin 2002), politics (e.g., Arwill-Nordbladh 2003), and ideology (e.g., Pollock 1991; Brumfiel 1996a).

Woman the Tool Maker and Tool User

The early challenges to feminist archaeology to "find women" in the archaeological record, and the continuing challenge to find "others" there as well, has brought a solid respect for materiality to not only the practice, but also to the theory, of feminist archaeologists. One could argue that this appreciation for the material context of our being is not exclusive to feminist archaeology, but rather it is shared more broadly with processualist middle-range research and with Childe's Marxist focus on "the wo/man that makes her/himself," for instance. However, in a theoretically powerful twist, the materiality of feminist archaeology, focused on the microscale of low-level theory and on seemingly mundane materials such as domestic structures, gardens, household debris, and spindle whorls, has challenged theoretical conclusions drawn from materials of monumental proportion. Feminist low-level theory has reverberated up from its base to bring high theories into question. Tringham in her study of Opovo, a late Neolithic village in the former Yugoslavia, for instance, says that the high theory of "large general trends and patterns of adaptive processes" (1991, 125) produce a "prehistory of genderless, faceless blobs" (1991, 97). She argues that the study of social relations of production in prehistory needs to be carried out at the microscale of archaeology. A "household scale of analysis" (1991, 101) that makes gender visible is necessary if we are to produce social archaeology that effectively explores "the trajectory of human transformations" (1991, 125) wherein women and others can be recognized as social agents. Watson and Kennedy (1991), by looking at the ethnohistoric record of women's work in the Eastern Woodlands of North America, call our attention to "woman the innovator" in the domains of activities culturally assigned to them, in this case, the gathering and harvesting of plants. This appreciation of the women of the Late Archaic and Early Woodlands period, along with an examination of archaeological and archaeobotanical data allows Watson and Kennedy to challenge the speculation/high-theory models for the origin of agriculture that would either privilege the role of the intelligent shaman domesticator and educator, or alternatively explain domestication as "unintentional." They present the more tenable hypothesis that women of the Eastern Woodlands, through their knowledge, skill, and intellect, as they went about the routine "women's business" (Watson and Kennedy 1991, 269) of working with food plants, made "a significant contribution to culture change, to innovation, and to cultural elaboration" (1991, 269), transforming gatherers into domesticators. Gero and Scattolin (2002) looked at household debris from the formative period in northwestern Argentina at the site of Yutopian. The intimate intermixing of evidence for grain grinding and "pyrotechnical processing to produce cooper artifacts" (Gero and Scattolin 2002, 168) in some households allows Gero and Scattolin to call into question simplistic high-theory models of binary genders and binary gender systems (i.e., complementary versus hierarchical systems) and to problematize a definition of craft specialization as "extrahousehold" (2002, 169) suggesting we need more work in "home economics" if we are to produce credible economic theory at larger scales. Brumfiel's "low-level research" with the household data of spindle whorls used by women under the Aztec state and early colonial power in Mexico (1996b) allowed her to refine her understanding of the relationship of domination and resistance in state societies so as to recognize the level of state coercion that could invade the household and the importance of coercion in maintaining compliance to state demands. Perhaps more important for the argument I am making in this chapter, her low-level research on women's work in the household allowed her to call into question the extreme relativist position of high postprocessualist theory that would not allow theories to be tested by data (1996b, 458) (gathered by workers in the trenches.)

Woman the Symbol User and Meaning Maker

Low-level studies of "women" in subsistence activities in the household have not only revealed "woman-the-tool-maker-and-user," but have also offered us glimpses of "woman-the-symbol-user-and-the-meaning-maker." Alongside her discussion of data from Opovo and its relevance to high theories involving discussion of households and economics, Tringham (1991) offers us a vision of the "end [of] the use-life of a house" and the beginning of a new episode in the life of a woman. Watson and Kennedy (1991) remind us that in such a repetitive gendered chore such as collecting plants, women were "bored, or curious, or saw some economic advantage in it, [and] they acted consciously with the full powers of human intellect" to contribute to "to culture change, to innovation, and to cultural elaboration" (1991, 269). Brumfiel takes the spindle whorl of material economic production and recalls for us its symbolic "weight" for women's identity and pride in their skills and products, because "Spinning and weaving served as metaphors for women's experiences with pregnancy and childbirth, and several of the female deities who embodied female authority bore spinning and weaving equipment as part of their costumes" (Brumfiel 1996b, 456). These tales, imaginings, and remarks are veracious, rather than fictional, because ethnographic sensitivity and breadth along with dirt-level work in archaeology makes that distinction possible. However, I would push the significance of these tales and remarks further, arguing that it is feminist archaeology's microscale materialist focus on the engaged and performing body (whether male, female, or other) within the physical context of ecology and material culture that offers us the possibility of revisiting the "symbolic" in a powerful way.

A Place at the Theoretical Table

As I see it, feminist archaeology as *archaeology by women, about prehistoric women and for everyone* has not only revealed for us wo/man the tool maker and wo/man the meaning maker, but offers the means to transcend that dichotomy in a powerful way that lays claim to "sensuous material practice" as a central focus of anthropological theory and to archaeology's critical place at the theoretical table. It allows us to transcend the limitations of abstract symbolism and to question the force of abstract theory; it allows us a powerful transcendence of the dichotomy of matter and symbol by referencing the iconic and the indexical and concomitantly by dismissing essentialist ideas of "woman."

Crossing subdisciplinary boundaries of archaeology, ethnohistory, and ethnography and working at low-level theory can incite one to theoretical bricolage, and feminist theory can be very provocative in a theoretical blend. There is a radicalism to the empiricism of feminist archaeologists that allows us—has allowed me—to appreciate that in order to understand the "efficaciousness" of the symbolic, we need to explore how our bodies in the contextualized acts of moving, sensing, and feeling, as well as in material creation, serve as cultural repositories not only of the "techniques of the body" but as the source of "embodied metaphors" that we employ in our philosophies of being (and becoming.) A brief moment from the Betsileo of the central highlands of Madagascar, a moment of routine and ritual, might allow me to illustrate this point.

Strands of Body, Sentiment, and Thought

The Betsileo live in the central highlands region of Madagascar. They number more than a million souls and are primarily wet-rice cultivators who also raise zebu oxen. It is easy enough to find in the literature classical, dry, and "objective" descriptions of what traditionally has been considered women's work by the Betsileo. Reading such descriptions one finds, not unexpectedly for agriculturalists, that women bear and socialize children, physically maintain the household through tasks including cooking, carrying water, and weaving, and contribute to agricultural labor. However, such a description of women's roles does not speak to how such a way of being in and engaging with the world is found compelling by most individual women in Betsileo society. Some appreciation for their cultural conviction comes from moments spent in the field and in their company.

The sensuous body, skilled as well as culturally "equipped," dressed, and decorated, defines age, social status, and gender. For the Betsileo, after passing stages of infancy, a girl "ages" with the acquisition of skills. In the classic work on Betsileo culture by DuBois, he presents a list of the terms used to designate the "ages of a girl child" (1938, 392–93). (A corresponding list exists for the male child.) Some of those terms include the following:

anakotene	"[a child] that is weaned"
atorankivoho	"[a child] that one carries on the back"
añindramandre	"who sleeps at the side of their mother"
songondande	"who has 3 locks [of hair]"
mahafotsy vary	"who knows how to pound rice"

mahandry kanakana	"who is capable of watching over the ducks"
maharay akalo	"who can lift the pestle"
mahazo rano amboboka	"who can carry water from the spring to the storage jar"
soamandrare	"who knows how to weave"

Women's identity as weavers is very culturally salient. What they weave is indispensable for agriculture, the household, social relations, and ritual activity. Women weave the various baskets and mats that are indispensable to agricultural and household tasks of transportation and storage. Women also produce the mats used during such rituals as marriage (e.g., as part of the wife's dowry) and funerals (e.g., traditionally used to wrap, transport, and bury the body), and they weave the decorated mats that are laid out to receive guests in the fostering and maintenance of social relations. Weaving is so commonplace and so essential to the functioning of everyday life, and at the same time so ritually critical, that it becomes a powerful and central metonym for the status and role of the adult female in Betsileo society. The ability to weave is an indexical sign as well as a metaphor for the eligibility of a young woman for marriage.

It is in the routine of life and its material accouterments that we build up a repository of habits of the body and sediments of sentiment that are sources of metonymy and mimesis that link areas of lived experience, underpin cultural conviction in both routine custom and esoteric belief, and create fields of philosophical rumination and moral codes. A concrete moment in the Betsileo marriage ritual will allow us to explore this abstract assertion.

During the lengthy marriage ceremony among the Betsileo, there is one short moment when the woman-to-become-wife is brought in among the elders who have been engaged, often for hours, in traditional dialogical speech exchanges. The woman-to-become-wife sits down and is given a basket to place on her head. This basket contains the monetary portion of her dowry contributed by members of her extended family. She is asked by the senior male representative of her family side: "An'iza ity ta(n)ty ity?" ("Whose basket is this?") She answers: "Amiko." ("It is mine.") Asked deliberately a second time: "Ta(n)tinao?" ("Is it your basket?"), she replies: "Ta(n)tiko!" ("It is my basket!") Such a simple gesture and exchange of words can easily slip by even a "trained anthropologist" attentive to ritual. Several Betsileo friends, however, made a point to explain the significance of the gesture and words, since most Betsileo appreciate a good play on and play with words. The word, "ta(n)ty" can be translated as the noun, "basket." It can also be translated as the verb to mean "support the weight," or "bear the burden [of responsibility]." The seeming repetition of the question, "Is it your basket?" "Ta(n)tinao?" can be understood as asking the more important question, "Can you bear the weight [of this new social responsibility]?" The woman-to-become-wife responds, "Ta(n)tiko!" affirming her willingness to bear the responsibility of this marriage, which includes the responsibilities of social obligations beyond the immediate responsibilities of the wife within the division of labor in the new household.

This ritual moment highlights the force of material symbols in their multireferentiality, multivocality, and multimodality, as well as in the sheer élan of the co-presence of significant items. The simple, undecorated basket of the marriage ritual resembles the many the wife-to-be will continue to make; baskets for storage and to carry; to carry on the head as she and other women have, do, and will carry other baskets to free their hands for other tasks; and to carry on the head as one renders honor to a gift by touching it to one's head. This basket and gesture become a metonym for the woman and for the product of adult female labor and a metaphor for the recognized central role of women in society. Her plain clothes are the iconic sign of gendered skills, and their grease stains and water marks are indexes of her skills, for just moments earlier she had been involved with other women in tasks of getting water, cooking food, and serving guests, the very tasks she will continue to perform as wife. The sedimentation of "habitus" both underlay the ordinariness of this woman in dress, in gesture, and in practice, and it underlay the deliberate gestural, linguistic, and material concurrence that sustains the ritual's "poetic" performative power to transform this woman into wife. Honoring her responsibility as sustainer of family and of social alliances she places the "weight of this responsibility" on her head, and in a performative (rather than a simple affirmative) speech act she acknowledges her acceptance of status and responsibility. The commonplace dress and the commonplace basket will find a reverberation in counterpoint later that day, in her celebratory dress as new wife and as she is accompanied by female friends who will carry on their heads decorated baskets filled with the household goods she brings to her new residence.

Conclusion

The Betsileo woman becomes wife both in ritual practice and in "practical, sensuous human activity" (one definition given by Marx to the term "praxis"). Concrete metaphors, underpinned by indexical and iconic "significants," in praxis and in ritual are "persuasively" transformative, capable of transforming woman into wife. Metaphor and routine ritual can move us, as Fernandez argues, in "quality space," accommodating us "in many subtle ways to our condition in all its contrarieties and complexities" (1986, 20). Perhaps it is this routine movement in "quality space" of our quotidian existence that we must first understand in order to speak of the symbolic domain in any "significant" way. The Betsileo example of a brief but powerful ordinary ritual moment should give us pause. It suggests that we should hone our middle-range theory to be able to appreciate the poetic economy of concrete gestures and words that are built upon an underlying strata of copious cultural embodied experience that invest material objects with meaning. Microscale observations of awls, plants, spindle whorls, cooking fires, domestic space, baskets, and other mundane materials in the archaeological record and in ethnoarchaeological studies, allow us to understand that not only is the private the political, but that technology and the quotidian are the materials of our poetries and our philosophies. This should also allow us to avoid falling into high theoretical traps of impoverished "prosaic readings" of other cultures' symbolic productions and alternative ways of (gendered) being in the world.

Epilogue: Being Washed over by the Breakers on Far Distant Shores

The Malagasy say: "Ny herikerika mahatonga ny tondradrano," "it is the drizzle or small drops that [eventually] bring the inundation."

Now that I am where the waves break rather than crest, now that I am on the far distant shores of a small liberal arts college, I am emboldened by feminist archaeology and anthropology. My presence in front of an undergraduate class in archaeology calls into question Indiana Jones, hirsute males, and white-haired elder males stereotypes as archaeologists. I relish the minor victory each semester when I stand in front of my class in Introduction to Anthropology or Introduction to Archaeology and explain that students must use gender-inclusive language in their writing assignments since the American Anthropological Association demands such in submissions for publication in the premier journal of the discipline, even though the students do not know that it is low-level theory that makes this inclusive language imperative.

Yet, what I relish most is that I can give range to my voice, a voice that that is embodied and sensuous and even humorous as a "woman writing culture." I have been empowered to use words as "magic," "mother," "audacity," "ethos," "body and soul," and most satisfyingly, "sensuous," in titles and texts of my presentations at the annual meetings of anthropologists and at the annual meetings of archaeologists. These are not just minor or private victories for those of us on distant shores. They inspire us to dream big. Even to dream that a worker, like me, in the low- and middle-range trenches and from a small liberal arts college, can one day aspire to become president—president of the American Anthropological Association.[4]

Chapter 7
Materiality and Social Change in the Practice of Feminist Anthropology

ELIZABETH M. PERRY AND JAMES M. POTTER

Performativity has recently emerged as an attractive conceptual frame-work for feminist archaeologists concerned with the materiality of gen-der in the past, particularly with respect to the work of Judith Butler (Joyce 1996, 2000a, 2001a; Knapp and Meskell 1997; Meskell 1999; Perry and Joyce 2001). However, feminist activists and anthropologists have heavily criticized Butler's discussions of gender and power. Nuss-baum (1999) feels Butler's characterization of the pervasive role of power in the reproduction of gender relegates all possibilities for resis-tance to discursive, sadomasochistic parodies of dominant categories. She concludes: "Judith Butler's hip quietism is a comprehensible re-sponse to the difficulty of realizing justice in America. But it is a bad response. It collaborates with evil. Feminism demands more and women deserve better" (Nussbaum 1999, 45).

In a poignant yet less vituperative critique, Alonso (2000) pointed out that contemporary feminists who are comfortable with the theoretical detachment of gender from biology represent those privileged enough to detach themselves from their own biology with the help of modern advancements in women's health and medicine brought about by ear-lier feminist movements. In contrast, "less privileged women—in this country and elsewhere—are much more aware of the materiality of the body because they have to struggle with the changes brought on by their cycles, pregnancies, and illnesses in ways that carry more sensory imme-diacy" (Alonso 2000, 223).

As feminist archaeologists committed to the idea of positive social change, as well as theorizing the history of the interaction between peo-ple and material in diverse phenomenological realms, we find ourselves motivated by the challenge presented by the difficulty of resolving bio-logical and material realities with the active processes of social construc-tion we observe across time and space. This chapter represents an example of our attempt to resolve our theoretical position on gender as a social phenomenon within our particular field (archaeology of the American Southwest) with our concern for social change and oppression in the contemporary world. We begin with a discussion of the particular model of gender performativity we employ in our research, followed by an example of the operation of gender within multiple social contexts in the pre-Hispanic American Southwest. We conclude with a suggestion of how theorizing prehistoric gender relations can potentially translate into more widely accessible mechanisms of contemporary social change.

Gender Performance and Archaeology

Broadly, performance refers to certain social processes that continuously construct gender difference. According to Butler (1990, 33), "Gender is the repeated stylization of the body, a set of repeated acts within a highly rigid regulatory frame that congeal over time to produce the appearance of substance, a natural sort of being." The concept of performativity is descended from anti-essentialism feminism and practice theory (Morris 1995) in its critical examination of the relationship between sex and gender and the importance of embodiment. In this analysis, sex is materialized through repetition of regulated practice (Butler 1993). Repetitive, structured practice and its material effects are accessible in the archaeological record, and thus we find the concept of performativity particularly compatible with archaeological knowledge. As Butler (1993, 2) pointed out, "performativity must be understood not as a singular or deliberate 'act,' but, rather, as the reiterative and citational practice by which discourse produces the effects that it names." From an archaeological research perspective, regulated reiterative practices result in the production of major classes of material culture—such as architecture, ceramics, worked stone, and agricultural products. Sex and gender are implicated in the production and distribution of material culture.

Some feminist theorists (e.g., Alonso 2000) object to the translation of the observation that gender is the social manifestation of sex into the suggestion that sex is discursively constructed by gender (Butler 1993; DeLauretis 1987b). Does this constitute a denial of the role of biology (women's biology, in particular) in shaping gender possibilities? Butler, for example, does not deny the existence of physical difference, but she is more concerned with the ways in which sexual differences are discursively constructed; "there is no reference to a pure body which is not at the same time a further formation of that body" (Butler 1993, 10). Theorizing elements of biological sexual difference in relation to socially performative elements is not an impossible project. While integrating the vocabulary of performativity, it is also possible to "engage fully with the concept of sexual difference and deliver a politics and ethics appropriate to the feminist agenda" (Shildrick and Price 1999, 7). A materialist discipline (such as archaeology) can contribute a critical involvement of biological variation and an improved mechanism for social change to performativity. Butler (1993, x) suggests that the repetition that is crucial to both gender performance and the materialization of sex can "also constitute the occasion for a critical reworking of apparently constitutive gender norms." This is where the time depth provided by archaeological investigations of gender is particularly useful. Drawing on the material manifestations of repetitive performance, archaeologists are in a position to document the regulatory structure that informs performance, as well as those areas where gender norms are indeed reworked through the agency of individuals over long periods of time.

THE ROLE OF ABJECTION IN PERFORMANCE

The concept of the abject (e.g., Butler 1993; Kristeva 1982) is employed as a heuristic device in this study to describe the formation and transformation of sex/gender manifestations in archaeological contexts. Julia Kristeva (1982) introduced this idea in *Powers of Horror: An Essay on Abjection* by describing the complex oppositional quality of the phenomenon that is "neither subject nor object." In Kristeva's (1982, 1) analysis, "The abject has only one quality of the object—that of being opposed to I." Kristeva's treatise on abjection is fundamentally psychoanalytic, concentrating on the forceful repudiation of elements of the self—the female and maternal body in particular. A quandary results in that the rejected elements are simultaneously constitutive of the self:

Not me. Not that. But not nothing, either. A "something" that I do not recognize as a thing. A weight of meaningless, about which there is nothing insignificant, and which crushes me. On the edge of nonexistence and hallucination, of a reality that, if I acknowledge it, annihilates me. There, abject and abjection are my safeguards. The primers of my culture. (Kristeva 1982, 2)

Shildrick and Price (1999, 7) stressed that Kristeva's view of the abject as the repudiated, unstable elements of self that are nonetheless intrinsic aspects of the body "resonates with the widespread cultural unease with bodily, and especially female bodily, fluids . . . in the effort to secure the 'clean and proper' male body, the body that is sealed and self-sufficient, it is women who are marked by the capacity of that which leaks from the body—menstrual blood is the best exemplar—to defile and contaminate."

Judith Butler (1993) articulates abjection within performativity as a potential context of agency within structured gender constraints. In this elaboration of the concept, the existence of the abject is a product of the instability of socially enforced gender norms—yet the very existence of the "not me" simultaneously bolsters normative gender categories. The habitual, embodied, performative processes that construct gender and other identities though time result in a certain dissonance in the form of abject or ambiguous individuals that fail—in some performative dimension—to achieve the ideal with respect to either the materiality of sex or the performance of gender. This failure to materialize the ideal sex/gender construct is a product of the dialectic between the composition and decomposition of gender difference in society. Gender difference decomposes in its composition because no one can actually exemplify the ideal, in body or action. The abjected self is both outside of (rejected from) and constitutive of the self. Butler (1993, xi) explains the process through which the rigid construction of gender produces the domain of the abject:

Thinking about the body as constructed demands a rethinking of the meaning of construction itself. And if certain constructions appear constitutive, that is, have this character of being that "without which" we could not think at all, we might suggest that bodies only appear, only endure, only live within the productive constraints of certain highly gendered regulatory schemas. Given this understanding of construction as constitutive constraint, it is still possible to raise the critical question of how such constraints not only produce the domain of intelligible bodies, but produce as well a domain of unthinkable, abject, unlivable bodies?

The role of the abject in performativity—those selves and aspects of the self that are inconsistent with the performative ideal—may be an avenue for reintegrating the materiality of the body into gender performance. This avoids the danger of implying that there is a basically invariable set of biological characteristics that separates male sex from female sex, which constrain the gender possibilities for femaleness and ultimately naturalizes gender asymmetry. We return the reality of the female body back to the theoretical fray by critically integrating measurable sex-linked characteristics into social performance. There is a great deal to be gained by looking at the relationship between performative gender possibilities and how they are socially constructed and biological possibilities. If gender constitutes sex, it follows that gender determines how certain biologically observable variables (sex-linked characteristics) are delimited such that a certain sex comes into being as a socially meaningful category associated with a set of variables that are ranked in order of importance. The ways in which race is described as a social construct may be translatable to sex: what we understand to be a biological sex is composed of a diverse set of variables that may not invariably pattern out into what we socially comprehend as male and female. As Shildrick and Price (1999, 3) explain, "Where the body is viewed though conventional biological and racial taxonomies that make appeal to a given nature, it is taken for granted that sexual and racial difference are inherent qualities of the corporeal, and, moreover, that male and female bodies, black and white bodies, may each respectively fit a universal category."

Laqueur's (1990) account of changing representations of the "natural" body in premodern Europe is instructive in this regard, as he demonstrates how the privileging of particular biological/genital characteristics (i.e., the phallus) relates to the construction of sexual categories. Laqueur (1990, 16) also notes that interrogating the constriction of sex characteristics into certain categories is an important political practice, pointing out that "the fact that pain and injustice are gendered and correspond to corporeal signs of sex is precisely what gives importance to an account of the making of sex."

The following discussion draws on the concepts of performativity and abjection to describe the construction and transformation of gender in a particular archaeological context—the Ancestral Puebloan communities of the North American Southwest.

Gender, Metaphor, and Performance in the Southwest

Gender as a social and behavioral construction, as an embodied category of identity, requires diverse discursive arenas and multiple spaces of production and ramification to become fixed in and internalized as practical consciousness. The embodiment of gender though reiterative practice and its underlying cultural logic depends upon certain metaphorical reifications operating at a variety of spatial and conceptual scales. As a result of their mutually reinforcing nature, elements of gender definition map onto multiple aspects of experienced reality, making them feel all the more natural, grounded, immutable. Their strength and resilience is determined by these imbricated sources of meaning, as the metaphorical associations between gender and other "natural" objects and phenomena compel the reiteration of normative gendered practice.

We see this multiscalar metaphorical system of gender construction in operation throughout the Puebloan world of the American Southwest. Femininity and masculinity are respectively linked to certain material realities and behavioral practices such that the gendered production of material culture and participation in ritualized gendered acts continually reproduces the relations upon which they depend. Potter (2004), for example, has discussed the metaphorical connection in Puebloan thought between the construction of maleness and the material and

spiritual implications of hunting. Hunting activities and rituals conceptually refer to the grounded literal landscape, including natural landscapes and architectural landscapes, to the landscape of the animal
carcass, reifying in the process the imbricated and natural disposition of
that which is masculine.

The major joints of large game, for instance, were places where spirits
emerged, openings into the spirit world, and techniques for butchering
incorporated the reality of this geography. These spirit portals were not
unlike sipapus, small openings in the floors of ceremonial rooms that
linked the spirit world below to the outer world. These ceremonial
rooms, or kivas, were the containers of male activities, such as the performance of secret rituals and weaving, which were generally not visible
to outsiders, particularly women (Potter 2004, 325).

Metaphorical connections between hunting and warfare, and game
animals and women, further provide for the conceptualization of what
is masculine. Femininity, on the other hand, is defined and produced
through activities such as ceramic manufacture and the preparation and
serving of food, primarily corn-based dishes. These practices tie women
conceptually and actually to the home and village and allow Puebloans
to metaphorically "imagine" (Isbell 2000) their community as a self-
contained whole. The village is a family, and the leader, although ob-
servably male, is referred to as the "mother of the village." For example,
the summer chief was referred to as "mother old-woman" at historic
Santa Clara Pueblo, despite being recognized as male (Parsons 1929,
109). These leaders ensured agricultural success through correct performance of rituals, and redistributed or "served" surpluses to the community in a central village. Feasting of this kind was a way for leaders to
demonstrate and perform their duties as the metaphorical "mothers" of
the village (Potter and Ortman 2002).

We thus have a multilevel metaphorical system of gender construction
operating in Puebloan society that rendered categories of femaleness
and maleness, and the social practice that represented them, seemingly
immutable. From the archaeological record of the ancestral Puebloan
Southwest, however, we see evidence of mutability. The actuality that
changes occur in gendered practice even in the face of a seemingly stable, self-reinforcing system that continually reproduces gender/sexual
norms is a paradox of performativity:

As a sedimented effect of a reiterative or ritual practice, sex acquires
its naturalized effect, and, yet, it is also by virtue of this reiteration that
gaps and fissures are opened up as the constitutive instabilities in such
constructions, as that which escapes or exceeds the norm, as that which
cannot be wholly defined or fixed by the repetitive labor of that norm.
This instability is the deconstituting possibility in the very process of

repetition, the power that undoes the very effects by which "sex" is stabilized, the possibility to put the consolidation of the norms of "sex" into a potentially productive crisis (Butler 1993, 10).

The instabilities produced through metaphorical and practical reiteration of gendered and sexed norms are evident in significant changes that occurred in the Puebloan world regarding the material representation and performance of gender. Kivas, for instance, prior to about A.D. 1300 were not primarily male ceremonial rooms but instead housed female labor, such as corn grinding (Ortman 1998). After 1300, grinding labor appears to have shifted out of kivas to public, plaza spaces. The intensity and duration of this labor increased with the formalization of largely male-dominated ritual spheres and practices, which involved a growing demand for finely ground corn (Crown 2000; Ortman 1998). Additionally, communities appear less well integrated before 1300 and competition for status among households is evident both architecturally and in the apparent lavishness of household sponsored feasts. Thus, the metaphorical association of "mothering" with village leadership, and the emergence of communal, redistributive feasting may not have been emphasized prior to this time. Finally, the yearly emergence of Katsinas from the San Francisco Peaks is also a post-1300 phenomenon (Adams 1991). Although the specific conceptual metaphors of gender construction prior to 1300 are not known, we do know that the "taskscape" (Ingolds 2001) of gender construction was very different than the system that developed after this date and that survived into the modern era. Those material representations of gender that are metaphorically associated with multiple areas of social and ritual life are subject to change. While the kiva may have been representative of femaleness and the site of domestic activity at one point in time, a noticeable performative shift renders the kiva exclusive masculine space, literally becoming the container of the ritual reproduction of maleness through the ceremonial initiations tied to those structures.

Thus the construction of gender norms that is heavily tied to ritual and metaphorical realms cannot so thoroughly occupy the field of gender possibilities as to preclude the existence of bodies that are unintelligible by the dominant cultural logic. The male-female dichotomy is continually reproduced, yet abjections of these representations leak from the system. As noted above, the masculine appearance of village leaders can be subordinated to their metaphorical position as mother/old woman. In this scenario, the materiality of sex is in conflict with the performance of gender—an event that destabilizes oppositional gender norms by presenting a body exhibiting the material signatures of maleness ritually performing femaleness. At the same time, the adherence to the metaphorical associations among food, village, mother, and femaleness

even in the face of a masculine body acting in that capacity effectively stabilizes gender norms by refusing to disrupt those associations.

The practice of active, daily gender transgression by some individuals
presents a different picture of abjection than the ceremonial and situa-
tional disruption of sex-gender norms discussed above. Such transgression has been observed in historic Puebloan society, where apparently
male- and female-bodied individuals have successfully performed genders that were not consistent with the morphological sex characteristics
perceived as more meaningful to European observers (Roscoe 1991;
Parsons 1939).

Although the frequency of such transgressive individuals though time
is unknown, the ability of the Puebloan cultural logic to accommodate
such practice points to the relative importance of metaphorical and performative constructions of gender. A well-documented example of performative gender transgression comes from the Pueblo of Zuni, where
the status of *lhamana*, or transgendered person, was tied up both in the
performance of domestic labor (which was infused with culturally specific
gender significance) and in the ritual performance of Kolhamana, the
transgendered Katsina.

Lhamanas were primarily identified by ethnographers and other observers at Zuni by dress and gesture. Parsons (1939, 338–39) referred to
lhamanas as transvestites, and described in detail the culturally specific
feminine clothing, jewelry, hairstyle, speech, and mannerisms of individuals who she perceived to be biologically male (Parsons 1916). Similarly,
some individuals perceived to be biologically female were described as
"girl-boys" primarily based on such characteristics as gait, movement,
and attitude (Parsons 1916, 525). Although individuals described as
lhamanas in the historic literature are almost without exception documented as participating regularly in the economic labor stereotypically
associated with the "opposite sex" at Zuni, it seems that there was a
tremendous amount of diversity in the types of labor performed by
lhamanas. The famous Zuni lhamana, We'wha, was documented as a
farmer, weaver, potter, and housekeeper—a mixture of occupations with
both female and male contextually contingent gender significance
(Roscoe 1991). Female-bodied lhamanas were described in a sweeping
manner as "mannish," but their labor tended to cross gender lines as
well (Roscoe 1991, 27).

By virtue of their transgressive gender performance in domestic settings, which in many cases at Zuni originated in childhood (Roscoe
1991, 145), lhamanas tended to take the role of Kolhamana, the transgendered Katsina, in public ritual performances (Parsons 1916, 525).
Kolhamana figures prominently in the Zuni origin story. Although Parsons (1916, 524) reported some dispute among her informants regard-

ing the specifics of Kolhamana's story, Cushing (1896, 401–13) documents Kolhamana as the first of ten supernatural offspring of a brother and sister who were chosen to lead the Zuni's to the "middle place." Due to his role in Katsina origin stories, Kolhamana figures in public ceremonial performance (Parsons 1916, 525).

It is noted above that Katsina religion likely crystallized after 1300 in the Ancestral Puebloan Southwest, specifically the public, performative aspects of formalized ritual as well as the importance of dualistic representations of gender. Given this, it is probable that the social status of lhamana may have its roots in this period as well. The near-simultaneous emergence of gender-transgressive performance (both ceremonial and domestic) and a highly structured ritual system tied to dualistic gendered societal organization exemplifies the paradox intrinsic to performativity and abjection: the existence and ritualized formalization of the lhamana, the "not me" of most gendered subjects that by its ritually contained existence safeguards the sanctity of the self. If the practice of the lhamana represents an abjected product of the construction of gendered norms and certain correlative manifestations of sex, it is potentially disruptive to the normative system; as Kristeva (1982, 2) wrote, the abject is "the jettisoned object (that) is radically excluded and draws me toward the place where meaning collapses." The association of the transgendered person with the spiritual and supernatural in the context of origin stories and ritual performance acts as a buffer to the potential collapse of everyday gendered meaning and practice: that which is unintelligible to a rigid dualistic gender/sex schema is intelligible parsed within the context of Katsina religion.

The association between transgendered individuals and the supernatural is not limited to Zuni history. For example, Sandra Hollimon (1997) has observed the role of transgendered or "Two-Spirit" individuals as undertakers, closely associated with the dead among the Chumash. The Navajo concept of *nádleehí* that describes gender or sexually transgressive individuals is a role understood to be "honored by the gods and to possess unusual mental capacity combining both male and female attributes" (Roscoe 1998, 47). It is possible that in such cases, hailing the supernatural in order to account for divergence from a gendered regulatory schema preserves the natural quality of the schema itself.

Descriptions of gender performativity in ethnohistoric and archaeological contexts have particular social value in that they document the variable and contingent conditions of the social construction of both the materiality of sex and the performance of gender, exposing areas of destabilization and thus introducing the possibility of social change. In this endeavor, however, it is crucial to recall that the social construction of gender roles can result in dangerous and oppressive material realities.

Recognizing the conditions of gender construction does not deny the material consequences of gender.

For example, women in the pre-Hispanic Southwest were likely responsible for the processing of corn, a practice strongly tied to the construction of femaleness in multiple metaphorical realms. Hegmon, Ortman, and Mobley-Tanaka (2000) have argued that such labor was physically debilitating to women and was not correlated to significant increases in social status. Thus the resilient metaphorical connection between women and food, while allowing male village leaders to effectively integrate their communities with redistributive feasting, produced tangible, material, and painful effects on the female body. As noted above, increases in the duration and intensity of grinding activities for women coincided with the elaboration of male-dominated ritual after A.D. 1300. Similarly, Debra Martin (1997, 2000) has documented disproportionate cranial and skeletal trauma, sprawled and haphazard burial positions, evidence of short life spans and infection, and extreme occupational stress on female skeletons recovered from two Southwestern Puebloan sites occupied from around A.D. 1000 to 1300. There may be variables other than gender contributing to the violence perpetuated against these women (ethnicity, the acquisition of "war captives"), but the association between women and abuse in this scenario is unquestionable. At these sites, it is possible that violence, low status, and intense labor were elements of the cultural construction of "femaleness." Clearly, the association of violence and low status with the experience of women is not limited to the archaeological evidence presented above. In the following section, we suggest the value of certain feminist perspectives on gender for addressing gender oppression in the contemporary world.

Social Change and Performativity

A question we view as key for the future of feminist archaeology is, can the observations driven by third wave feminist theories regarding the social construction of sex/gender through time and space (such as we have offered above) translate into the language of social change? We believe there is theoretical value in embracing the notion of the social construction of sex, as it can expand our understanding of the ways in which human biology interacts with gender construction under contingent social circumstances. It is important to further the exposure of sexual variability (as well as gender variability), and the relationship of that variability to social construction, in order to liberate and give voice to people whose biology is considered contextually abject. The common response to this suggestion is that the frequency of intersexed or hermaphroditic people is so low through time that analysis only serves to elucidate a few extraordinary cases, such as Foucault's (1980) illumination of the memoirs of Herculine Barbin, an eighteenth-century hermaphrodite. This may indeed be an extraordinary case, but there is a range of biological abjection to which no one is immune, and even relatively minor conditions of such abjection may combine with cultural contexts of gender to amplify them.[1] Outwardly visible secondary sex characteristics, such as voice, body and facial hair, body size, and breast development are extremely variable and subject to a range of endocrine and genetic variation (Worthman 1995). In the attempt to reintroduce the significance of women's health and biology into feminist theories of performativity, we need to address biological variability in the category of "woman." Theories of performativity that integrate the complexities of biology can speak to the experience of a "woman" who exhibits extremely masculine secondary sex characteristics (not just the residuals of habitual "performance") attempting to access gynecological heath care in a public clinic. To quote Leslie Feinberg, a well-known transgender activist: "More exists among human beings than can be answered by the simplistic question I'm hit with every day of my life: 'Are you a man or a woman?' " (Feinberg 1998, 1). In her brand of feminist activism, Feinberg engages "the links between lesbian, gay, bi and trans desires and the desire for education, food, and shelter" (Feinberg 1998).

Social contexts of gender and sexual ambiguity and indeterminacy can be addressed within performative modes without reducing these elements to nihilistic social constructions. A focus on the performative contexts in which observable attributes of sex, gender, class, age, ethnicity, politics, and religion are configured and organized into socially meaningful categories can enable researchers and activists to model variable contexts of oppression. Documentation of the mutable conditions of gender construction across time and space can potentially generate conceptual possibilities for social change; as this exercise illuminates the contingent character of gendered relations and challenges their "naturalness." The mechanisms of power through which variability is reined in and structured can be evaluated through performative frameworks. In theory, effecting change in one performative realm will impact other realms. If we have some basis for understanding how these multiple reams interact under certain circumstances, we have an opportunity to positively guide social transformation.

Part IV
Grounding Feminist Theories in Educational and Professional Settings

Chapter 8

Feminist Perspectives and the Teaching of Archaeology: Implications from the Inadvertent Ethnography of the Classroom

JULIA A. HENDON

In this chapter I address the contributions of feminism to archaeology in the context of the classroom. We often think of archaeology in terms of fieldwork and research. Many professional archaeologists in North America work outside the academy. At the same time, education of the "public," people who are not and never will be professional archaeologists, is firmly embedded in the mission of archaeology as defined by the major professional organizations to which academic and nonacademic archaeologists belong (Table 1). The reasons for the concern with public outreach and education are obvious. We need the support of people who are *not* archaeologists but who are sympathetic to archaeology's goals of preserving the physical remains of the past, developing knowledge about the past, and understanding the processes and events shaping the past. Archaeologists and the archaeological societies to which they belong are thus interested in promulgating a set of values that they hold dear (it is worthwhile to know about the past; material remains and information should be recovered and preserved; such remains should not be looted or sold; archaeologists have effective ways of studying the past) in ways that will allow us not only to achieve this goal but also allow us to reproduce ourselves as a profession through the continued recruitment of supporters as well as new members.

At the same time, like many scientific or science-like disciplines (Lloyd 1996), archaeology faces, or appears to face, new challenges to its authority and disciplinary unity. Some of these challenges, such as those raised by Native Americans and other descendents of the people archaeologists study, have, after considerable debate and anxiety, been embraced and incorporated into the discipline's self-definition and ethical stance (Bender 2000; Dongoske, Aldenderfer, and Doehner

TABLE 1. PROFESSIONAL ORGANIZATIONS AND EDUCATION

Professional organization	Extracts of statements on education
American Anthropological Association: Code of Ethics Part II, Introduction, Paragraph 3.[a]	"The mission of American Anthropological Association is to advance all aspects of anthropological research and to foster dissemination of anthropological knowledge through publications, teaching, public education, and application."
Archaeological Institute of America: Mission Statement, Paragraph 3.[b]	"The AIA exists to promote archaeological inquiry and public understanding of the material record of the human past worldwide...Believing that greater understanding of the past enhances our shared sense of humanity and enriches our existence, the AIA seeks to educate people of all ages about the significance of archaeological discovery."
Society for American Archaeology: Principles of Archaeological Ethics Principle No. 4, Public Education and Outreach.[c]	"Archaeologists should reach out to, and participate in cooperative efforts with others interested in the archaeological record with the aim of improving the preservation, protection, and interpretation of the record. In particular, archaeologists should undertake to: 1) enlist public support for the stewardship of the archaeological record; 2) explain and promote the use of archaeological methods and techniques in understanding human behavior and culture; and 3) communicate archaeological interpretations of the past."
Society for Historical Archaeology: Principles of Archaeological Ethics Principle 7.[d]	"Members of the Society for Historical Archaeology encourage education about archaeology, strive to engage citizens in the research process and publicly disseminate the major findings of their research, to the extent compatible with resource protection and legal obligations."

[a] http://www.aaanet.org/committees/ethics/ethcode.htm (accessed 3 September 2004).
[b] http://www.archaeological.org/webinfo.php?page=10027 (accessed 3 September 2004).
[c] http://www.saa.org/aboutSAA/ethics.html (accessed 3 September 2004).
[d] http://www.sha.org/About/ethics.htm (accessed 3 September 2004).

2000; see also websites listed in Table 1). A second area of ferment in recent years has been the critique of processual archaeology that has developed along several theoretical and methodological lines, generally lumped together as postprocessual approaches (see Preucel 1991, 1995; Shanks and Hodder 1995; Wylie 2000). Other challenges to archaeology's authority, such as creationism, hyperdiffusionism, alien origins of civilization, and lost tribes, continue to be rejected as acceptable alternative ways of understanding the past or the archaeological record.

Achieving Archaeology's Educational Mission

Archaeologists feel a strong sense of mission to preserve, conserve, and learn about the past. They recognize the importance of sharing this knowledge and sense of mission with others. They feel that to do so it is necessary to take on the role of teacher, a role that may be enacted in many different settings, such as the classroom, the museum, the field school, or the national park. I suggest that incorporating a feminist perspective and research on gender into *what* we teach and feminist or critical pedagogy into *how* we teach will allow us to achieve the educational goals of the discipline more effectively. Feminist-inspired pedagogy and content will advance the broader educational project of anthropology, such as destabilizing common sense (i.e., culture-bound) notions of the human condition and its origins; developing an awareness of ethnocentrism, androcentrism, sexism, racism, and other consciously and unconsciously held perspectives; separating analysis (what do others do, why, and with what consequences) from assessment (these practices are wrong, bizarre, primitive); and the social construction of identity and difference. By accepting a role as teachers (people who educate), we create new opportunities for testing and reflecting on our own received ideas and pet theories. We can also serve the greater social good of helping our students develop into critical learners who, through exposure to archaeology's questions, data, and methods, transform their naïve curiosity, their fascination with the subject, into "epistemological curiosity," a transformation that retains the eagerness to know but equips the student with better ways of knowing and of evaluating that knowledge (Freire 1970, 1998). If we really want our public, who are also members of the same local and global communities that we inhabit as archaeologists and citizens, to be able to evaluate arguments, assess the internal logic of truth claims, decide if proposals are adequately supported by information, and identify tendentious or false claims, then we need to consider carefully our pedagogical practice and our own epistemologies.

But why feminist approaches? Feminism, or to be more precise, feminist critiques of science, have been implicated in the challenges to scientific authority (Kohlstedt and Longino 1997; Lloyd 1996). They have typically been placed under the post-processualist umbrella by archaeologists. Since I find convincing Alison Wylie's argument that feminist approaches are neither processual nor postprocessual, the full panoply of perspectives lumped into the postprocessual category does not concern me here (see Preucel 1995; VanPool and VanPool 1999; Wylie 2002). Feminist approaches represent a third set that "exemplify a critical engagement of claims to objectivity that refuses constructivism as firmly as it rejects unreflective objectivism" (Wylie 1997a, 80–81). My main point in this chapter is that archaeology's educational project is best served by exposing students to perspectives that have an identifiable research question and point of view that represents an underlying theoretical framework because all of our analyses and interpretations of the archaeological record and past societies are theorized or "theory-laden" (Wylie 2002). The kinds of observations that we make of our archaeological record are shaped by our knowledge of what is likely to be useful and by our research interests. "It is only with a theoretical system that a problem can be addressed so that important observations can be identified" (VanPool and VanPool 1999, 41).

I base my argument that feminist perspectives represent a *good*, and in fact a *better* way to teach about archaeology on my experiences teaching in continuing education and, most recently, at a four-year liberal arts college in the United States. Through these experiences I have come to realize that such a perspective has improved my research and thus my teaching. Some have claimed that the connection between good teaching and good research is not obvious or inevitable (Eble 1988) but I disagree. "To teach is not *to transfer knowledge* but to create possibilities in the production or construction of knowledge" (Freire 1998, 30; emphasis original), possibilities that exist in equal part for the teacher and the student. While professional organizations such as the Society for American Archaeology have rightly emphasized that many archaeologists practice outside the academy, this should not obscure the fact that the most sustained contact, both temporally and intellectually, with archaeology's public takes place in a classroom setting at the college level and that this setting offers one of the best opportunities for the kind of interaction between teacher and student likely to result in a transformative experience.

The opportunity to engage students in a process of learning centered on archaeology and to reflect on that process has involved me in a kind of inadvertent ethnographic experience. This intensive participant-observation experience forms the underlying framework on which I have constructed the analysis presented here. My inadvertent ethnography has both synchronic and diachronic dimensions. As the only archaeologist in a combined department of sociology and anthropology, I have taught introductory courses on archaeology and on significant world areas every semester since 1996 and will do so for the foreseeable future until retirement. Thus in any given semester my introduction to archaeology courses presents me with thirty-five or more naïve thinkers grappling with the process of becoming epistemological thinkers. I also encounter students more than once over the "life course" of their undergraduate career as they take more advanced courses with me or become anthropology majors.

How to Conceptualize Feminism?

Some commentators on the archaeological literature of gender have noted its rapid growth and diversity after a relatively late introduction of the topic (Conkey 2003; Wylie 2001; Joyce and Claassen 1997; but see Sørensen 2000). They have also noted that the authors of many of these papers and publications do not label themselves or their work as feminist. This failure to self-identify raises the possibility that not all archaeological research on women or gender is feminist (Conkey 2003; Gilchrist 1999). Interviewing and surveying of participants at a 1989 conference on the archaeology of gender, one of the first of its kind, indicated that at least some of those not labeling themselves feminists wished to avoid being so designated (Hanen and Kelley 1992; Wylie 2001). Although it is troubling that some archaeologists concerned with women and gender may think that feminist theories have nothing to offer, it is difficult to know how to generalize these results to more recent writings on women and gender. Attempts to exclude those who do not self-label are equally troubling. While such work is often undertheorized, it must be remembered that despite a great deal of discussion of theory in archaeology over the last forty years, "most mainstream archaeology has not been very reflective about method, underlying assumptions or epistemic commitments" (Hanen and Kelley 1992, 196).

Myriad disciplinary, historical, political, social, and theoretical strands make up contemporary feminism. It is social and political movements, bodies of theory, philosophies of knowledge and of life, and moral dispositions (di Leonardo 1991a; hooks 2000; Wylie 1997b). Thus no single unitary body of theory exists that can be labeled as feminist. Different academic disciplines have developed bodies of theory and focused on distinct research questions. In my own work I have drawn on feminist research in sociocultural anthropology, sociology, economics, history of technology, and philosophy (see Hendon 1996, 1997, 1999, 2002). Other archaeologists have drawn ideas from other strands of the feminist tapestry (Conkey 2003; Gilchrist 1999; Joyce 2001a; Klein 2001; Meskell 1999; Nelson 1997; Sørensen 2000; Wylie 1997a).

Such diversity needs to be respected. Is it possible, though, to find some common elements within this diversity? I am not concerned to define a unitary feminist archaeological theory that will constrain research within the discipline. But common elements may serve as a useful starting point. In the classroom, they give students the beginnings of a conceptual vocabulary. They also provide students with something to analyze, evaluate, disagree with, and expand upon. Wylie (2001) has suggested that at its most fundamental, a feminist approach would argue that gender be part of the discussion of social relations, social structure, and of society, that it not be consciously suppressed or unconsciously ignored. This baseline may be applied to reconstructions of past societies or, in line with feminist critiques of science, to the history and practice of archaeology. Wylie notes that if research on women and gender that does not label itself as feminist is held to this "bottom-line" standard, a good deal of it would exemplify such an approach. However, if by making gender visible one does not challenge or at least question "the use of sex-gender ideologies to justify things as they are" (Hartman and Messer-Davidow 1991, 2) then visibility does not move us very far along (hooks 2000). Commonly shared core tenets of a more-developed feminist perspective identified by Wylie (2001) include (1) starting with the premise that gender, however socially constructed, represents one of several dimensions of organization in society; (2) recognizing the hierarchical nature of gender roles and relations and that such relations have tended to disadvantage women (as socially defined) systematically; and (3) recognizing that relations that produce systematic disadvantage are unjust and should be changed.

Debates and questions about society that connect to gender may be traced back to the nineteenth-century emergence of the discipline. Arguments about original forms of kinship, marriage, sexual relations, and ultimately, control (e.g., primitive matriarchy, patriarchy, or equality) raised the possibility that current conditions were historical and could be changed. These ideas helped to shape and were shaped by contemporary feminism of the time (so-called "first wave" feminism) (di Leonardo 1991; Visweswaran 1998). Since the 1970s, sociocultural anthropologists have grappled at length with the cultural construction of gender and its social consequences. Abandoning efforts to develop a universal explanation for women's secondary status, many feminist anthropologists have focused on documenting the varieties of women's perceptions and experiences, and how these perceptions and experiences intersect with other dimensions of difference such as race or class. This has placed increased emphasis on women's agency, a perspective that sees women as "social actors working in structured ways to achieve desired ends" (Rosaldo in di Leonardo 1991, 142) without assuming that all women are the same or that oppression is universal or universally constructed or experienced. "Oppression," "status," "prestige," and other such terms need to be defined within the context of gender and other dimensions of difference (di Leonardo 1991; Hoodfar 1992; hooks 2000). These conditions or relationships then become something to be investigated, not assumed (see, e.g., Joyce 2002).

Feminist Pedagogy in Practice: Teaching Archaeology

A feminist approach encompasses a way of looking at all things archaeological. It is not a specific set of research methods or techniques although it is or has the potential to be an epistemology (Harding 1987; Wylie 2001). It is a "world view that will operate most visibly in problem selection, espousal of a feminist perspective, and in a form of skepticism that questions received views and acts to expose hidden biases in previously held views" (Hanen and Kelley 1992, 213).

During my eight years at Gettysburg College I have used at least one gender-focused archaeological analysis describing research informed by feminist theory in my introduction to archaeology course and in other courses offered to students with no or minimal background in anthropology. I have also used readings or presentations in other media such as film that are not overtly feminist but discuss gender or men and women and are thus susceptible to feminist analysis. More broadly, I have made questions of how archaeologists study social difference and hierarchy one of the central themes of these courses. Publications that I have used at least once in introduction to archaeology and that have been successful in provoking thinking and discussing are listed in Table 2. All concern themselves with gender as a social construction that has implications for people in society, and particularly those categorized as women. They differ in the degree to which they see gender as separable from biological sex, in their assessment of the social function of gender,

TABLE 2. READINGS THAT PROMOTE DISCUSSION OF GENDER OR FEMINIST PERSPECTIVES USED IN INTRODUCTION TO ARCHAEOLOGY

"The Development of Horticulture in the Eastern Woodlands of North America: Women's Role" by Patty Jo Watson and Mary C. Kennedy. *Engendering Archaeology: Women and Prehistory.*, ed J. M. Gero and M. W. Conkey (Oxford: Basil Blackwell, 1991).

"The Domestication of Europe" by Ian Hodder. *Archaeological Theory and Practice* (London: Routledge, 1992).

"The Eloquent Bones of Abu Hureyra" by Theya Molleson. *Scientific American* 271 2 (1994).

"Pounding Acorn: Women's Production as Social and Economic Focus" by Thomas L. Jackson *Engendering Archaeology: Women and Prehistory.*

What this Awl Means: Feminist Archaeology at a Wahpeton Dakota Village by Janet D. Spector (St. Paul: Minnesota Historical Society Press, 1993).

and in their theoretical framework. In this sense, they are examples of the diversity of research on gender in archaeology today (see Claassen and Joyce 1997).

Feminist archaeological research offers a way of introducing students to the realities of archaeological knowledge production because it can combine a well-articulated set of theoretical perspectives that not only generate ideas about social identities, relationships, structures, and consequences but also show a commitment to making clear the researcher's point of view. At the same time, feminist archaeological research has demonstrated great fidelity to empirical analysis based on some body of data (Wylie 1997a). This combination allows for greater discussion of the relationship between theory, data, and interpretation within the context of a peopled and embodied past. A feminist approach can contribute to the problematization of accepted notions about past societies and, in the process, make archaeological research more productive, significant, and potentially of greater interest to the general public. Feminist perspectives have enlarged our discussions of social identity and relations by requiring archaeologists to move beyond the ungendered, disembodied type of "person" defined by social status ("elite") or economic role ("farmer"). The apparent indeterminacy that some claim has resulted from the desire to consider social identity as multifaceted is really the positive effect of the disruption of simplistic models of human behavior as ungendered, social differentiation as hierarchy, and hierarchies as resulting only from differences in wealth.

I am also advocating adoption of pedagogical techniques and philosophies developed in critical and feminist pedagogies. Feminist pedagogy, like feminism itself, is a diverse and dynamic area of thought and practice (Briskin and Coulter 1992; Hoodfar 1992). It emphasizes self-reflexivity while holding up for scrutiny conventional ideas about how and why people learn. Some have conceived of feminist teaching as nurturing but others have challenged this maternal metaphor, arguing that the classroom is where teachers and students engage in difficult work (Martindale 1992). This work is both intellectual and political in that it tries to construct new knowledge in a setting marked by differences in authority, power, experience, and engagement (Hoodfar 1992; hooks 1994).

Archaeology is more impoverished than some academic disciplines in the production of accessible case studies or articles for students that address the issues of interpretation, epistemology, and practice that archaeologists contend with and that have informed current debates. This is partly a problem of presentation and partly of the reward structure for academic promotion and tenure that most academic institutions employ, which values research and publications aimed at fellow specialists over the development of pedagogical tools (Fagan 2004). In this context, the few articles published on teaching archaeology in a feminist context or on bringing issues of concern to feminism into the teaching of archaeology represent an unusual concern with pedagogy. Conkey and Tringham (1996) discussed a coaching approach to teaching as a feminist pedagogical alternative to merely depositing knowledge in students. Romanowicz and Wright (1996) examined why gender issues should be part of courses taught at the undergraduate and graduate level. Spector and Whelan (1989) also support the inclusion of questions about gender in archaeology courses and offered some tools for doing so. Claassen (1992b) presented a transcript of a discussion of teaching about gender among conference participants at the 1991 Boone Conference and some examples of syllabi. Since these articles were published, introductory textbooks have made an effort to include discussions of feminism and gender. Thus, the subject is not as invisible as was formerly the case but is still treated as a "topic" or an example of a particular set of research questions centering on women, the mixing of politics and research comparable to claims made by descendent communities for control of the past, or the less scientific and more empathetic turn in the discipline with postprocessualism (see, e.g., Ashmore and Sharer 2000; Fagan 2004; Praetzellis 2000; Renfrew and Bahn 2004 for good attempts).

What this small literature on pedagogy and my own experience make clear is that the benefits to the student, the teacher, and the discipline are most likely to emerge in a context of inquiry, problem-solving, and dialogue. Teaching archaeology, as with teaching any subject, proceeds most effectively when the instructor rejects the dominant banking approach to education in order to embrace the problem-posing or inquiry approach (Freire 1970; hooks 1994; see also Conkey and Tringham 1996). It is possible to teach as if one were depositing knowledge into the empty bank accounts of students, who then try and show how successfully they have received this information and how full their account is by returning the right answer in some standardized format. But such an approach discourages critical understanding, fails to spark intellectual creativity, and does not lead to the production of new or expanded knowledge. Nor does it offer any opportunity to destabilize a student's commonsense notions of the world, whether those notions stem from a position of privilege or exclusion. The necessity of recognizing that both students and teacher come to the classroom knowing things also occupies a central place in the inquiry model (Freire 1998; hooks 1994). Recognizing that students know things does not preclude the possibility of transforming, extending, or changing that knowledge, in fact, quite the opposite. It facilitates these processes of transformation and change.

Throughout the semester, I ask my students to reflect on the kind of archaeology they would like to do based on the examples of archaeological practice presented in the readings, videos, class discussions, and a computer simulation, *Adventures in Fugawiland* (Price and Gebauer 2002). These reflections take the form of small-group work in which each student works out and defends her or his opinion through discussion and debate, short in-class writing assignments, and more formally as part of the research design each student develops for the simulated excavation. I have found that they are quite uninterested in large-scale social evolutionary processes, environmental adaptation, or the function of abstracted social units. What they want to know, at least at the beginning level, is what life was like in ancient societies, how people did things, what they believed in, and other such highly social topics. They want a peopled past, a sense of the day-to-day, an understanding of the ability of individuals to make and carry out decisions, and a sense of the texture of social, political, and economic relations—what we might call an "experience near" kind of archaeology. This was brought home to me when I began using a text called *Discovering Our Past* (Ashmore and Sharer 2000), which makes an honest attempt to explain the differences between cultural-historical, processual, and postprocessual archaeology in a way that is aware of their historical relationship and respectful of the contributions of all three. What struck me about the students' responses was the degree to which they found postprocessual approaches (which includes feminist and gender-focused approaches in this text) as more interesting. When asked which set of approaches they would adopt as an archaeologist, the consensus was that while establishment of time-space systematics was an important beginning point and while an understanding of technology, environment, and other material factors would have its uses, it was the postprocessual focus on agency, gender, symbolism and meaning, and everyday life that had the potential to produced the most interesting research results.

Perhaps because of this, I have found that research that is either explicitly feminist or at least focused on a peopled and gendered past to be among the most effective case studies in moving students towards a better understanding of archaeological practice and of how theory informs data and interpretation. In the introduction to his textbook, Patterson (2005, 6) writes, "archaeologists rely on the same social theoretical traditions that historians, anthropologists, economists, or political scientists employ. Sometimes, they are explicit about their ideas and beliefs; in other instances, the social theory they use is implicit or only vaguely formed; in still other instances, their ideas are eclectic mixes of different theoretical strands." Even when archaeologists state their ideas, beliefs, or theoretical orientation, it can be difficult to connect grand statements of "Theory" with what actually follows. What do all those artifact categories have to do with origins of the state?

The majority of textbooks aimed at undergraduates do a competent job explaining our discipline's most basic methods such as relative and absolute dating techniques, stratigraphy, and typology, but understanding the rules of superposition or the temporal limits of radiocarbon dating is not an adequate basis for understanding the theory-laden nature of most archaeological evidence or for carrying out the kinds of systematic, analytical, and critical thinking that we, as a profession, identify as part of the value of studying archaeology. Where textbooks, documentaries, and other kinds of presentations generally fall short is in convincing their readers that the explanations presented are either verifiable or subject to evaluation. In other words, the explanations offered of how archaeologists use such data-gathering and analysis methods to present and support a coherent description of past human or proto-human behavior, society, and culture are either viewed as fact or as speculation by students. Such explanations are fact if only one narrative is given and if that narrative is presented as unproblematic. Such explanations are speculation if alternatives are given, particularly if presented as opposites or part of a debate. Even when different kinds of data are described as part of a discussion of how one might test or choose among these alternative explanations, many nonspecialists see the entire enterprise as hopelessly relative, since it appears that one can pick and choose one's evidence as well as one's story.

Our data are indeterminate to some degree, but most archaeologists, including many postprocessualists and feminists, would not agree that all explanations are equally likely or valid (VanPool and VanPool 1999; Wylie 1997a, 2002). Nor can we retreat from grappling with these issues into "'hyperscience,' where the focus of archaeological inquiry has been narrowed down to such a small scale that . . . one loses sight of the essential human aspect of the discipline" (Majewski 2000, 17). To take an example from the works listed in Table 2, *What This Awl Means* provides a good beginning point for discussion. Spector states her dissatisfaction with archaeology as practiced and couples that with the development of her interest in women's roles as part of a commitment to feminism. In the process, she not only situates herself, but provides the reader with a definition of feminism. I have used this short work many times in introductory archaeology courses. Many of my students' initial reactions to this book are strongly negative, based solely on the presence of the word "feminist" in the title. Some have very positive feelings to the title. The fact that there is a reaction at all is because they all come to this book with an opinion, a theory of what feminism is. Their understanding of feminism is often of the "fem-nazi" type: anti-male, political correctness at its worst, and so on. Another common understanding is of the "woman's culture" type: women as always nurturing, egalitarian, and morally superior to men, a concept much criticized as essentializing women by ignoring cross-cultural, historical, and sociological differences (di Leonardo 1991; hooks 2000). Sometimes I encounter a more informed perspective developed through exposure to women's studies, sociology, or anthropology but that still tends to distinguish between what is seen as a justifiable critique of social injustice and the possibility of systematic analysis.

I encourage students to bring out these opinions, often through small-group discussions or ungraded writing exercises, even if many of them make me cringe. But transformation and a more informed understanding cannot happen if existing perspectives are not acknowledged. Students can see the ways that Spector demonstrates how her theoretical and political stance raised new questions, led her to develop a particular kind of analysis, that of gender task, and contributed to her desire to move beyond such an analysis. Spector presents herself as someone with a point of view that is based on experience but grounded in theory. The concept of feminism, which initially seems entirely political to my students, becomes now something that relates directly and legitimately to a research process.

Contributing to my students' unease with the idea of a feminist approach to studying archaeology is their fear of bias. This concern has been instilled in them through their educational experiences. A common theme of most if not all state-mandated academic standards in the United States is developing the capacity to differentiate fact from opinion. Students should also be able to identify bias and propaganda, where present, and to evaluate an author's effectiveness (Pennsylvania Department of Education 2004). When asked to explain what typifies a biased argument or interpretation, the most frequent response is that it lacks objectivity. Objectivity and not being biased are synonymous; by being objective one arrives at truth. My students display here a fidelity to the "legendary view of science" described more fully by VanPool and VanPool (1999).

But, in fact, there are at least four definitions of objectivity that can be extracted from philosophy and science (Lloyd 1995). These definitions are given in Table 3. Not only are these definitions different, they stem from different premises or states. Clearly, the first one most closely matches my students' perception, a perception that many archaeologists share (VanPool and VanPool 1999). Definition 1 says something about the person making a claim or statement: the author exhibits objectivity, which is supposed to tell us something positive about the work or conclusions. The attempt to create a detached or unbiased observer, however, is

TABLE 3. DEFINITIONS OF OBJECTIVITY[a]

Definition 1	"detached, disinterested, unbiased, impersonal, invested in no particular point of view (or not having a point of view)." Refers to the attitude of a person, such as an archaeologist writing a report.
Definition 2	"public, publicly available, observable, or accessible (at least in principle)." Posits a relationship between a person, such as an archaeologist, and reality. Implies that observations of some phenomenon made by one archaeologist should be repeatable by another archaeologist.
Definition 3	"existing independently or separately from us." Also posits a relationship between a person, such as an archaeologist, and reality. Assumes that the data are not entirely a construction of the archaeologist's imagination or point of view.
Definition 4	"really existing, Really Real, the way things really are."

[a] Source; Lloyd 1995, 354.

doomed to fail. Having a point of view is inevitable; what counts is to be aware of it and to make it evident to others. Even so, "scientific knowledge can still be viewed as empirical in the sense that experience is its basis; but reasoning from evidence to hypotheses is always contextual" (Hanen and Kelley 1992, 203).

The second and third definitions focus on describing a relationship, one that exists between reality and a person, a *knower*, in Lloyd's terminology. The final definition is a statement about reality that is independent of any relationship with a knower. If, as VanPool and VanPool (1999 36) claim, many archaeologists including many postprocessualists, "recognize that the archaeological record does exist and that it can be studied," then Definition 3 would seem to be the most relevant meaning of objectivity. Analyzing and evaluating a feminist perspective can be a way for students to move from a naïve assumption of bias to an epistemologically sophisticated recognition of the relationship between evidence, questions, and interpretation. This is much harder to do when lack of bias is presumed on the basis of language or author's authority. Once this presumption is made, one is predisposed to take statements and claims at face value.

These examples only touch on the ways that critical feminist pedagogy can inform and improve our teaching and thus contribute to our discipline's educational mission. Giving students some sense of how archaeology works as a way of knowing about the past requires more than simplistic or glamorized stories of heroic scientists creeping into tombs to discover the truth. As part of our storytelling, we need to introduce students to the scaffolding and the integuments supporting and constraining that story. By looking at theorized research that is also profoundly empirical, and by acknowledging the researcher's, the teacher's, and the students' situated perspectives, we will not only create an informed public but also a more creative, reflective, and valid archaeology.

This essay is a substantial revision of a paper given at the 101st annual meeting of the American Anthropological Association in a session organized by the two editors of this volume. I would like to thank Pamela Geller and Miranda Stockett for inviting me to participate in that session. My development as an archaeologist and a teacher has benefited from conversations with Rosemary Joyce, Jean Potuchek, GailAnn Rickert, Marta Robertson, and my students and advisees; all of whom, of course are absolved from any responsibility for the ideas expressed in this essay or any errors it may contain.

Chapter 9
Toward a (More) Feminist Pedagogy in Biological Anthropology: Ethnographic Reflections and Classroom Strategies

Ann M. Kakaliouras

> *The knowing self is partial in all its guises, never finished, whole, simply there and original; it is always constructed and stitched together imperfectly, and therefore able to join with another, to see together without claiming to be another.*
> —Haraway 1991, 193

> *Feminist education—the feminist classroom—is and should be a place where there is a sense of struggle, where there is visible acknowledgement of the union of theory and practice, where we work together as teachers and students to overcome the estrangement and alienation that have become so much the norm in the contemporary university.*
> —hooks 1989, 51

Annette Weiner (1995), in her science studies-positive 1993 presidential address to the American Anthropological Association, encouraged biological anthropology graduate students to explore the socially constructed nature of genetics, among other reflexive pursuits. She also called for sociocultural anthropologists to turn their analytical gazes toward the culture of science in biological anthropology. Some of us were and are struggling to heed those kinds of calls in our research and teaching. In the early 1990s in particular we were experiencing our training in biological anthropology in a new way, informed in part by feminism, antiracism, queer theory, and science studies. The split between biological and cultural anthropology was certainly as palpable as it ever had been, yet the emergence of science studies in anthropology provided a conceptual space for feminist students like me to critically and reflexively place ourselves within our chosen disciplinary specializations in biological anthropology.[1] The possible paths to follow or blaze were already modeled in the literature by feminist scientists and critics in and out of anthropology, such as Donna Haraway (1989), Janet Spector (1993), Evelyn Fox Keller (1985), Anne Fausto-Sterling (1985), Micaela di Leonardo (1991), and Lori Hager (1997), among others.[2]

Even more urgently, though, in the late 1980s and early 1990s my undergraduate mentors in biological anthropology were already in a partnership with Native American groups and the state of Minnesota to repatriate and rebury thousands of ancestral Native skeletal remains. They taught me by gentle example and experience that my fascination with the aesthetics and interpretive possibilities of skeletal remains was rightfully secondary to Native American calls for justice and the basic human rights to control the disposition of their dead. Thanks not directly to science studies theory then, but to the reburial movement and the passage of NAGPRA (the Native American Graves Protection and Repatriation Act, PL 101–601), American physical anthropologists were boldly confronted with the culturally situated nature of our practice. While a good deal of osteologists, bioarchaeologists, and ancient DNA geneticists resisted reburial and continued (and continue) to pursue scientific business as usual, others of us have paused to consider the ethics of our practice.[3] Further, my burgeoning research program focuses on the critical reevaluation of classification in American biological anthropology and bioarchaeology, though such work is rarely considered central to my discipline (Kakaliouras 2003).[4]

Returning to Weiner's address for a moment, she saw science studies in anthropology as a key way to "develop . . . the kinds of critiques that will embody scientific knowledge with the stuff of lived experiences as people everywhere are faced with growing contradictions about the way they have named and come to know the natural world." One of these contradictions was evident in what I learned as an undergraduate of the history of anthropology, namely the Western scientific notion that some peoples were best seen as biological and ethnological objects, bound to "nature" in a way that "we" were not. Some, myself recently included, were in positions to build careers on the study of these Other people, their cultures, their bodies, and their pasts. To further contextualize my specific experience in bioarchaeology (the study of human remains from archaeological sites), my subdiscipline had at its base a conceptual separation of the objects of its study from their living descendents, claiming human skeletal remains as part of a larger history that only we were qualified to interpret and present to an interested American public. How is it possible, then, to reconcile scientific views of Native pasts, based largely on the etic analysis of their material remains, with diverse Native voices who find our work irrelevant or objectionable, and who call for the cessation of all such study (Riding In 1992)? While my advisors included such conflicts in their curriculum and practice, in the two hottest decades of the reburial debate within American physical anthropology there are still no straightforward answers, and further, little open discourse within the discipline that refuses to privilege other perspectives over the powerful trope of scientific authority.

Consequently, my individual struggle for what bell hooks (1994, 15–17) described as "self-actualization" within biological anthropology continues. In the sense hooks promotes the process in her discussion of engaged pedagogy, it is the dual project of resisting intellectual objectification and alienation in the academy, and striving to be a whole person. She insists on self-actualization for teachers "if they are to teach in a manner that empowers students" (15). My own striving for a kind of wholeness as a professional in biological anthropology is not currently limited to engaging my peers and students in discussions of repatriation and reburial, or attempting to pursue my own research in an ethical and responsible way. As a white, (visibly) queer woman, a scientist, and a feminist, how is it that I can in good conscience, for example, teach material in biological anthropology from primate studies and evolutionary psychology whose best explanations of the existence of homosexuality are often hopelessly androcentric and pathologizing (e.g., de Waal 2001, 41–68)? Even more importantly, though, how can I work to construct an anti-authoritarian classroom, yet teach evolution, an all-encompassing, classically grand, and authoritative scientific narrative? How can I teach, in introductory biological anthropology, that race is not a valid biological category using the logic of human variation, yet stress that race and racism are perhaps the most crucial social and cultural relationships my students will experience in their twenty-first-century North American lives? How can I teach evolution using hunter-gatherer groups as analogues for early hominid behavioral patterns when such a strategy commits the symbolic violence of denying those peoples' colonial histories and increasingly globalized presents?[5]

I did not come to tackle these questions easily, even though I possessed the theoretical grounding to ask them. In graduate school, I initially conceived and cultivated a fragmentation between my critical research interests and the material I knew, or mistakenly thought, I would be required to teach. I argued in discussions with my sociocultural peers—rather naively in retrospect—for the retention of a traditional four-field approach to anthropological education. Steadfastly holding onto the notion that students must learn "the basics" before they can integrate critical or reflexive perspectives into their practice, I effectively denied the currency of my earlier theoretical and practical ethnographic experiences to my emerging pedagogical practice. The painful experience of instructing students in ways that ensured my (and their) self-erasure in the classroom quickly disabused me of the notion that I could lead a kind of "double-disciplinary life."[6] I realized that teaching biological anthropology from an uncritical scientific perspective only perpetuated disciplinary defensiveness among my students, and between myself and graduate school colleagues and mentors, whose critique and counsel I was in danger of squandering.

I began, therefore, to address the questions I posed above in my introductory biological anthropology classroom. Slowly and sometimes fitfully, I started to engage my students in discussions of how Westerners are acculturated to think in certain ways about human biology and evolution, while still teaching the basic details of hominid evolution and behavior. I included detailed treatments of Social Darwinist thinking, the eugenics movement, and racist anthropology to bring home the point that how Americans have been taught to think about biological difference has had tragic historical and material effects on politically and economically disenfranchised people. Through moving myself and my classes through these sorts of very basic anthropological exercises, I created opportunities for more pedagogical risk-taking. I now readily challenge myself and my students to interrogate the very basis of narrative construction in paleoanthropology and biological anthropology, examples of which I detail in the rest of this chapter. I am admittedly more skeptical of the possibilities for wholeness and self-actualization for the so-called "sciences" (a space biological anthropology endeavors to occupy) in the powerful way hooks engages the concept for teaching in the humanities. For now, I am inclined to remain located within a Harawayian space of partial perspective, using my specialization in human osteology and bioarchaeology to ask critical questions of myself and my students about the construction of interpretation and the disciplinary culture within biological anthropology.

Some of my peers, sociocultural and biological anthropologists alike, do not think such integration of research and pedagogical pursuits is possible, or even desirable in the context of either transforming a traditional scientific anthropology or enhancing a postmodern or poststructuralist anthropology. Others of my colleagues and mentors sympathize or empathize with my particular version and personal incarnation of these disciplinary conflicts, and have constructed feminist and nonhegemonic research and teaching strategies in fields that may not lend themselves easily to such practice (e.g., human osteology and bioarchaeology, forensic anthropology, human behavioral ecology, and evolutionary theory). I have also brought this sense of disciplinary conflict and struggle to my teaching, not just in the courses that speak directly to my research, but to the introductory biological anthropology classes I teach every term. Like Annette Weiner advised, I see science studies as an important reflexive framework for my entire disciplinary worldview; further, I see feminist pedagogy as one of the central vehicles for crafting a classroom space where students are invited and encouraged to question singular and authoritative views of the human biocultural world (hooks 1994; Omolade 1987; Weiler 1991).

As I continue to transition from student to teacher, an awesome and intimidating change in and of itself, I see my students grappling with some of the same contradictions and conflicts I am now committed to face, some of which I will document here in three related classroom vignettes from my introductory biological anthropology courses. In the examples and selected strategies I will discuss, I endeavor to character- ize my students' perspectives in an honest and ethnographically sound way; to overgeneralize about their values or political orientations would disrespect the diversity of voices I have witnessed and cultivated in my last few years of teaching. Likewise, more experienced feminist peda- gogues may see the gaps and weaknesses in my methods. I do not claim to be an expert in feminist pedagogy, nor do I always succeed in creat- ing a completely feminist classroom; my process of designing and imple- menting constructive feminist pedagogical strategies is ongoing. I welcome, therefore, these kinds of critical discussions as opportunities to hone and improve my classroom practice.

Evolution Versus Christian Creationism: Engaging the Narratives

At the Southern public university where I teach, I experience intense defensiveness from students as we engage the very first topic of my Bio- logical Anthropology introductory course, the contemporary political and policy debate between Christian creationism and evolution. Many of my students, most of whom are white and middle or lower middle class, were raised in households steeped in a deep and often conserva- tive Christian faith. These students bristle at and resist any nonbiblical framework for understanding how humans came to inhabit the earth. More theologically open students, however, also voice their disquiet with the whole controversy, reacting against both extremes of literal six-day creation and atheistic evolutionism. Also, many of the agnostics, athe- ists, and evolutionists who show up in my class take it on themselves to impugn any kind of religious understanding of the world as often as possible.[7] Biological anthropology, grounded in the grand narrative of evolution, traditionally offers students as holistic and arguably deter- ministic a framework as creationism for understanding their place in the social and natural world. Rather than ignore their views or present evolution as a logical and rational replacement for their ignorance (an accusation one of my students leveled against "other professors"), we take the conflict apart and try to understand the increasingly acrimonious public debate between creationists and evolutionists. Additionally, rather than let the class be satisfied with so-called compromise solutions right away, I try to get each student to place themselves as specifically as possible within a recognized creationist or evolutionist viewpoint. Then we can start to play with the categories.[8]

I deliver a few lectures describing in detail various strains of creationism and evolutionism, as well as the current tenor and policy status of the debate.[9] I invite students to place themselves within defined viewpoints, such as "gap creationist," "day-age creationist," "young earth creationist," "theistic evolutionist," and "intelligent design proponent" during future discussions, both in class and, often, on a Web-based discussion board. The use of these distinct perspectives, and discussions around the limitations of these categories, is typically helpful to both the creationists and evolutionists in class. I draw from Steven Schacht's (2000) use of feminist pedagogy: "When each individual's experiences and outlooks are limited, as [Donna] Haraway argues, when partial and situated knowledges are recognized and explored, better, more comprehensive accounts of the world are possible . . . I not only recognize that the classroom is a political context, but further acknowledge both the possibilities and limits of my own situated knowledge and partial perspective." Being able to place themselves into a meaningful category allows students to more abstractly and critically look at the way their belief system organizes their thoughts about human origins. They also tend to become very curious about what I think and where I would place myself. I answer them honestly and tell them how I came to think the way I do; this is a dangerous moment though, because some students will often displace their own voice to assimilate one they feel comes from a place of scientific authority. Therefore I often share some of my doubts, or frame my self-explanation in as nonscientific a way possible. In any event, because the categories around which we align ourselves are highly specific and novel to most people in the class, there is typically both an imperative to accurately represent a particular viewpoint and a relative personal distance from the new labels. A devout Baptist and a nonpracticing Catholic could find themselves sharing the view that geological time is a phenomenon they agreed with, and that a biblically literal creation account did not sync with their views on the origin of life and of the human species.

Furthermore, I find that allowing a discussion of creation and evolution to continue all semester on a Web-based discussion board that I participate in has distinct pedagogical advantages. First, in larger classes interactive in-class discussion is not always possible, and many students are reluctant to state their personal beliefs so publicly. I offer an anonymous option on the board, where students email their posts to me and I then post them on their behalf. Additionally, students will often formulate their arguments and responses to the threads on the board on their own time and back them up with both online and textual sources, adding texture to the classroom discussions.

In some of my introductory biological anthropology courses I have also used a library and online exercise that requires students to research and read the "origin stories" of a number of different non-Western cultures and religious traditions. I supply a list of ethnographies and other sources where such information can be found, and I set up another online board where students then post the origin stories verbatim. One term, this process resulted in a student-initiated discussion of the contrasts and parallels between the Christian creation story, where the origin of humans is pinpointed to two individuals, and the idea that it is possible to find a single origin for hominids in the fossil record. That is, they critically related the idea that "we" (a Western scientific "we") will someday discover the ultimate origin of the human species in the fossil record to the search for a mythical Adam and Eve, an analytically interesting and insightful parallel.

Engaging the creation versus evolution debate brings many students out in class discussions sooner in the semester, especially those who are intimidated (or annoyed, like many of my sociocultural anthropology students, who are required to take biological anthropology for the major) at the idea of taking a science class. When I have committed to taking the time to flesh out the debate and its diverse perspectives, I've also experienced a comparatively greater student interest in the curricular material to follow—genetics, the basis for evolutionary theory, mechanisms of evolution, and primate analogues for human evolution. Some students have attested that these topics feel more intimately grounded in their process of evaluating evolutionary perspectives as a result of our earlier discussions.

The First Hominid . . . Family?

Since features critical to behavior do not fossilize, and since behavior is precisely what must be explained, imaginative reconstruction was explicitly legitimated as part of the scientific craft. (Haraway 1989, 214)

In many ways, Haraway's chapter in *Primate Visions*—"Remodeling the Human Way of Life: Sherwood Washburn and the New Physical Anthropology"—is as current an analysis of paleoanthropological narrative and reconstruction as it was when my students were in elementary school. Biological anthropology's "Man the Hunter" and "universal man" tropes continue to suffuse the way in which my students initially come to the topics of early hominids and their possible social behavior, though they may not communicate these views with such exacting terminology. I have designed a group exercise to specifically bring out student assumptions (and imaginations) about the very first hominids, one that we return to frequently for further evaluation and discussion as we learn about humanity's more recent hominid ancestors.

We do this exercise right after we have spent an entire unit on living and fossil nonhuman primates—examining the wide morphological, behavioral, and social plasticity of lemurs, monkeys, and apes—and before we have spent any class time on the evolution of the hominid lines from apelike ancestors. I break the class into groups of three to five, give them a poster-sized sheet of paper, and instruct them to imagine what the first hominids would have looked and acted like based on what they know about the morphology and social systems of nonhuman primates. The categories of the "first hominid" they are charged to address are

- Bones and bodies: What was their morphology like? How did their skulls and faces look? How big or small were they? How did they get around? What did they eat and how might that behavior have shown up on their remains?
- Material culture: Could they make and use tools? If so, of what sort and for which kinds of activities?
- Intelligence and creative capacity: What kinds of problems would they have had and/or been able to solve socially, or in their environments?
- Group size and composition: How did they organize their social relationships? How big were their groups and of what ages and sexes were their groups composed?

They can draw their "first hominids," or write out detailed descriptions. During the next class we then discuss their pictorial or textual reconstructions.

The astonishing result of this exercise is not—as I initially expected—the diversity of reconstructions they collectively produce, but the consistent way they imagine the makeup of the first hominid social groups. I say openly that I want them to stretch their imaginations, especially since they have not approached the archaeological and paleontological evidence for early hominid evolution at this point in the term. Therefore I expected that different groups would come up with different if not wildly incorrect details, especially in the nonfossilizing categories of intelligence, creativity, and material culture. Yet over two-thirds of my students will consistently describe the groups (or even troops) as "family" groups, composed of one male, one female, and their young, or larger groups composed of a few discrete families, but rarely topping more than twenty or thirty individuals. There is no apparent pattern to how this feature relates to any of the other factors they may have imagined; socially intelligent, creative, and chimplike bipeds, as well as isolationist, combative, human-looking toolmakers will all come in family packages. Gone then, for the majority of my students, is all consideration of polygynous social systems, one-male groups, or the diverse sexual behavior of chimpanzees and bonobos that they were so fascinated with during the previous week of class.

In the process of both validating and challenging their reconstructions, I ask my students why families were such prominent features in their descriptions. Invariably in their responses they ascribe a new quality of humanness to their first hominids, one implicitly associated with nuclear family groups and, as a matter of fact, male dominance. They readily accept vast morphological and behavioral differences between early hominids and our species, but the fuzzy line between hominoids and hominids deserves, for many of them, an important conceptual social break, one that persists in our discussions of later hominid evolution. The fixity of sex/gender roles, the dynamism of male hunting activities and the necessity for female security at some sort of stable "home" location are continual themes my students return to, no matter what hominid species we are discussing. It is a particular challenge to encourage students to imagine hominid social life outside of these organizing principles, since "Man is self-made, father of the species and the guarantor of human nature. The family of man depended on the human family, an indispensable ambiguity facilitating the junction of discourses of technology, heterosexuality and reproduction. Not about maternal function except derivatively and dependently, 'the family' is about the Father, an independent variable, a cause, not a function" (Haraway 1989, 220).

I return to our class memory of the above exercise frequently to try to complicate my students' notions of the biological and cultural possibilities of "family" and hominid social organization. I cite ethnographic examples and even challenge them to explain the diversity of the functioning twenty-first-century American family. Their equating of what is natural or evolved, however, to a nuclear family construct is a particularly entrenched conception within American culture as a whole, and in biological anthropology in particular, as Haraway so pointedly reminds us. Similarly, as my last class examples illustrate, this vice grip on an idealized family can be encompassed within a more powerful notion my students carry with them, one that I have become acutely aware of as I pursue a more feminist classroom—the perception that sameness and normality, not variation, is an inevitable and even desirable result of human evolution.

Biological Anthropology and the Pathologization of Difference

But what about hermaphrodites? (question posed in my classes every semester)
Intersexuality is primarily a problem of stigma and trauma, not gender. (Intersex Society of North America, www.isna.org)

One of the consequences of opening a classroom to all student voices, of encouraging everyone to pose questions coming directly from our experiences, is the display in those questions of prejudice, ignorance, and especially, racism. I invite my students to ask any question in or out of class related to human evolution, human biology, and the meaning(s) of biological difference. I am happy that they take these opportunities, though I have often been unhappily surprised at some of their queries. Specifically, I am often asked questions about race that my students say are "out there," such as: Do people of African descent have thicker bones and more muscles than "other people" (these questions are nearly always asked in vague generalities by students of all ethnicities)? Unfortunately, after encouraging them to give voice to their core beliefs and experiences and to lend their imaginations and skepticism to human evolutionary reconstructions, I must then re-don the hat of scientific authority and tell them what is really *right*, although certainly it is my responsibility to provide them with as accurate an account of human biological difference as possible. I hope I am getting more skilled, as well, at taking biological race apart in class in a dialogic, not pedantic, fashion.

More often than not, however, my very individualistic students have problems connecting these kinds of distortions about race to any larger cultural, historical, or societal processes. Certain, usually unnamed individuals have told them these things and their curiosity led them to ask their questions. This is a moment for me when it becomes plain that they have rarely had conversations about race beyond receiving or arguing about its social construction.

Similarly, the social construction of gender and a continuum of gender expression readily present in their everyday experiences, and most of my students are quite astute and critical of gender norms. However, any suggestion of biological sex difference that goes beyond categories of unambiguously male and female is met with disbelief, open protest, or stunned silence. I am usually given an opening early in the semester to discuss a continuum of biological sex through a general lecture on chromosomal variation (i.e., Fausto-Sterling 2000). I then straightforwardly tell them about the different ways in which people may be intersexed, with or without possessing a "normal" chromosomal complement of XX and XY. As much as I attempt to present genetic, chromosomal, or uterine environmental sex variation in the human species in a non-pathologizing way, the "hermaphrodite" question is always just around the corner. Where their sense of respect for race differences, or even their notion of "political correctness," leads them to ask questions about race using more respectful terminology, no such allowance is made for intersexed people.[10]

Yet, to my students' credit, traditional modes of teaching about evolution and natural selection have implied to them that adaptability and fitness equals biological normalcy, sameness within groups, and that a person cannot possibly be evolutionarily fit if they desire the "wrong" sex (despite the fact that fitness is passing ones genes into the next generation as often as possible, a feature one can accomplish without respect to the construction of their desires). Even more commonly, evolutionary theory that appears in college biological anthropology textbooks is silent with respect to how students could conceptually approach intersexed people, people born with disabilities, and the possible meanings of biological difference beyond dichotomous notions of race and sex.

Evolutionary theory's and biological anthropology's erasure and denial of these differences contribute to their continued invisibility in my students' social experiences. Students initially recognize themselves as "evolved" insofar as they are normal morphologically and have the ability to reproduce, a rather cold and unsatisfying way to conceive of oneself, in any event. Similarly, there is a danger that they would mistakenly recognize other people and other cultures as biological objects to ultimately be eliminated by natural selection if they do not measure up to some standard of normalcy. This is the case even before the seductive field of evolutionary psychology suggests that women who are not hourglass-shaped are less fit, and men must endeavor to be sugar daddies to pass on their genes (Buss 1994).[11]

Coda

I use the term [experience] not in the individualistic, idiosyncratic sense of something belonging to one and exclusively her own even though others might have "similar" experiences; but rather in the general sense of a process by which, for all social beings, subjectivity is constructed. Through that process one places oneself or is placed in social reality, and so perceives and comprehends as subjective (referring to, even originating in, oneself) those relations—material, economic and interpersonal—which are in fact social, and in a larger perspective, historical. (de Lauretis 1987, 159)

The desire to place oneself—while preserving one's unique sense of individuality—into a framework that generically explains the existence of the human species may be a specific Western and scientific imperative. My use of feminist pedagogical strategies in the classroom has helped me tease out this search for individual meaning among my students, time and time again. Students at all levels often mark their individuality through the evolutionarily distancing and pathologization of other people and entire contemporary human populations, while they also fail to recognize that they are part of, and responsible for acting within, a social structure that shapes their perceptions of biological difference.

As a final example, I highlight this contradiction in class by presenting the Neanderthals as a kind of hominid Other, a species (or subspecies as the case may be) of humans who coexisted with our species in space and time, yet who are envisioned by some paleoanthropologists as critically different morphologically and culturally from "ourselves." I present the history of how Neanderthals have been conceptualized differently at unique points in the development of interpretation in biological anthropology. Transformed from brutish "cavemen" to caring people in the span of a disciplinary generation in the mid-twentieth century, Neanderthals have occupied a number of spaces on a continuum of what it means to be human. When students see that even professionals in biological anthropology have envisioned hominid species in wildly different ways using the same evidence, it does not take long for them to start imagining Neanderthals as people equivalent to themselves, but people they may not easily be able to understand without a good deal of conceptual work. Similar to our experience of exploring the transition from apeness to hominidness, though, my classes must often be reminded of this exercise to apply their insights to the experiences of people different from themselves who are living in the world right now.

The particular struggle I invite students to share with me—to honestly and respectfully confront the way our cultural lenses inform our understanding of evolution and biological difference—has resulted in as many light moments of laughing at our assumptions as it has brought out our frustrations, impatience, and defensiveness. Likewise, I will no doubt continue to imagine how, as a biological anthropologist, I can teach that humans are an evolved, adaptable, and biologically diverse species. Much to my students' dismay, I still make them responsible for understanding the derived morphological features that distinguish *Homo habilis* from the Australopithecines, or the biological consequences of transitioning from a foraging to an agricultural lifeway. We are all called to balance the responsibilities of training students in the substance of our discipline by encouraging their critical thinking and analytical skills; these kinds of pedagogical struggles are certainly not new. In my case, the additional responsibility of engaging students in a biological anthropology that interrogates its own social and cultural assumptions simultaneously validates and challenges my own disciplinary subject position. At this point in my continuing process of learning to be a biological anthropologist, I would not proceed in any other way.

Chapter 10
The Professional Is Political

Sarah M. Nelson

This chapter branches off from the feminist slogan that "the personal is political" to consider ways in which the professional is also political. This expression is meant to convey the notion that women's professional lives should be lived as feminists in addition to infusing feminist ideals in our scholarly work. It should not be forgotten that feminism is about women, although men can also profit from feminist successes. In the long run, relationship between the genders is what requires both action and analysis.

It is important to consider exactly what ways the professional is also political. I will argue that, while what we do, say, and even wear is political, what we teach and publish as professional archaeologists and anthropologists is likewise political. The words we use are political choices. The success or failure of the attempt to have gender recognized as an important facet of archaeological interpretation is dependent on the awareness of its advocates that we may be judged both as archaeologists and as women, and the ability to behave in politically astute ways is paramount.

I am personally and professionally pleased that this book concerns feminist theory in anthropology. Some women archaeologists have been notoriously timid about using the "F" word, and have even wished to disassociate themselves from any such ideas. Even the category "women" seems to have acquired bad karma. It is much more common for archaeologists to use the word "gender" than "feminist," at least partly for reasons of protecting their careers (which demonstrates that the feminist agenda has been partially successful). Possibly the reluctance to use the word feminist is because the media have turned it into a loaded word (Faludi 1991), made to mean covertly (and sometimes overtly) shrill, man-hating, selfish, and anti-child. These descriptions are inaccurate and even inverted, but they nevertheless have been repeated often enough that they stick. I suspect that this interpretation is behind the use of the "wave" theory of feminism, with the implication that "third wave" women are not like the (bad old) feminists of the past. I argue that this rendering of the past needs to be deconstructed before we can focus on any unifying feminist theory for anthropology as a whole, or even for archaeology.

The "Waves" of Feminism

I find that the construct of waves of feminism not only is not helpful for understanding the development of feminist theories and actions in archaeology, but it is inaccurate, mostly applied by those who are self-described as "third wave," and effectively a self-congratulatory concept. "Wave" theory has taken up media notions that distort the Women's Movement. It is particularly inappropriate to imply that the feminism of the 1960s and 1970s was only about selfish upper-middle-class white women getting their share of the male pie. Since the Women's Movement arose out of the Civil Rights Movement, this is particularly ludicrous, and even offensive.

Another accusation aimed at the feminism of the 1960s and 1970s is that it assumed all American women were alike. This is nonsense. Part of the point of "women's liberation" was that the laws treated all women the same, whereas women's experiences and desires are diverse. "Choices for women" was the watchword.

Another mistaken assumption is that the Women's Movement took no notion of the women of the rest of the world. No one who has ever read, or even heard of, Robin Morgan's *Sisterhood Is Global* (1984) could share that view. In this book, Morgan showcases the varieties of women's issues being tackled by women around the world. The Women's Movement confronts both local and global issues.

Two recent books provide histories of the Women's Movement as it was lived in the 1960s and 1970s. (This is usually described as the "second wave," with the push for the vote earlier in the twentieth century occupying the first "wave.") These two books are different in their perspectives, showing different faces of feminism as it was lived in the last half of the century. Ruth Rosen, in *The World Split Open: How the Modern Women's Movement Changed America*, concentrated on changes in federal laws, in which effort she played an important part. She pointed out that she herself is astonished in retrospect to realize that changes in women's lives have been "so deep, so wide-ranging, so transformative" (Rosen 2000, xii). Her definition of feminism is simple: "Addressing the world's problems as if women mattered" (Rosen 2000, 341).

Brenda Feigen, in *Not One of the Boys: Living Life as a Feminist* (2000), took a more cultural view of what the women's movement produced in twentieth-century America. She, too, is a lawyer, but in addition to legal issues, she shows the reader the cultural wars as they were being played out in Hollywood. What happens on the big screen is not an accident; we learn from the inside that it is grounded in attitudes toward women, with an eye on the box office.

Thus the wave "theory" is not a theory, only an attempted description. As a description it is unproductive: what do we think we know when we have described feminism in waves? The problem is that "waves" never existed, especially in archaeology, as I will show. Apparently the notion that is behind the ideas of waves of feminism is that it comes and goes, and then another wave comes in.

I will not address this metaphor for all of feminism, but for archaeology I will demonstrate its flaws. The problems fall into two categories. First is the implication that with each wave something new arrives, while in contrast the new builds on the old, but does not replace it or supplant it. The second is the suggestion that the projects of the past are finished. But they are not, especially in archaeology. Furthermore, feminist gains need to be continuously guarded against erosion by opposing forces.

In thinking about the development of feminism in archaeology, I have conceived it as layers. This layering is only meant to be a device for separating the strands of gender archaeology, not a metaphor. It is in archaeological order, that is, the oldest approaches are on the bottom. I present the issues that attracted the attention of women and feminists, in the order that they began to be tackled in archaeology. I do not mean to imply a rigid sequence; many of these approaches to gender in archaeology began to be developed more or less simultaneously, but they nevertheless build on each other. They each continue to be relevant and to become more sophisticated as each genre is more deeply probed in the light of further work.

EQUITY ISSUES

Equity issues form the bottom layer. The problems for women archaeologists have been profound, and while conditions for women in archaeology have improved, there is still work to be done to achieve real equality. Before the Women's Movement, women students were rarely mentored as well as men, and received less support in graduate school. Gender stereotypes interfered with work, and created difficulties for women who wanted to network. Women's writing was belittled, and women were discouraged from continuing their studies. As equity issues began to be addressed, the relatively small size of the cohort of women in archaeology made naming the issues slow and finding remedies difficult (Nelson, Nelson, and Wylie 1994). Women mostly stuck to the male script in order to succeed.

Impediments to doing feminist archaeology, and having it taken seriously within the discipline, are encountered on a variety of levels. A truly basic level is the ability to do field archeology and research without harassment. This includes sexual harassment, which many of my women students tell me has not disappeared, although it may be sometimes less public, or more subtle. This kind of situation is not only personally debilitating, but also unfair, because it subjects women to less favorable working conditions.

Other inequities still occur in terms of appointments, salaries, promotions, and perks. Recent studies show that women scientists, even at so prestigious an institution as MIT, have not been treated equally (Zernike 1999). These factors are often discussed in terms of the "chilly climate," including small slights as well as larger issues. The daily putting down of women, or their work, has been called a "ton of feathers," because while each event may be relatively trivial, a ton of feathers still weighs a ton. A study at the University of Michigan, noted in *Science*, found that women scientists were 3.5 times more likely to find the climate chilly than men scientists were (Mervis 2002).

The chilly climate for archaeologists includes trivializing of gender archaeology, and any attempt to consider women of the past. Several feminist archaeologists have argued that some archaeological practices made it difficult to do gender archaeology (e.g., Brumfiel 1992), but it appears that gender in archaeology is being taken more seriously in the past decade, as a part of the move toward "postprocessual" archeology. It is my observation, however, that gender archaeology can fit into any paradigm—as can be seen by any close looks at edited volumes (e.g., Kent 1998; Nelson and Rosen-Ayalon 2001; and see Bacus et. al 1993 for critiques of the early volumes). The processes through which archeologists study the past, interpretations of the past, and standards of professional practice are inextricably intertwined with gender. Gendered assumptions about society and the gender of archaeologists are not unrelated phenomena. Much ground has been gained in revealing the gender biases about the ancient past in the recent past, and in making research into gender acceptable practice in archeology.

CRITIQUES OF ANDROCENTRISM

A psychologist, Sandra Bem (1993), wrote clearly about the ways that our current culture influences our perspectives on women and men, calling these causes of distortion the "lenses of gender." She isolated three forms of distortion caused by these lenses.

The first problem Bem isolated is androcentrism, by which she means the assumption that men are in the center of cultures, and that women are the other, to be measured against a male standard. It is only by destabilizing this idea that women's contributions can be fully appreciated. Some groups of women, especially those who emphasize women's spirituality, wanted to move women to the center to replace men, but this strategy fails, partly because it substitutes wishful thinking for descriptions of reality.

Early contributions to the gender in archaeology included some strange bedfellows. The goddess movement uses female figurines from the distant past, glossed as "goddesses," as an inspiration for the present in the women's spirituality movement. Some archaeologists aided the quest for past goddesses (Gimbutas 1982), but most felt this was a misuse of archaeology (Conkey and Tringham 1995). Another strand of the use of archaeology by nonarchaeologists was the attempt to support Engels' (1972) testable assertion that women lost their own rights and became men's property with the rise of the state. Explorations by archaeologists have shown that there is no universal rule (e.g., chapters in Nelson, ed. 2003).

Instead of looking for status universals, we can recognize that where one is situated is partly responsible for one's viewpoints. One of the stumbling blocks for women was the notion that women were all alike in being inferior to men (Gould 1981; Tavris 1992). Standpoint theory, which allows for perspectives arising from many traits of individuals, including age, skin color, and ethnicity, not just gender, was an important move toward deconstructing an essentialist view of women.

Biological essentialism is another stumbling block, making women's reproductive and sexual functions stand for the whole of what women are and do. Social constructivism was one response to that distortion, as was the creation of the concept of the sex/gender system. This concept is not intended to reify gender; it is simply a theoretical construct. The point is that gender is a social/cultural construct, in that women and men learn to be gendered. Thus gender is not in our genes, hormones, brains, or sexual organs. Although I have heard feminists speak of "testosterone poisoning" when explaining extreme violence by men, it is the masculine admiration for violence (a cultural trait not found everywhere) that is at fault (Morgan 2001).

Finally, Bem took to task gender polarization, in which men and women are perceived as opposites in all things. This is silly on the face of it; there are many shades of gray and much overlap, even in what American culture of the 1950s decided to call masculine and feminine. The notion of "androgeny," in which individuals could have traits from both genders, was developed to combat gender polarization. Cultural anthropology has long taught us that gender expectations differ from one society to another. For a simple and obvious example (and one with relevance to archaeology and material culture), in some cultures the men dress up like peacocks, in others it is the women who deck themselves out for display. The flexibility of definitions of what women and men do, how they should behave, and what they are like, is a basic tenet of anthropology.

Archaeologists continue to note these forms of gender distortions, plus another that is endemic to our discipline: the tendency to interpret the past in terms of present gender arrangements that are so familiar to the archaeologist that they seem natural. In deconstructing these ideas, representations of men and women in the past, especially in museums and textbooks, receive close scrutiny. Some of these representations have been memorably named. My personal favorite is Diane Gifford-Gonzalez's (1993) expression for the little woman scraping hides in the background of many depictions of the past. Haven't we all seen "the drudge on the hide" in some museum display or another?

RETRIEVING WOMEN ARCHAEOLOGISTS FROM THE PAST

It has been important to note that this generation of women archaeologists is not the first to have braved overt masculinity in archaeology by insisting on doing what they desired to do (Levine 1991; Claassen 1994; Parezo 1993; Diaz-Andreu and Sorenson 1998). That some women were able to achieve in spite of the barriers placed in their way is a tribute to their dedication and persistence.

One of the difficulties for women archaeologists was (and still is?) the fact that what is "manly" has tended to define the field of archaeology—especially fieldwork. Male images in archaeology have been well-demonstrated—archaeologists as a "band of brothers" or the "cowboys of science" (Gero 1983), the "trowel holsters" emphasizing the Wild West theme, and not least, archaeologists as belonging to one of two groups—the hairy-chested or the hairy-chinned (Kidder 1949). These images are not just from long ago, a kind of relic of what archaeology used to be. They are still very much with us (Nelson 2003).

These tough women were also challenged by conditions of work, in which women were paid less for the same work, or worse, were expected to work for nothing. They were often taken to the field as cooks. They functioned as secretaries rather than as principal investigators, and often had their work coopted by a man (Cordell 1993). As Linda Cordell has noted, a woman who claimed her rights was labeled a "pain in the ass," and might henceforth not be welcome in archaeology.

Our archaeological foremothers were challenged in these and other ways by the male establishment, but they persisted. Some continued and made important discoveries; some struggled for a while and then ceded the field to men. Either way, these women are important as role models for young aspiring women archaeologists, as well as provide historical continuity for women. But the last words have not been said. Retrieving "lost" women archaeologists is not a finished work, and the rigors of the recent past are not as far behind us as some students appear to believe.

RECLAIMING THE DRUDGE ON THE HIDE

Diane Gifford-Gonzalez brought to our attention the phenomenon of the "drudge on the hide," in which museum displays and artist's renderings in books tend to depict men engaged in prominent actions, while women are in the background scraping hides. This is a way of rendering women invisible, which feminist archaeologists have exposed in various ways.

In addition to reclaiming early women archaeologists, it was important to learn to see women in the past. Margaret Ehrenberg (1989) wrote the first attempt at an extended view of women through time. She concentrated on Europe, since that was where most data could be teased out. The book was a welcome antidote to the persistent theme that it was not possible to find women in the past.

One reason that women in the past had been invisible was the belief that women's work was the same through time and space. Instead, there were many variants of women's lives, in different cultures as well as within the same culture—and they are worth discovering and telling. All culture change did not come about because of men.

One of the first coherent attempts to consider women in the past seriously was a conference in Norway in 1979 titled "Were They All Men?" (Bertelson, Lillehammer, and Naess 1987). This title ironically reflected the way that archaeology is written, as if only males existed in the past. The papers all showed that women could be made visible in archaeology, just by looking, and that what was seen was far from trivial.

Making women visible took a lot of work—male archaeologists did not immediately say, "oh, yes, that's right," and change their ways. It was necessary to demonstrate the many ways the women in the past had been overlooked. It was especially important to critique the way explanatory criteria often shifted, depending on whether men or women were being described (Conkey and Spector 1984).

Other critiques of unspoken assumptions were more specific. Why have we assumed that hunters and stone toolmakers were all men? Did women hunt in any cultures (Wadley 1998)? What is considered "hunting" in different cultures—is the wielder of the weapon the only hunter (Brumback and Jarvenpa 1997)? Did men actually make all the stone tools while the little woman waited for a man to come home and chip her a knife so she could chop up dinner (Gero 1991)?

It has become clear as a result of these and other studies that the division of labor by gender is rarely absolute. Even tasks that are generally performed by one gender or another could be done by the other gender. Furthermore, women were part of the evolution of culture, and as such should not be neglected or trivialized in any archaeological site description or interpretation. They were not all men.

GENDER AS RELATIONAL

As the demand to take women seriously as participants in the making of the past began to be heard, it became obvious that men had to be part of the equation as well. People were not the topic of most archaeology. We were digging up "faceless blobs," not active human beings (Tringham 1991). Clearly, the intention behind using the term "gender" and taking the focus off women was partly strategic and partly political. Even the path-breaking *Engendering Archaeology* (Gero and Conkey 1991) was subtitled, *Women and Prehistory*, as if the notion of adding gender to archaeology needed further explanation.

It was obvious that all societies that reproduced themselves had to have both women and men, but how did they interact (Wylie 1992)? Looking at constructed roles and behaviors, instead of sexed bodies, made it possible to demand balanced attention to male and female.

Furthermore, studying gender instead of only women opened up the possibility of studying other genders, a space that is being occupied with increasing sophistication. The very idea of talking about gender instead of sex was based on the insistence that the designation of specific gender roles and ideologies is cultural, and does not inhere in bodies.

BODIES AND SEXUALITY

Archaeologists often have bodies available to study, both in the form of human remains and representations of humans in a variety of media. These two versions of human bodies have both required thinking in new ways in order to come to grips with gender. If gender is not sex, then what do we do with sexed bodies?

Mortuary analysis has a long tradition in archaeology, including analyzing bodies in a cemetery according to sex and age. Demographics can thus be deduced, as well as gendered customs such as female infanticide or wife-beating. Less deliberately harmful results of the kinds of labor that the different sexes have performed in their lifetimes can be deduced (Peterson 2002).

Problems arise, however, when bodies are missing or ambiguous as to sex. Along with the actual bodies are adornments, clothing, and body alterations. In some archaeological circles it was customary to sex un-known graves by means of the associated artifacts. Often, spindle whorls were equated to women, and weapons equated to men. This process clearly shortcuts attention to gender.

With the theoretical attention to gender, mortuary study has become more sophisticated, and far more aware of the pitfalls of assuming gen-der (Arnold and Wicker 2001a). Other dimensions of bodies, such as age, class, and ethnicity, can also be studied using these more advanced methods. The selection of categories to marked death can reveal the im-portant distinctions within a particular culture (Joyce 2001a).

Depictions of men and women can also be used to make statements about gender in the past (Hamilikas, Pluciennik, and Tarlow 2002b). Sometimes the assumptions about depictions of sexed bodies have been theoretically underdeveloped, but attention to gender critiques has helped to make such studies more nuanced. Not all the newer studies of bodies are feminist, but their subject matter is grist for the archaeolo-gists' mill.

While there are those who appear to believe that the study of sexuality in archaeology is quite new, it has in fact been a topic approachable for some time in branches other than prehistoric archaeology, such as clas-sical archaeology (Pomeroy 1974) and historic archaeology (Schmidt and Voss 2000a) for some time. Sexuality reared its head in prehistoric archaeology, when female figurines were found. Assertions regarding sexuality and the ancient figurines were wildly speculative. Some claimed that the figurines represented either the objects of men's de-sires or nurturing mother figures. The imbalance in the interpretation arose from the fact that the figurines were assumed to have been made by men and for men (Nelson 1990).

But archaeologists were late to join the feminist debates about sexual-ity. Feminists of the 1960s and 1970s hotly debated questions of female sexuality. One side insisted that women's sexuality had been repressed, and women had a right to express their sexuality however they wished. The other side worried about the effects of pornography on limiting women's freedom of movement, and the degrading of women who were expected to please men and not themselves. These thorny issues have not often been approached with archaeological data, although histori-cal archaeologists are beginning to address them.

Some sexuality studies point out the variations within a single sex and ridicule the idea of a dichotomy between males and females. While this may be true at a molecular level, ancient societies did not know about chromosomes, they named the sexes by the shape of a newborn's geni-tals, and made the child into a man or a woman or another gender by cultural means. We should be careful not to saddle past societies with what science "knows" today.

Important ways to study sexuality in the past include putting aside our own cultural notions, and working with the data to deduce what sexuality, its expression and its control, might have meant to the people we are studying.

STORIES

Using fiction as a device to understand the past is certainly not new, but it is a useful tool in the hands of feminist archaeologists. Stories are ways of putting people back in the past, in all their complexity. They require the archaeologist to think about gendered parts of culture not obviously represented in the material record. But fictionalizing sites is not unproblematic. For example, many stories could be generated from the same set of archaeological data. Does writing one story preclude or preempt all the other possible stories? Multiple interpretations of the past are encouraged in some circles, including open-ended stories (Tringham 1991).

Postprocessualism has freed archaeology from its reliance on ecological factors as explanatory devices, and to some extent from the rigidity of cultural evolutionary stages. It is possible to see people as actors in the past, to view people as agents.

Experimenting with other media, such as art, music, and literature, is beginning to produce some useful ways to think about archaeological sites (J. Jameson 2003).

Doing Gendered Archaeology

Gendered archaeology is an activity, not a thing. By considering gender in all facets of archaeological work, from fieldwork to laboratory analysis to site interpretations, archaeologists can make great strides in peopling their sites.

Several approaches have been productive in doing gendered archaeology. Ethnoarchaeology provides valuable lessons in possibilities and realities in actual situations. Realizing that bodies, images, space, technology, and everything else related to material culture can be gendered leads to asking gendered questions of the present as well as of the past. But using multiple lines of evidence strengthens any inference, because in most cases the archaeological record is impoverished.

Feminist-inspired archaeology has contributed to the discipline of anthropology by exposing many biases and destabilizing present gender attitudes and arrangements. It creates more honest approaches to the present and the past. But do we have any effect on public perceptions?

Brenda Feigen (2000, 281) takes academic feminism to task: "by now women who are interested in women's studies, which today has almost universally transformed into 'gender' studies, have gone on to advanced degrees that require them to speak in a jargon understandable only to themselves." Are we as archaeologists also at fault? Feigen asserts that academics are not trying to solve the problems of the world's women. She says further that, "As far as I am concerned, feminist theory is only valuable if it sheds insight on how to better women's lives" (Feigen 2000, 282). We could consider gender archaeology as improving at least some women's lives, if only by broadening the choice of models for women, and demonstrating that societies can have a great variety of gender arrangements. Clearing up past distortions is an important goal. The gender concept has been transformative for archaeology, and archaeology contributes to a wider anthropological perspective that adds the dimension of time to gender arrangements.

The ways of approaching gender in archaeology outlined in this chapter are additive, not replacing each other in a wavelike fashion. There is much more to do on each topic, from equity issues to stories. These are not "old-fashioned" ideas from a previous "wave" but important, live problems that are continually being addressed and partial solutions found.

Afterword: On Waves

ALISON WYLIE

A decade ago Linda Alcoff and Elizabeth Potter opened a collection of essays on feminist epistemologies with the question, why "retain the adjective 'feminist'?" (1993, 4). By the early 1990s a number of convergent strands of philosophical analysis had reinforced awareness that a great many factors structure cognitive authority: "gender hierarchies are not the only ones that influence the production of knowledge" (1993, 3). Feminist theorists had likewise argued, trenchantly and in connection with a wide range of fields of research and activism, that gender cannot be posited as an autonomous variable "separable from other axes of oppression and susceptible to a unique analysis"; gender identity "cannot be adequately understood—or even perceived—except as a component of complex interrelationships with other systems of identification and hierarchy" (Alcoff and Potter 1993, 3–4). This was the juncture, described here by Henrietta Moore, at which feminists took a decisive turn away from binary, single-dimension conceptions of gender difference (as difference between men and women), and focused instead on differences that operate multidimensionally and intersectionally. The precarious point of departure for Alcoff and Potter in defining a mandate for feminist epistemology in the mid-1990s was, then, an appreciation that gender, the defining category of analysis for feminist epistemology, could not be assumed to be primary "in any sense of primary"; it is just one among many different kinds of "political relationships (that is, disparate power relations)" that must be taken into account (Alcoff and Potter 1993, 3). Alcoff and Potter's answer to the question "why retain the adjective 'feminist'?" was that it marks where they were coming from, if not necessarily where they are going; it "correctly identifies the history of this work" (3–4).

The question Alcoff and Potter articulate is the central problematic engaged by contributors to this collection: what does it mean to say that a body of anthropological work is feminist, or that one is doing feminist anthropology, at this juncture, given all the ways an earlier focus on women and gender has been reframed, expanded, fragmented, and problematized? Is it just a matter of marking a past trajectory? What does this past imply for the future?

Where the past is concerned, despite sharp disagreement about the value of the wave metaphor that Geller and Stockett use to frame the collection, there is considerable convergence in what contributors identify as important reference points in the feminist legacy on which they draw. The roots of feminist anthropology, as elsewhere, lie in an activist commitment to document—to bear witness to—to understand, and ultimately to change sex/gender inequalities that have real political and material implications for lives and bodies, personal and social/cultural identities, public institutions, and forms of intimacy. The mandate for feminist research in the social sciences was characterized, in the context of the "feminist method debate" of the 1970s and 1980s, by several core values and broad methodological guidelines that reflect these activist roots (Wylie 1995): feminists should do research by and for women; they should ground research in women's experience; they should ensure that feminist research is not exploitative or demeaning of its subjects; and they should institute reflexivity (see also introductory discussions in Hesse-Biber and Yaiser 2004; Reinharz 1992; and a classic statement by Ehrlich 1975). In its canonical form, feminist research of this kind was marked by an extreme "literalism of the referent" (to use a term of Povinelli's, from the AAA session that gave rise to this collection); it was characterized by community self-studies, by research on "women worthies," "women's contributions," and "women victims" (Harding 1986, 30–31), on women's distinct voices and cultures, and on continuities across difference (e.g., Rich 1983).

Almost immediately, in every context where feminist research was undertaken, things got complicated along exactly the lines illustrated and described by contributors to this collection. Feminist anthropology is particularly striking for the depth and sophistication of the autocritiques that emerged within a decade of its first major publications. Two examples that anticipate the critique of heteronormative assumptions developed here by Blackwood and by Dowson are Michelle Rosaldo's early and deeply critical assessment of the "reverse discourse" (in Dowson's sense) in which she and other feminist anthropologists had engaged (1980), and Gayle Rubin's challenges to the heterosexism inherent in much feminist theorizing (1984), including her own influential feminist appropriation of kinship theory in "Traffic in Women" (1975). Although the focus and substance of their critiques is very different, Rosaldo and Rubin both detailed ways in which feminists had inverted and revalued conventional gender categories but left intact an underlying structure of binaries and hierarchies derived from nineteenth-century middle-class (Western and European) assumptions about the division of public from private, the normative family form, and the conventions that structure sexual identity, behavior, and the direction of desire.

In the same period, the crisis of interpretation taking shape in cultural anthropology anticipated and fueled internal criticism of an early enthusiasm, among feminists in a wide range of fields, for ethnographic and ethnohistorical forms of practice. For many, especially feminists working in highly quantitative social sciences, these qualitative, negotiative approaches seemed uniquely congenial to feminist goals and values; they held the promise of leveling the power hierarchies associated with self-consciously scientific social science, and of restoring to the subject an autonomous voice, epistemic authority, and the prospect of coproducing (feminist) knowledge (e.g., Mies 1983; Oakley 1981; D. Smith 1974). But it quickly became clear that these research practices carry their own liabilities (Stacey 1988), and that they could not be expected to serve all the research goals important to feminists (Jayaratne 1983; Harding 1987). In response to this debate, Longino rejects the quest for a "feminist science," and explores, instead, the question of what it means to "do science as a feminist" (Longino 1987). With critical and constructive challenges of this sort, significant pressure was brought to bear on the central tenets of feminist research: the ways in which its primary referents were conceived (sex/gender systems, identities, roles, and relations), its goals, and its methodological guidelines.

These substantial shifts in feminist thinking were not just a matter of changes in intellectual fashion, an outgrowth of pressures to speciate within academia. They constitute significant accomplishments, empirically and conceptually. What began as a remedial program of research generated a number of transformative insights: about the complexity and diversity of the lives, the forms of experience feminists initially set out to recover; about the deeply contextual, intersectional nature of gender roles and relations; about the opportunistic fluidity of the forms of oppression that operate along gendered lines of social differentiation; and about the possibilities for "doing research as a feminist." The upshot was an appreciation that nothing unifies the domain of feminist inquiry as a whole: neither the subjects that interest feminists nor the forms of research practice required to understand them.

The question, then, is: what follows? There can be no doubt that this "dilution of specificity" (as Meskell put it in the original AAA session) is profoundly destabilizing; with no distinctive feminist method and no distinctive feminist subject, what remains for a feminist qua feminist to engage, either as an activist or as a scholar?

I urge a response that takes as its ground the social relations and conditions of life with which we and our ethnographic subjects grapple.

Feminist perspectives would certainly be irrelevant to anthropological inquiry, and to much else, if sex/gender systems were no longer a powerful force in differentiating social agents, structuring their opportunities, identities, relationships in symbolically and materially consequential ways. Feminism is an oppositional stance and if the conditions of inequality that have given rise to wave after wave of feminism no longer obtain, we should be happy to dismantle the intellectual and political armature of feminism. But we are nowhere near realizing such a happy condition. To extend a point Kakaliouras makes with respect to race categories, even though conventional, naturalizing conceptions of sex/gender difference may be unsustainable, they have enormous impact on our lives; there is much to be done and anthropology has a crucial role to play.

This does not mean that we can return to (feminist) business as usual. What the recent history of feminist activism and scholarship makes clear is that the inequalities with which we must concern ourselves are complex, ramifying, and multiply embedded in ways that demand rather different approaches than (many) feminists had imagined. The question is how to refocus: what possibilities, what directions forward emerge in the essays assembled here? I identify four broad themes crosscutting the contributions to this volume that suggest some promising ways of grounding in and building beyond the past named by the contested adjective feminist.

One is a resolution to change the question that animates research as a feminist in anthropology. If anything survives of the mandate to do anthropology as a feminist it is, I suggest, a version of Longino's "bottom line maxim": as a feminist one should be minimally committed to ensuring that the research strategies or assumptions you adopt (in activism or in research) do not preemptively disappear gender (Longino 1994; Wylie 1995). Combined with a commitment to reflexivity (in Longino's terms, "provisionality") this means that, while you cannot assume in advance that gender will be a relevant category of analysis, much less how it should be conceptualized in any particular context of study, you can never assume that it is irrelevant. Dowson's arguments for queering archaeology, both informed by and in tension with feminist initiatives, draw attention to a range of interpretive possibilities that have not been explored because this bottom-line maxim has been enacted with little reflexive attention to naturalizing assumptions that persist about sex/gender categories; feminists have countered the assumption that gender can be disappeared, but not always the assumption that gender roles and relations, sexual identity, the direction of desire in the distant (and not-so-distant) cultural past may radically disrupt familiar heteronormative conventions. Kakaliouras observes that nowhere are such conventions more deeply entrenched among the undergraduate students she teaches than in normative conceptions of family structure; Blackwood and Walrath trace the legacy of these assumptions in the interpretive practices of professional anthropologists. Blackwood details ways in which the treatment of Afro-Caribbean family relationships reproduce a narrative of difference and blame in contexts where domestic relations do not conform to the "safe, bounded, familiar" categories of middle-class, Euro-American kinship ideals, while Walrath finds evolutionary narratives about adaptation to childbirth constrained by gender-conventional assumptions about the origins of sexual dimorphism and the challenge of an "obstetrical dilemma" that reflects historically specific conventions of medical practice. In these cases a number of interpretive, investigative paths open up when the feminist impetus to change the question takes a reflexive turn.

In similar spirit, several contributors who have drawn inspiration from Butler's account of gender performance suggest strategies for creatively, reflexively, reframing this theory. They insist on the need to keep sharply in focus the material conditions and consequences of gender constructs; an emphasis on agency and ideation, on performativity, should not obscure the real difference that these make in people's lives. Moore's argument runs along these lines, while Joyce, Perry and Potter, and Kus all argue the case for thinking beyond the oppositional categories of recent debate in which constructivist analyses are presumed to trivialize the material dimensions of gendered performance. Kus proposes a nondualistic "radical empiricism" that focuses attention on the ways in which the slippery play of metaphoric meaning is both grounded in and also figures (sexed and gendered) bodies. In a parallel analysis, Perry and Potter argue that gender symbolism is often more salient, culturally, than observable sex characteristics, but insist that this is not a brief for erasing the physical experience and the consequences of sedimented performance. Both draw inspiration from Joyce's highly productive use of performance theory to reframe archaeological analysis, shifting the interpretive emphasis from decoding a record presumed to reflect social realities, to questions that presuppose a dynamic of embodiment in which (social, symbolic) regulatory regimes both shape, and are shaped by, their material articulation.

A second, related theme is the caution not to lose sight of systemic structures of social differentiation in the course of refocusing attention on fluidity, contingency, and particularity. Moore argues, in this connection, that the academic turn to ambiguity and pluralism resonates with popular discourses that articulate an insistent, if anxious, "individualization"; a preoccupation with self-realization—a "tyranny of choice"—that fosters a myopic politics of personal self-help, obscuring discriminatory effects of the "longer running . . . larger scale structures." Kakaliouras and Hendon both register this concern with reference to classroom dynamics, and the demands of communicating with a range of publics. A crucial insight Kakaliouras draws from the literature on feminist pedagogy is that the classroom is itself a political context, structured by race and class as well as gender politics that persistently figure the individual as a primary locus of agency and opportunity, obscuring the systemic conditions that reproduce inequitable power relations. She urges, with Hendon, strategies of direct engagement, not evasion and not recapitulation.

A third theme is the insistence, especially clear in Hendon's chapter, that feminists should not allow dominant norms of epistemic authority to set the terms of their engagement in the classroom and with the wider public or, indeed, within their own research community: their research agenda and their relationship with research subjects. Substantive assumptions about sex/gender systems that have long since been subjected to trenchant critique will continue to circulate, impervious to counterevidence and critical argument, unless we directly the entrenched assumptions of a "folk epistemology" that stabilizes them, that renders them authoritative, and that marginalizes, as mere speculation, any interpretive options that do not conform to expectation. Dowson makes a similar case with reference to the epistemic privilege enjoyed by museum representations that reproduce heteronormative wisdom about first families and domestic relations in prehistory. If these taken-for-granteds are to be destabilized, Hendon argues, it will be crucial to resist the false dichotomies that posit facts (theory free, interpretively neutral) as sharply separable from speculation, that align theory with speculation, and that assimilate conventional wisdom about sex and gender to the realm of fact. The combined effect is to obscure the contingent, speculative elements of familiar narratives and foreclose any nuanced adjudication of interpretive options that depart from them. Feminists must resist ubiquitous pressures to deliver bite-sized packets of authoritative knowledge and must systematically question the epistemic standards that underpin these demands for closure and for certitude, the elision of ambiguity, the denial of partiality. At the same time, Hendon rejects the option of a lazy relativism, so often presented as the only alternative to the positivist convictions of folk epistemology. Here her analysis converges on Walrath's and Joyce's; these arguments go well beyond feminist interests, narrowly construed, but they build on the hard won wisdom of feminist struggle with the procrustean categories of the science wars.

Fourth and finally, a persistent theme running through these contributions is the injunction not to lose sight of the possibilities for feminist praxis, starting where we live and work as anthropological scholars and teachers. Feminist archaeologists and physical anthropologists—as described by Hendon, Kus, Kakaliouras, and Joyce—have been especially creative in integrating a commitment to accountability into their practice, both in the classroom and in communicating the point and the value of anthropological research to wider publics. Perry and Potter urge a broad vision of the relevance of anthropological theorizing for understanding and ultimately changing current realities of exploitation. The wisdom here seems to be to work locally but think globally, in the process recognizing that feminist sensibilities are a point of departure that inevitably open up beyond themselves.

Consider, then, some ways of thinking about the contentious metaphor of waves that refocuses attention on what needs to be done, inspired by Kus's meditation on the Malagasy image of "moving water." In fact, waves do not so much overtake and succeed/supercede one another as rise and fall again and again in the same place, transmitting and diffusing energy in complicated ways. They have troughs as deep as their crests, but they are resurgent, insistent in their recurrence. When they break against a shore again and again they are powerful erosional forces.

If these aspects of waves are held in focus, the metaphor of waves in feminism draws attention to the vulnerability of our gains politically and intellectually; we are engaged in a long struggle marked by significant ebbs as well as swells. The feminists now canonized as "first wave," in Anglo-American contexts, took seventy years to win the vote and to gain access to educational institutions and employment opportunities that had been closed to women (longer in some jurisdictions). We postsuffrage feminists have retained the vote but we lost heavily on other fronts in the postwar era. Indeed, in university and college education, it was not until the 1970s and 1980s that women recovered levels of representation they had realized in the 1920s and 1930s. To secure any of these gains we must be prepared to rise again and again: resurgent, insistent mobilization.

Note, too, the complexity of waves, and of feminism. Resurgence never takes quite the same form from one swell to the next. For one thing, waves propagate and interact even in the simplest of circumstances: drop a pebble and radiating circles of waves ramify through a pool or a bowl and then reflect off the edges; drop several pebbles and you set up interference patterns. In bodies of water that are not artificially contained, waves are generated in many different ways: by river or tidal currents, by snags and obstructions under water, by wind and by traffic on the surface, and, on rare and catastrophic occasion, by grinding shifts in tectonic plates. When we look back on first wave feminism it is painful to realize the cost of the singular focus that ultimately won the vote, however positive its long-term effects. In a compelling interrogation of this history, Jakobsen details the vibrant diversity that gave rise to first wave feminism: the engagement of its early proponents with abolitionist and class politics and with a range of competing conceptions of (gendered) moral and political agency. She is particularly interested in how this rich complexity was displaced by a strategic narrowing of focus, a sundering of alliances that entrenched deep and destructive contradictions at the heart of feminist activism. She sees a similar pattern reenacted in the mid-twentieth century. Once again a broad-based women's movement was "born out of the work of diverse movements and alliances" (1998, 57): civil rights activism of the 1950s and 1960s; antipoverty and class-based activism in the 1960s and 1970s; liberationist challenges to hetero-sexism in the 1970s. But the movement came to be, and to be seen as, predominantly white and middle class. By the 1980s, "difference" reappeared as a problematic in a context dominated by historical narratives that systematically erased the multifaceted alliances and debates that gave it impetus in the 1960s and 1970s: in its standard use the wave metaphor is understood "to imply that, if the 1970s was the decade of monolithic feminism, and the 1980s brought differences to the fore, then perhaps the 1990s will be a decade of alliances" (1998, 61).

In scrutinizing this "narrative of progression"—a narrative of transcendence, of movement from simple, unsophisticated origins—Jakobsen's aim is not so much to question its accuracy as to raise probing and strategically consequential questions about the political conditions and social forces—the "dominative practices"—that "led to the forgetting of race [and heteronormativity and class] as an issue of feminist theory" (1998, 62), sharply narrowing the vision of mid-twentieth-century feminism. Why are movements that are formed in "the crucible of alliance" so often reduced to "singular issues and communities" (1998, 58)? Why do their proponents so quickly forget "the lessons of alliance" that were their impetus and inspiration (1998, 58)? Beyond the politics of naming, which are not trivial in themselves, there is much to learn from the history of struggle that informs contemporary feminist anthropology, much to learn by "correctly identify[ing] the history of this work" (Alcoff and Potter 1993, 4). The failures as much as the successes make clear the complex forces of subversion and dissipation with which we must reckon, rising again in a place deeply structured by "dominative practices" that condition our own most intimate sense of self and agency. These are the "master's tools" so precisely delineated by Audre Lorde: the internalized reflexes of identification with the masters' interests, the social and psychological mechanisms that foster fear of difference and divide us against one another (1984a, b).

Second and third wave feminism, reexamined in this light, has been a sustained lesson in the complexity of fluid dynamics. We are not swimming against a single strong current of unchanging sexism; singularity of focus is a luxury we cannot afford. A condition of all our practice, scholarly and activist, is the friction, interference, amplification—the continually shifting snags and crosscutting currents—we must work against if we are to sustain working alliances. Historical amnesia obscures the conditions that so persistently undermine the fragile alliances through which our waves of mobilization have taken shape. A more promising alternative to a false universalism, as the ground for working alliances, is not solipsistic relativism but what Jakobsen describes as relationalism (1998, 150). To enact these possibilities requires a long view and the kind of expansive, intersectional vision articulated by contributors to this volume.

Notes

Introduction

1. The deployment of dichotomies persists in popular feminist dialogues as well. Ecofeminism, for example, propagates the nature : culture is equal to female : male binary in its consideration of the environment, animal rights, the military, and capitalism. Scholars have criticized this "feminist" approach for essentialist and denigrating conceptions of gender roles and relations, as well as its unconscious reproduction of a male-dominated ideology (Alaimo 1994; Meskell 1995, 1999, 56–58).

Chapter 1

1. The Fifth Ministerial Conference of the World Trade Organization took place in Cancún, Mexico, September 10–14, 2003. The aim of the summit was to further implement the Doha agenda on world trade. However, its outcome was widely considered as a significant failure, after the richer countries failed to respond the requests of poorer countries for a drastic reform of their agricultural subsidies.

Chapter 4

1. The status of kinship and marriage has been part of a prolonged debate, but some of the key critical texts include Needham 1971; Schneider 1984; Yanagisako 1979; and Yanagisako and Collier 1987.

2. This discussion disregards for the moment the problem of viewing societies as cohesive wholes, given that my interest here is to examine why particular concepts are developed.

3. See Yanagisako's (1977) critique of the emphasis on the affective bond between mothers and their children as the key to matrifocal households.

4. I am not suggesting that researchers should ignore the poverty of many such households but that the correlation of woman-headed households with poverty misdirects attention away from political, social, and global processes that leave women undereducated, underskilled, and undervalued for the work they do.

5. See Barrow 1986, 1996; Bolles 1996; Mohammed 1986; and Monagan 1985 for a more extensive history and critique of these issues.

6. The experience of slavery has also been considered a contributing factor to the development of matrifocality. This brief recitation cannot do justice to the complexity of the debates. I am interested here primarily in the way the discussion was framed, rather than in seeking underlying causes.

7. But see Elliston 1997, which recoups the term as a way to signify the balance of power between women and men within households.

8. Lack of recognition of the diverse relationships in Afro-Caribbean households was due in large part to colonial and racist attitudes toward African Americans and Afro-Caribbeans. Many researchers claimed that extended kin relations were adaptations to poverty, stress, and outside forces, in effect, invalidating these cultural practices across a large part of the United States and Caribbean region.

9. Some exceptions include Cornwall and Lindisfarne 1994, Peletz 1996, Weismantel 1995, and studies that explore the differences between dominant and nondominant forms of masculinities, such as Lancaster 1992 and Manalansan 2003.

10. See Blackwood and Wieringa 1999a on the heterosexual deprivation theory.

11. See Elwin 1997 and Silvera 1992. For studies of women's same-sex relations in other areas of the world, see Blackwood and Wieringa 1999b.

12. My use of the term "matrilineal" here is not meant to reify a particular form of kinship structure over actual relations. See Blackwood 2000.

13. The Minangkabau living in West Sumatra numbered approximately 4.2 million in 2000. Citizens of the Indonesian state, they are the largest matrilineal group in the world.

14. Adat refers generally to a set of local customs, beliefs, and practices concerning matrilineal kinship and inheritance, but it is more than rules of kinship and behavior or prescriptions for ceremonies. It constitutes the foundational discourse for Minangkabau identity and ethnicity (see Kato 1982; Sanday 1990a). Adat "rules" were codified by the Dutch in the 1800s.

15. My research was conducted during 1989–90 and 1996 in the wet-rice farming village of Taram in the easternmost district of West Sumatra. Taram's population in 1989 was approximately 6,800. I focused on one hamlet of 125 households with a population of 583, which I call Tanjung Batang. Not all rice-farming villages in West Sumatra experience the same conditions; some may have more migration if there is less land available for farming.

16. Figures are based on my 1989 survey of 115 farm households, which were dependent primarily on income from rice fields.

17. Other researchers have also discussed the duality of men's position as husband and brother, including Prindiville 1985; Reenen 1996; Sanday 2002; and Tanner 1971. I do so here to demonstrate the subordinate position of the conjugal couple.

18. Extended households of three or more generations make up 26 percent of all households, nuclear households 35 percent. Another 29 percent are a diverse group of two-generation, nonnuclear households, and the remainder are single-generation.

19. I use "household" here to refer to the individuals residing in a particular house, but I do not mean to suggest that only members of individual households count as kin or family. Kin and affinal networks are quite extensive in West Sumatra.

20. In 43 percent of single-family households (23 percent of all households) both husband and wife contribute equally to household income and decision making about household resources. But even in these households, matrilineal relations structure production, access to resources, and lineal affairs.

21. See, for example, Krier 2000; Peletz 1987, 1996; and Sanday 2002 regarding the significance of groom exchange for the Minangkabau and culturally similar people of Negeri Sembilan.

22. There is some debate as to the significance of groom price, but I would agree with Sanday 2002 that the exchange signifies the rights of the matrilineage in the groom

23. Other societies without marriage include the Nayar (see Schneider and Gough 1961) and the Moso of China (Shih 2001).

24. This also recalls Rubin's (1975) argument about compulsory heterosexuality.

Chapter 5

1. Cliff Richard is a well-known British pop singer, and the Village People an all male American pop group popular at the beginning of the 1980s.

2. The term "Berdache" has long been used in anthropological literature as a term for male and female native Americans who assume the dress and duties of their opposite sex—also known as third and fourth gender people. Contemporary gay and lesbian natives have adopted the term 'two-spirits' to reflect the non-Western roots of their identities.

Chapter 6

1. For instance, Berg (1985) has argued that the number of European muskets that were introduced originally into the highlands area of the island in the seventeenth century were of such limited number that it was their symbolic significance that was most critical for local political development rather than any military advantage that they conferred.

2. This notion of "empirical responsibility" is borrowed from Lakoff and Johnson (1999). They argue that philosophy and philosophers need to be "empirically responsible" toward contemporary findings of psychology, physiology, and neuroscience. In the similar fashion, middle-range theory calls for empirical responsibility toward the natural and cultural forces that pattern the archaeological record.

3. "What will consign some of the output of today's most visible postprocessualists to early obscurity is their choice of fundamentally irrelevant, at times, even ludicrous, subjects for analysis" (Kohl 1993, 16).

4. At the time of the original writing of this text, Dr. Elizabeth Brumfiel, a feminist archaeologist from a small liberal arts college in the Midwest, was president designate of the American Anthropological Association.

Chapter 7

1. Such connections may be seen as including the diversity in the contemporary American "Trans" community, which Leslie Feinberg (1998) described as

"Trans Liberation," the phrase that has come to refer to all those who blur or bridge the boundary of the sex or gender expression they were assigned at birth: cross-dressers, transsexuals, intersex people, Two Spirits, bearded females, masculine females and feminine males, drag kings and drag queens.

Chapter 9

1. At the same time the synthetic discipline of biocultural anthropology was gaining currency within the discipline as a whole. My particular project here, though, is to stress that even those of us who were on a path to careers in traditional scientific anthropology found a place to include critique of the disciplinary culture of biological anthropology in our theoretical and analytical development.

2. These texts represent some key and classic works that fueled my self-reflexive trajectory in bioarchaeology and science.

3. For the most part, archaeologists have been at the forefront of contributing to the reburial literature, while pro-reburial biological anthropologists have not as readily embraced repatriation and reburial issues as part of their scientific research and publications. The most visible biological anthropologists have been those initially protesting reburial and others who have been involved as plaintiffs in the Ancient One/Kennewick Man case, suing to study and curate the controversial ancient skeleton. For more information, Kathleen Fine-Dare (2002) has written a fairly comprehensive history of the reburial movement. For more on the varied responses of archaeologists and bioarchaeologists to repatriation and reburial, see sources such as: Mihesuah (2000), Buikstra (1983), Owsley and Jantz (2001), and Meighan (1992). Also see comments on the "Draft Principles of Agreement Regarding the Disposition of Culturally Unidentifiable Human Remains" submitted by the American Association of Physical Anthropologists to the Native American Graves Protection and Repatriation Act Review Committee. Electronic document, http://www.physanth.org/positions/cuhr .htm, accessed 10 October 2004; Society for American Archaeology (SAA). Repatriation Archive. Electronic document, http://www.saa.org/repatriation/ index.html, accessed 10 October 2004; "Friends of America's Past," http:// www.friendsofpast.org/, Electronic document, accessed 5 November 2004.

4. For the most part, published work in bioarchaeology follows a stringent scientific paradigm of interpretive hypothesis-testing based on osteological analyses, usually performed by the principal author or authors. Reevaluative work and theoretical critiques are rare in the literature. Exceptions include "The Osteological Paradox" (Wood et al. 1992) and an exchange in the *American Anthropologist* between researchers over reanalyses of some of Franz Boas's immigrant cranial data (see especially Gravlee, Bernard, and Leonard 2003). Examination and critique of the underlying logic or methodology of the discipline, though, is not typically on-topic for journal publications such as the *American Journal of Physical Anthropology* or the *International Journal of Osteoarchaeology*. Recent critiques do include Alan Goodman's (1997) exhortation to stop using racial categories and Cathy Gere's (1999) interrogation of sex determination.

5. Historical processes do not necessarily produce results that are congruent with traditional themes in biological anthropology. Many well-known examples of human variability and human adaptations to diverse environments are presented in physical anthropology classes and texts from data that is no longer

current, where peoples have been displaced or affected politically and economically by larger historical and social forces. Examples such as the San and the Inuit can be useful illustrations of an "ethnographic present," but they must be acknowledged and taught as such. Moreover, some populations have been and are impacted culturally, politically, and economically to such an extent that the possibilities for biological "adaptation," strictly speaking, are greatly compromised. The physical anthropological focus on origins and species-wide patterns of behavior can leave us unequipped to deal with the biological effects of regionally and historically specific examples of the exercise of human power and agency. This is especially the case when many of our introductory courses end at the transition from foraging to agriculture. I believe that when we attempt to teach what motivates various human behaviors, biological anthropology instructors should look to recent ethnography and medical anthropology as quickly as we look to sociobiology and evolutionary psychology.

6. In a rather ironic "Epistemology of the Closet" twist (Sedgwick 1990), my stilted insistence on a split between research and teaching paralleled my earlier emergence from the contradiction of the closet.

7. Nonreligious students in my classes are often anthropology majors with strident critiques of Christianity. In their wholesale condemnation of creationist viewpoints, however, they often fail to see aspects of their own ethnocentrism. Likewise, science majors from other disciplines are also attracted to biological anthropology, and I try to communicate to them that because they are in an anthropology course, one very important feature of their experience in my class will be a consideration of the cultural aspects of this particular science. Students being trained in scientific disciplines who cross over into the anthropology department are a particular challenge; they are often some of the more vocal and resistant voices to examining any scientific interests and frameworks as culturally situated.

8. I have them participate in this very specific identification exercise because at the start of a semester I have observed that many students will quickly concur with each other that extreme views are rarely useful simply to dampen conflict or to not be accused of challenging each other. Since I am attempting to open my classroom to argumentation, I also attempt to move away from that kind of conflict avoidance.

9. The substance for these lectures came from both National Center for Science Education (Electronic document, http://www.ncseweb.org/article.asp, accessed 10 December 2004) and the online Talk.Origins archive (http://www.talkorigins.org/faqs/faq-god.html, accessed 10 December 2004)

10. While my students are generally sensitized to the presence of queer people in their class, or queer people teaching their classes for that matter, they rarely consider the possibility that intersexed people could be present or in fact could exist at all. Likewise, people with disabilities are often conceived of as different in a way not allowable in the normalizing process of evolution.

11. For an engaging deconstruction of evolutionary psychology see McCaughey (1996). I often encounter students in my classes who have taken our psychology department's Evolutionary Psychology seminar. Such students often have accepted a premise that all individual human desires are the same—deep, universal, and evolutionarily produced—making any deconstruction of social assumptions within evolutionary theory even more challenging.

Bibliography

Abelove, Henry, Michèle Aina Barale, and David M. Halperin, eds. 1993. *The Lesbian and Gay Studies Reader*. London: Routledge.

Abu-Lughod, Lila. 1990. The Romance of Resistance: Tracing Transformations of Power Through Bedouin Women. *American Ethnologist* 17 (1): 41–55.

Adams, E. Charles. 1991 *The Origin and Development of the Pueblo Katsina Cult*. Tucson: University of Arizona Press.

Alaimo, Stacy. 1994 Cyborg and Ecofeminist Interventions: Challenges for an Environmental Feminism. *Feminist Studies* 20 (1): 133–49.

Alberti, Bemjamin 2001a. Faience Goddesses and Ivory Bull-Leapers: The Aesthetics of Sexual Difference at Late Bronze Age Knossos. *World Archaeology* 33: 189–205.

———. 2001b. De género a cuerpo: una reconceptualización y sus implicaciones para la interpretación arqueológica. *Intersecciones en antropología* 2: 61–72.

Alcoff, Linda and Elizabeth Potter. 1993. Introduction: When Feminisms Intersect Epistemology. In *Feminist Epistemologies*, ed. Linda Alcoff and Elizabeth Potter. 1–14. New York: Routledge.

Alonso, Ana M. 2000. The Use and Abuse of Feminist Theory: Fear, Dust, and Commensality. In *Gender Matters: Rereading Michelle Z. Rosaldo*, ed. Alejandro Lugo and Bill Maurer. 221–32. Ann Arbor: University of Michigan Press.

Angel, John L. 1978. Pelvic Inlet Form: A Neglected Index of Nutritional Status. *American Journal of Physical Anthropology* 48: 378.

Appadurai, Arjun. 1996. *Modernity at Large: Cultural Dimensions of Globalization*. Minneapolis: University of Minnesota Press.

Arnold, Bettina and Nancy L. Wicker, eds. 2001a. *Gender and the Archaeology of Death*. Walnut Creek, Calif.: AltaMira Press.

———. 2001b. Introduction. In *Gender and the Archaeology of Death*, ed. Bettina Arnold and Nancy L. Wicker. vii–xxi. Walnut Creek, Calif.: AltaMira Press.

Arwill-Nordbladh, Elisabeth. 2003. A Reigning Queen or the Wife of a King Only? Gender Politics in the Scandinavian Viking Age. In *Ancient Queens*, ed. Sarah M. Nelson. 19–40. Walnut Creek, Calif.: AltaMira Press.

Ashmore, Wendy and Robert J. Sharer. 2000. *Discovering Our Past: A Brief Introduction to Archaeology*. 3rd ed. Mountain View, Calif.: Mayfield.

Bachand, Holly, Rosemary A. Joyce, and Julia A. Hendon. 2003. Bodies Moving in Space: Ancient Mesoamerican Human Sculpture and Embodiment. *Cambridge Archaeological Journal* 13: 238–47.

Bachelard, Gaston. 1994. *The Poetics of Space*. Boston: Beacon Press.
Bacus, E. A., A. W. Barker, J. D. Bonevich, S. L. Dunavan, D. L. Gold, N. S. Goldman-Finn, W. Griffin, and K. M. Mudar. 1993. *A Gendered Past: A Critical Bibliography of Gender in Archaeology*. Ann Arbor: University of Michigan Museum of Archaeology.
Baines, John. 1985. Egyptian Twins. *Orientalia* 54: 461–82.
Baker, M. 1997. Invisibility as a Symptom of Gender Categories in Archaeology. In *Invisible People and Processes: Writing Gender and Childhood into European Archaeology*, ed. Jenny Moore and Eleanor Scott. 183–91. London: Leicester University Press.
Ball, R. P. 1938. Pelvicephalometry. *Radiology* 31: 188–97.
Banks, Maggie. 1998. *Breech Birth Woman-Wise*. Hamilton, New Zealand: Birthspirit Books.
Bar On, Bat-Ami. 1993. Marginality and Epistemic Privilege. In *Feminist Epistemologies*, ed. Linda Alcoff and Elizabeth Potter. 83–100. New York: Routledge.
Barfield, Thomas, ed. 1997. *The Dictionary of Anthropology*. Oxford: Blackwell.
Barkley Brown, Elsa. 1989. Womanist Consciousness: Maggie Lena Walker and the Independent Order of Saint Luke. *Signs* 14 (3): 610–33.
Barrow, Christine. 1986. Anthropology, the Family and Women in the Caribbean. In *Gender in Caribbean Development*, ed. Patricia Mohammed and Catherine Shepherd. 156–69. Mona, Jamaica: University of the West Indies.
———. 1996. *Family in the Caribbean: Themes and Perspectives*. Kingston: Ian Randle.
Basta, Mounir. 1979. Preliminary Report on the Excavation at Saqqara (1964) and the Discovery of a Tomb from the 5th Dynasty. *Annales du Service des Antiquités de l'Égypte* 63: 631–50.
Bauman, Zygmunt. 1998. On Postmodern Uses of Sex. *Theory, Culture and Society* 15 (3–4): 19–34.
———. 2000a. *Liquid Modernity*. Cambridge: Polity Press.
———. 2000b. *The Individualised Society*. Cambridge: Polity Press.
———. 2001. *Liquid Love*. Cambridge: Polity Press.
Beck-Gernsheim, Elizabeth. 1998. On the Way to a Post-Familial Family: From a Community of Need to Elective Affinities. *Theory, Culture and Society* 15 (3–4): 53–70.
Beck, Ulrich and Elizabeth Beck-Gernsheim. 2001. *Individualization: Institutionalized Individualism and Its Social and Political Consequences*. London: Sage.
Behar, Ruth. 1993. *Translated Woman: Crossing the Border with Esperanza's Story*. Boston: Beacon Press.
Behar, Ruth and Deborah A. Gordon, eds. 1995. *Women Writing Culture*. Berkeley: University of California Press.
Bem, Sandra. 1993. *The Lenses of Gender: Transforming the Debate on Sexual Inequality*. New Haven, Conn.: Yale University Press.
Bender, Susan J. 2000. A Proposal to Guide Curricular Reform for the Twenty-First Century. In *Teaching Archaeology in the Twenty-First Century*, ed. Susan J. Bender and George S. Smith. 31–48. Washington, D.C.: Society for American Archaeology.
Benhabib, Seyla, Judith Butler, Drucilla Cornell, and Nancy Fraser. 1995. *Feminist Contentions: A Philosophical Exchange*. London: Routledge.
Berg, Gerald. 1985. The Sacred Musket: Tactics, Technology, and Power in Eighteenth Century Madagascar. *Comparative Studies in Society and History* 27: 261–79.
Bergstrom, W. H. 1991. Twenty Ways to Get Rickets in the 1990s. *Contemporary Pediatrics* 8: 88–106.

Bertelson, Reidar, Arnvid Lillehammer, and Jenny-Rita Naess. 1987. *Were They All Men? An Examination of Sex Roles in Prehistoric Society*. Stavanger, Norway: Arkeologisk Museum I Stavanger.

Blackwood, Evelyn. 1999. Big Houses and Small Houses: Doing Matriliny in West Sumatra. *Ethnos* 64 (1): 32–56.

———. 2000. *Webs of Power: Women, Kin, and Community in a Sumatran Village*. Lanham, Md.: Rowman and Littlefield.

———. 2001. Representing Women: The Politics of Minangkabau *Adat* Writings. *Journal of Asian Studies* 60 (1): 125–49.

———. 2002. Heteronormativity and Family in Anthropology. Paper presented at the 101st Annual American Anthropological Association Meetings, November 2001, New Orleans.

Blackwood, Evelyn and Saskia E. Wieringa, eds. 1999a. *Female Desires: Same-Sex Relations and Transgender Practices Across Cultures*. New York: Columbia University Press.

———. 1999b. Sapphic Shadows: Challenging the Silence in the Study of Sexuality. In *Female Desires: Same-Sex Relations and Transgender Practices Across Cultures*, ed. Evelyn Blackwood and Saskia E. Wieringa. 39–63. New York: Columbia University Press.

Bleier, Ruth. 1984. *Science and Gender: A Critique of Biology and Its Theories on Women*. New York: Pergamon Press.

Boas, Franz. 1905. Race and Progress. *Science* 74 (1931): 1–8.

Bolles, A. Lynn. 1996. *Sister Jamaica: A Study of Women, Work, and Households in Kingston*. Lanham, Md.: University Press of America.

Bordo, Susan. 1993. *Unbearable Weight: Feminism, Western Culture, and the Body*. Berkeley: University of California Press.

Borneman, John. 1996. Until Death Do Us Part: Marriage/Death in Anthropological Discourse. *American Ethnologist* 23 (2): 215–35.

Boucher, Joanne. 2003. Betty Friedan and the Radical Past of Liberal Feminism. *New Politics* 9 (35): 23–32.

Bourdieu, Pierre. 1995. *Outline of a Theory of Practice*. Cambridge: Cambridge University Press.

Braidotti, Rosi. 1991. *Patterns of Dissonance*. Cambridge: Polity Press.

Brewer, Rose M. 1993. Theorizing Race, Class and Gender: The New Scholarship of Black Feminist Intellectuals and Black Women's Labour. In *Theorizing Black Feminisms: The Visionary Pragmatism of Black Women*, ed. Stanlie M. James and Abena P. A. Busia. 13–30. London: Routledge.

Briskin, Linda and Rebecca P. Coulter. 1992. Feminist Pedagogy: Challenging the Normative. *Canadian Journal of Education* 17: 247–63.

Brode, Harry. 1987. The Case for Men's Studies. In *The Making of Masculinities: The New Men's Studies*, ed. Harry Brode. 39–47. London: Routledge.

Brumbach, Hetty J. and Robert Jarvenpa. 1997. Woman the Hunter: Ethnoarchaeological Lessons from Chipewyan Life-Cycle Dynamics. In *Women in Prehistory: North American and Mesoamerica*, ed. Cheryl Claassen and Rosemary A. Joyce. 17–32. Philadelphia: University of Pennsylvania Press.

Brumfiel, Elizabeth M. 1992. Distinguished Lecture in Archaeology: Breaking and Entering the Eco-System: Gender, Class, and Faction Steal the Show. *American Anthropologist* 94: 551–67.

Brumfiel, Elizabeth M. 1996a. Figurines and the Aztec State: Testing the Effectiveness of Ideological Domination. In *Gender and Archaeology*, ed. Rita P. Wright. 143–66. Philadelphia: University of Pennsylvania Press.

————. 1996b. The Quality of Tribute Cloth: The Place of Evidence in Archaeological Argument. *American Antiquity* 61 (3): 453–62.

Buikstra, Jane E. 1983. Reburial: How We All Lose. *Society for California Newsletter* 17 (1): 2–5.

Buss, David M. 1994. *The Evolution of Desire: Strategies of Human Mating.* New York: Basic Books.

Butler, Judith. 1990. *Gender Trouble: Feminism and the Subversion of Identity.* New York: Routledge.

————. 1993. *Bodies That Matter: On the Discursive Limits of "Sex".* New York: Routledge.

————. 1997a. *Excitable Speech: A Politics of the Performative.* New York: Routledge.

————. 1997b. *The Psychic Life of Power.* Stanford, Calif.: Stanford University Press.

————. 1997c. Merely Cultural. *New Left Review* 22: 733–44.

Bynum, Caroline Walker. 1991. The Female Body and Religious Practice in the Later Middle Ages. In Bynum, *Fragmentation and Redemption: Essays on Gender and the Human Body in Medieval Religion.* 181–238. New York: Zone Books.

Caldwell, William E. and Howard C. Moloy. 1933. Anatomical Variations in the Female Pelvis and Their Effect in Labor with a Suggested Classification. *American Journal of Obstetrics and Gynecology* 26: 479–505.

Caldwell, William E., Howard C. Moloy, and D. A. D'Esopo. 1934. A Roentgenologic Study of the Mechanism of Engagement of the Fetal Head. *American Journal of Obstetrics and Gynecology* 28: 824–41.

————. 1939. Studies on Pelvic Arrests. *American Journal of Obstetrics and Gynecology* 36: 928–61.

Campbell, Beatrice. 1993. *Goliath: Britain's Dangerous Places.* London: Methuen.

Cashmore, Ellis. 2003. *Beckham.* Cambridge: Polity Press.

Chamberlain, N. L., E. D. Driver, and R. L. Miesfeld. 1994. The Length and Location of CAG Trinucleotide Repeats in the Androgen Receptor N-Terminal Domain Affect Transactivation Function. *Nucleic Acids Research* 22 (15): 3181–86.

Cheah Pheng and Bruce Robbins. 1998. *Cosmopolitics: Thinking and Feeling Beyond the Nation.* Minneapolis: University of Minnesota Press.

Cherpion, Nadine. 1995. Sentiment conjugal et figuration à l'Ancien Empire. In *Kunst des Alten Reiches (Symposium im Deutschen Archäologischen Institut, Kairo, Oktober 1991).* 34–45. Mainz am Rhein: Verlag Phillipp von Zabern.

Claassen, Cheryl, ed. 1992a. *Exploring Gender Through Archaeology: Selected Papers from the 1991 Boone Conference.* Madison, Wis.: Prehistory Press.

————. 1992b. Workshop 3: Teaching and Seeing Gender. In *Exploring Gender Through Archaeology: Selected Papers from the 1991 Boone Conference,* ed. Cheryl Claassen. 137–53. Madison, Wis.: Prehistory Press.

————, ed. 1994. *Women in Archaeology.* Philadelphia: University of Pennsylvania Press.

————. 2000. Homophobia and Women Archaeologists. *World Archaeology* 32 (2): 173–79.

Clutton-Brock, Tim H. 1985. Size, Sexual Dimorphism, and Polygyny in Primates. In *Size and Scaling in Primate Biology,* ed. William L. Jungers. 51–60. New York: Plenum Press.

Cobble, Dorothy S. 2004. *The Other Women's Movement: Workplace Justice and Social Rights in Modern America.* Princeton, N.J.: Princeton University Press.

Cohen, Yehudi A. 1953. A Study of Interpersonal Relations in a Jamaican Community. Ph.D. dissertation, Department of Anthropology, Yale University.

Cole, Johnnetta B., ed. 1986. *All American Women: Lines That Divide, Ties That Bind*. New York: Free Press.

Collier, Jane F. and Sylvia Junko Yanagisako, eds. 1987a. *Gender and Kinship: Essays Toward a Unified Analysis*. Stanford, Calif.: Stanford University Press.

———. 1987b. Toward a Unified Analysis of Gender and Kinship. In *Gender and Kinship: Essays Toward a Unified Analysis*, ed. Jane F. Collier and Sylvia Junko Yanagisako. 14–52. Stanford, Calif.: Stanford University Press.

Comaroff, Jean and John L. Comaroff. 2000. Millennial Capitalism: First Thoughts on a Second Coming. *Public Culture* 12 (2): 291–343.

Conkey, Margaret W. 2003. Has Feminism Changed Archaeology? *Signs* 28: 867–80.

Conkey, Margaret W. and Joan M. Gero. 1991. Tensions, Pluralities, and Engendering Archaeology: An Introduction to Women and Prehistory. In *Engendering Archaeology: Women and Prehistory*, ed. Joan M. Gero and Margaret W. Conkey. 3–30. Cambridge: Blackwell.

———. 1997. Programme to Practice: Gender and Feminism in Archaeology. *Annual Review of Anthropology* 26: 411–37.

Conkey, Margaret W. and Janet D. Spector. 1984. Archaeology and the Study of Gender. *Advances in Archaeological Method and Theory* 7: 1–38.

Conkey, Margaret W. and Ruth E. Tringham. 1995. Archaeology and the Goddess: Exploring the Contours of Feminist Archaeology. In *Feminisms in the Academy*, ed. Domna C. Stanton and Abigail J. Stewart. 199–247. Ann Arbor: University of Michigan Press.

———. 1996. Cultivating Thinking/Challenging Authority: Some Experiments in Feminist Pedagogy in Archaeology. In *Gender and Archaeology*, ed. Rita P. Wright. 224–50. Philadelphia: University of Pennsylvania Press.

Conkey, Margaret W. and Sarah H. Williams. 1991. Original Narratives: The Political Economy of Gender in Archaeology. In *Gender at the Crossroads of Knowledge: Feminist Anthropology in the Postmodern Era*, ed. Micaela di Leonardo. 102–39. Berkeley: University of California Press.

Connell, Robert W. 1995 *Masculinities*. Berkeley: University of California Press.

Cordell, Linda. 1993. Women Archaeologists in the Southwest. In *Hidden Scholars: Women Anthropologists and the Native American Southwest*, ed. Nancy J. Parezo. 202–45. Albuquerque: University of New Mexico Press.

Cornwall, Andrea and Nancy Lindisfarne. 1994. *Dislocating Masculinity: Comparative Ethnographies*. New York: Routledge.

Cosinsky, Sheila. 1976. Cross Cultural Perspectives on Midwifery. In *Medical Anthropology*, ed. Francix X. Grollig and Harold B. Haley. 229–49. The Hague: Mouton.

Cott, Nancy F. 1987. *The Grounding of Modern Feminism*. New Haven, Conn.: Yale University Press.

Crown, Patricia L. 2000. Women's Role in Changing Cuisine. In *Women and Men in the Prehispanic Southwest: Labor, Power, and Prestige*, ed. Patricia L. Crown. 221–66. Santa Fe, N.M.: School of American Research Press.

Csordas, Thomas J. 1994. Introduction: The Body as Representation and Being-in-the-World. In *Embodiment and Experience: The Existential Ground of Culture and Self*, ed. Thomas J. Csordas. 1–24. Cambridge: Cambridge University Press.

Cunningham F. G., N. F. Gant, K. J. Leveno, L. C. Gilstrap III, J. C. Hauth, and K. D. Wenstrom. 2001. *Williams Obstetrics*. 21st ed. New York: McGraw-Hill.

Cushing, Frank Hamilton. 1896. Outlines of Zuni Creation Myths. In *Thirteenth Annual Report of the Bureau of Ethnology, 1891–1892.* 321–447. Washington, D.C.: U.S. Government Printing Office.

Dahlberg, Frances, ed. 1981. *Woman the Gatherer.* New Haven, Conn.: Yale University Press.

Danielsson, Ing-Marie B. 2002. (Un)masking Gender-Gold Foil (Dis)embodiments in Late Iron Age Scandinavia. In *Thinking Through the Body: Archaeologies of Corporeality,* ed. Yannis Hamilakis, Mark Pluciennik, and Sarah Tarlow. 179–99. New York: Kluwer Academic.

Darwin, Charles. 1871. *The Descent of Man and Selection in Relation to Sex.* New York: D. Appleton.

Davis-Floyd, Robbie E. 1992. *Birth as an American Rite of Passage.* Berkeley: University of California Press.

Davis-Floyd, Robbie E. and Carolyn F. Sargent, eds. 1997. *Childbirth and Authoritative Knowledge: Cross-Cultural Perspectives.* Berkeley: University of California Press.

Dawkins, Richard. 1976. *The Selfish Gene.* New York: Oxford University Press.

De Lauretis, Teresa. 1987a. *Alice Doesn't: Feminism, Semiotics, Cinema.* London: Macmillan.

————. 1987b. The Technology of Gender. In de Lauretis, *Technologies of Gender: Essays on Theory, Film, and Fiction.* 1–30. Bloomington: Indiana University Press.

de Waal, Frans B. M. 2001. Apes from Venus: Bonobos and Human Social Evolution. In *Tree of Origin: What Primate Behavior Can Tell Us About Human Social Evolution,* ed. Frans B. M. de Waal. 41–68. Cambridge, Mass.: Harvard University Press.

del Valle, Teresa, ed. 1993. *Gendered Anthropology.* London: Routledge.

di Leonardo, Micaela. 1991a. Contingencies of Value in Feminist Anthropology. In *(En)Gendering Knowledge: Feminists in Academe,* ed. Joan E. Hartman and Ellen Messer-Davidow. 140–58. Knoxville: University of Tennessee Press.

————, ed. 1991b. *Gender at the Crossroads of Knowledge: Feminist Anthropology in the Postmodern Era.* Berkeley: University of California Press.

————. 1991c. Introduction: Gender, Culture, and Political Economy: Feminist Anthropology in Historical Perspective, in *Gender at the Crossroads of Knowledge: Feminist Anthropology in the Postmodern Era,* ed. Micaela di Leonardo. 1–48. Berkeley: University of California Press.

Diáz-Andreu, Margarita and Marie Louise Stig Sørenson, eds. 1998. *Excavating Women: A History of Women in European Archaeology.* London: Routledge.

Dirlik, Arif. 1994. *After the Revolution: Waking to Global Capitalism.* Hanover, N.H.: Wesleyan University Press.

Dobres, Marcia-Anne. 1995. Gender and Prehistoric Technology: On the Social Agency of Technical Strategies. *World Archaeology* 27 (1): 25–49.

Dongoske, Kurt E., Mark Aldenderfer, and Karen Doehner, eds. 2000. *Working Together: Native Americans and Archaeologists.* Washington, D.C.: Society for American Archaeology.

Dowson, Thomas A. 1998. Homosexualitat, teoria queer i arqueologia. *Cota Zero* 14: 81–87.

————. 2000a. Homosexuality, Queer Theory and Archaeology. In *Interpretive Archaeology: A Reader,* ed. Julien Thomas. 283–89. London: Leicester University Press.

————, ed. 2000b. Queer Archaeologies. *World Archaeology* 32 (2).

————. 2000c. Why Queer Archaeology? An Introduction. *World Archaeology* 32 (2): 161–65.

————. 2001. Queer Theory and Feminist Theory: Towards a Sociology of Sexual Politics in Rock Art Research. In *Theoretical Perspectives in Rock Art Research: ACRA: The Alta Conference on Rock Art*, ed. Knut Helskog. 312–29. Oslo: Novus.

DuBois, Henri M. 1938. *Monographie des Betsileo.* Paris: Institut d'Ethnologie.

Eble, Kenneth. 1988. *The Craft of Teaching: A Guide to Mastering the Professor's Art.* 2nd ed. San Francisco: Jossey-Bass.

Ehrenberg, Margaret. 1989. *Women in Prehistory.* Norman: University of Oklahoma Press.

Ehrenreich, Barbara. 2001. *Nickel and Dimed: Undercover in Low-Wage USA.* London: Granta.

Ehrlich, Carol. 1975. *The Conditions of Feminist Research.* Baltimore: Vacant Lots Press.

Elliston, Deborah A. 1997. En/Gendering Nationalism: Colonialism, Sex, and Independence in French Polynesia. Ph.D. dissertation, Department of Anthropology, New York University.

Elwin, Rosamund. 1997. *Tongues on Fire: Caribbean Lesbian Lives and Stories.* Toronto: Women's Press.

Engels, Frederich. 1972. *The Origin of the Family, Private Property, and the State.* New York: International Publishers.

Errington, Shelly. 1990. Recasting Sex, Gender, and Power: A Theoretical and Regional Overview. In *Power and Difference: Gender in Island Southeast Asia*, ed. J. Atkinson and Shelly Errington. 1–58. Stanford, Calif.: Stanford University Press.

Evans-Pritchard, E. E. 1940. *The Nuer.* Oxford: Oxford University Press.

————. 1951. *Kinship and Marriage Among the Nuer.* Oxford: Oxford University Press.

Fagan, Brian M. 2000. Education Is What's Left: Some Thoughts on Introductory Archaeology. *Antiquity* 74: 190–94.

————. 2004. *Ancient Lives: An Introduction to Archaeology and Prehistory.* 2nd ed. Upper Saddle River, N.J.: Prentice-Hall.

Falk, Dean. 1997. Brain Evolution in Females: An Answer to Mr. Lovejoy. In *Women in Human Evolution*, ed. Lori D. Hager. 114–36. London: Routledge.

Faludi, Susan. 1991. *Backlash: The Undeclared War Against American Women.* New York: Crown.

Fanshawe, Simon. 2004. You Don't Have to Play It Straight. *The Guardian*, August 11.

Fausto-Sterling, Anne. 1985. *Myths of Gender: Biological Theories About Men and Women.* New York: Basic Books.

————. 2000. *Sexing the Body: Gender Politics and the Construction of Sexuality.* New York: Basic Books.

Featherstone, Mike. 1991. *Postmodernism and Consumer Culture.* London: Sage.

Fedigan, Linda M. 1982. *Primate Paradigms: Sex Roles and Social Bonds.* Chicago: University of Chicago Press.

————. 1986. The Changing Role of Women in Models of Human Evolution. *Annual Review of Anthropology* 15: 25–66.

————. 1997. Is Primatology a Feminist Science. In *Women in Human Evolution*, ed. Lori D. Hager. 56–75. London: Routledge.

Feigen, Brenda. 2000. *Not One of the Boys: Living Life as a Feminist.* New York: Knopf.

Feinberg, Leslie. 1998. *Trans Liberation: Beyond Pink or Blue.* Boston: Beacon Press.

Fernandez, James. 1986. *Persuasions and Performances: The Play of Tropes in Culture.* Bloomington: Indiana University Press.

Fine-Dare, Kathleen. 2002. *Grave Injustice: The American Indian Repatriation Movement and NAGPRA.* Lincoln: University of Nebraska Press.

Finn, Janet L. 1995. Ella Cara Deloria and Mourning Dove: Writing for Cultures, Writing Against the Grain. In *Women Writing Culture,* ed. Ruth Behar and Deborah A. Gordon. 131–47. Berkeley: University of California Press.

Foucault, Michel. 1977. *Discipline and Punish: The Birth of the Prison.* New York: Random House.

———. 1980. Truth and Power. In Foucault, *Power/Knowledge: Selected Interviews and Other Writings, 1972–1977.* Ed. and trans. Colin Gordon. 109–33. New York: Pantheon.

Fowler, Chris. 2002. Body Parts: Personhood and Materiality in the Earlier Manx Neolithic. In *Thinking Through the Body: Archaeologies of Corporeality,* ed. Yannis Hamilakis, Mark Pluciennik, and Sarah Tarlow. 47–69. New York: Kluwer Academic.

Fraser, Nancy. 1997 *Justice Interruptus: Critical Reflections on the "Postsocialist" Condition.* London: Routledge.

———. 1998. Heterosexism, Misrecognition, and Capitalism: A Response to Judith Butler. *New Left Review* 22: 8140–49.

———. 2000. Rethinking Recognition. *New Left Review* 3: 107–20.

Fraser, Nancy and Linda J. Nicholson. 1988. Social Criticism Without Philosophy: An Encounter Between Feminism and Postmodernism. In *Universal Abandon? The Politics of Postmodernism,* ed. Andrew Ross. 83–104. Minneapolis: University of Minnesota Press.

Freire, Paulo. 1970. *Pedagogy of the Oppressed.* New York: Continuum.

———. 1998. *Pedagogy of Freedom: Ethics, Democracy, and Civic Courage.* Lanham, Md.: Rowman and Littlefield.

Friedan, Betty. 1963. *The Feminine Mystique.* New York: Norton.

Frisch, Rose E. 1988. Fatness and Fertility. *Scientific American* 258 (3): 88–95.

Gacs, Ute, Aisha Khan, Jerrie McIntyre, and Ruth Weinberg, eds. 1988. *Women Anthropologists: A Biographical Dictionary.* New York: Greenwood Press.

Gaskin, Ina M. 1990. *Spiritual Midwifery.* Summertown, Tenn.: Book Publishing Company.

Gatens, Moira. 1992. Power, Bodies and Difference. In *Destabilizing Theory: Contemporary Feminist Debates,* ed. Michèle Barrett and Anne Phillips. 120–37. Stanford, Calif.: Stanford University Press.

Geisler, Gisela. 1993. Silences Speak Louder Than Claims: Gender, Household, and Agricultural Development in Southern Africa. *World Development* 21 (12): 1965–80.

Gere, Cathy. 1999. Bones That Matter: Sex Determination in Paleodemography, 1948–1995. *Studies in the History and Philosophy of Biology and the Biomedical Sciences* 30 (4): 455–71.

Gero, Joan M. 1983. Gender Bias in Archaeology: A Cross-Cultural Perspective. In *The Socio-Politics of Archaeology,* ed. Joan M. Gero, David M. Lacey, and Michael L. Blakey. 51–57. Amherst: University of Massachusetts Department of Anthropology.

———. 1985 Sociopolitics of Archaeology and the Woman-at-Home Ideology. *American Antiquity* 50: 342–50.

———. 1991. Genderlithics: Women's Roles in Stone Tool Production. In *Engendering Archaeology: Women and Prehistory*, ed. Joan M. Gero and Margaret W. Conkey. 163–93. Cambridge, Mass.: Blackwell.

———. 1993. The Social World of Prehistoric Facts: Gender and Power in Paleoindian Research. In *Women in Archaeology: A Feminist Critique*, ed. Hilary du Cros and Laurajane Smith. 31–40. Occasional Papers in Prehistory 23. Canberra: Australian National University.

Gero, Joan M. and Margaret W. Conkey, eds. 1991 *Engendering Archaeology: Women and Prehistory*. Cambridge, Mass.: Blackwell.

Gero, Joan M. and M. Cristina Scattolin. 2002. Beyond Complementarity and Hierarchy: New Definitions for Archaeological Gender Relations. In *In Pursuit of Gender: Worldwide Archaeological Approaches*, ed. Sarah Milledge Nelson and Myriam Rosen-Ayalon. 155–71. Walnut Creek, Calif.: AltaMira Press.

Gevisser, Mark and Edwin Cameron, eds. 1994. *Defiant Desire: Gay and Lesbian Lives in South Africa*. Johannesburg: Raven Press.

Giddens, Anthony. 1992. *The Transformation of Intimacy: Sexuality, Love and Eroticism in Modern Societies*. Stanford, Calif.: Stanford University Press.

———. 1994. *Beyond Left and Right: The Future of Radical Politics*. Cambridge: Polity Press.

Gifford-Gonzalez, Diane. 1993. Gaps in Zooarchaeology Analyses of Butchery: Is Gender an Issue? In *From Bones to Behavior: Ethnoarchaeological and Experimental Contributions to the Interpretation of Faunal Remains*, ed. Jean Hudson. 181–99. Carbondale: Center for Archaeological Investigations, Southern Illinois University.

Gilchrist, Roberta. 1994. *Gender and Material Culture: The Archaeology of Religious Women*. London: Routledge.

———. 1997. Ambivalent Bodies: Gender and Medieval Archaeology. In *Invisible People and Processes: Writing Gender and Childhood into European Archaeology*, ed. Jenny Moore and Eleanor Scott. 42–58. London: Leicester University Press.

———. 1999. *Gender and Archaeology: Contesting the Past*. London: Routledge.

———. 2000a. Archaeological Biographies: Realizing Human Lifecycles, Courses and Histories. *World Archaeology* 31 (3): 325–28.

———. 2000b. Unsexing the Body: The Interior Sexuality of Medieval Religious Women. In *Archaeologies of Sexuality*, ed. Robert A. Schmidt and Barbara L. Voss. 89–103. London: Routledge.

Gilroy, Paul. 1987. *There Ain't No Black in the Union Jack: The Cultural Politics of Race and Nation*. London: Hutchinson.

Gimbutas, Marija. 1982. *The Goddesses and Gods of Old Europe: Myths and Cult Images*. Berkeley: University of California Press.

Gimovsky M. and C. Hennigan. 1995. Abnormal Fetal Presentations. *Current Opinion in Obstetrics and Gynecology* 7 (6): 482–85.

Ginsburg, Faye D. and Rayna Rapp. 1991. The Politics of Reproduction. *Annual Review of Anthropology* 20: 311–43.

Giovannucci E., M. J. Stampfer, K. Krithivas, M. Brown, A. Brufsky, J. Talcott, C. H. Hennekens, and P. W. Kantoff., 1997. The CAG Repeat Within the Androgen Receptor and Its Relationship to Prostate Cancer. *Proceedings of the National Academy of Sciences, USA* 94 (7): 3320–23.

Gluckman, Max. 1956. *Custom and Conflict in Africa*. Oxford: Basil Blackwell.

Goer, Henci. 1995. *Obstetric Myths Versus Research Realities: A Guide to the Medical Literature*. Westport, Conn.: Bergin and Garvey.

Gonzalez, Nancie L. 1984. Rethinking the Consanguineal Household and Matrifocality. *Ethnology* 23 (1): 1–12.

Goodall, Jane. 1986. *The Chimpanzees of Gombe.* Cambridge, Mass.: Belknap Press of Harvard University Press.

Goodman, Alan. 1997. Bred in the Bone? *The Sciences* 37: 20–25.

Gough, Kathleen. 1971. Nuer Kinship: A Re-Examination. In *The Translation of Culture: Essays to E. E. Evans-Pritchard,* ed. T. O. Beidelman. 79–121. London: Tavistock.

Gould, Stephen J. 1981. *The Mismeasure of Man.* New York: Norton.

Gravlee, Clarence C., H. Russell Bernard, and William R. Leonard. 2003. Heredity, Environment and Cranial Form: A Re-Analysis of Boas' Immigrant Data. *American Anthropologist* 105: 125–38.

Gray, John N. 1995. *The Householder's World: Purity, Power and Dominance in a Nepali Village.* Delhi: Oxford University Press.

Grosz, Elizabeth A. 1994. *Volatile Bodies: Toward a Corporeal Feminism.* Bloomington: Indiana University Press.

———. 1995. *Space, Time and Perversion: Essays on the Politics of Bodies.* New York: Routledge.

Gupta, Akhil and James Ferguson. 1992. Beyond "Culture": Space, Identity and the Politics of Difference. *Cultural Anthropology* 7: 6–23.

Gutmann, Matthew C. 1997. Trafficking in Men: The Anthropology of Masculinity. *Annual Review of Anthropology* 26: 385–409.

Hager, Lori D., ed. 1997. *Women in Human Evolution.* London: Routledge.

———. 1989. The Evolution of Sex Differences in the Hominid Bony Pelvis. Ph.D. dissertation, Department of Anthropology University of California at Berkeley.

Hall, Donald E. 2003. *Queer Theories.* Basingstoke: Palgrave Macmillan.

Halperin, David. 1995. *Saint Foucault: Towards a Gay Hagiography.* Oxford: Oxford University Press.

Hamilakis, Yannis, Mark Pluciennik, and Sarah Tarlow. 2002a. Introduction: Thinking Through the Body. In *Thinking Through the Body: Archaeologies of Corporeality,* ed. Yannis Hamilakis, Mark Pluciennik, and Sarah Tarlow. 1–21. New York: Kluwer Academic.

———, eds. 2002b. *Thinking Through the Body: Archaeologies of Corporeality.* New York: Kluwer Academic.

Hanen, Marsha and Jane Kelley. 1992. Gender and Archaeological Knowledge. In *Metaarchaeology: Reflections by Archaeologists and Philosophers,* ed. Lester Embree. 195–225. Dordrecht: Kluwer Academic.

Haraway, Donna J. 1989. *Primate Visions: Gender, Race and Nature in the World of Modern Science.* New York: Routledge.

———. 1991. *Simians, Cyborgs and Women: The Reinvention of Nature.* New York: Routledge.

———. 1999. Situated Knowledges: The Science Question in Feminism and the Privilege of Partial Perspective. In *The Science Studies Reader,* ed. M. Biagioli. 172–188. New York: Routledge.

Harding, Sandra. 1986. *The Science Question in Feminism.* Ithaca, N.Y.: Cornell University Press.

———. 1987. Introduction: Is There a Feminist Method? In *Feminism and Methodology: Social Science Issues,* ed. Sandra Harding. 1–14. Bloomington: Indiana University Press.

————. 1993. Rethinking Standpoint Epistemology: What Is "Strong Objectivity"? In *Feminist Epistemologies*, ed. Linda Alcoff and Elizabeth Potter. 49–82. New York: Routledge.

Harris, E. 1998. Going Post-al. *Out* 58: 82–87.

Harrison, Faye V. 1997. The Gendered Politics and Violence of Structural Violence: A View from Jamaica. In *Situated Lives: Gender and Culture in Everyday Life*, ed. Louise Lamphere, Helena Ragoné, and Patricia Zavella. 451–68. New York: Routledge.

Harrison, Faye V. and Ira E. Harrison, eds. 1999. *African-American Pioneers in Anthropology*. Urbana: University of Illinois Press.

Hartman, Joan E. and Ellen Messer-Davidow. 1991. Introduction: A Position Statement. In *(En)Gendering Knowledge: Feminists in Academe*, ed. Joan E. Hartman and Ellen Messer-Davidow. 1–7. Knoxville: University of Tennessee Press.

Hastorf, Christine A. 1991. Gender, Space, and Food in Prehistory. In *Engendering Archaeology: Women and Prehistory*, ed. Joan M. Gero and Margaret W. Conkey. 132–62. Cambridge, Mass.: Blackwell.

Hawkes, Jacquetta. 1951. The Origin of the British People: Archaeology and the Festival of Britain. *Antiquity* 25: 4–8.

Hayden, Brian. 1992. Observing Prehistoric Women. In *Exploring Gender Through Archaeology: Selected Papers from the 1991 Boone Conference*, ed. Cheryl Claassen. 33–47. Madison, Wis.: Prehistory Press.

Hegmon, Michelle, Scott G. Ortman, and Jeannette L. Mobley-Tanaka. 2000. Women, Men, and the Organization of Space. In *Women and Men in the Prehispanic Southwest: Labor, Power and Prestige*, ed. Patricia L. Crown. 43–90. Santa Fe, N.M.: School of American Research Press.

Hendon, Julia A. 1991. Status and Power in Classic Maya Society: An Archaeological Study. *American Anthropologist* 93: 894–918.

————. 1996. Archaeological Approaches to the Organization of Domestic Labor: Household Practice and Domestic Relations. *Annual Review of Anthropology* 25: 45–61.

————. 1997. Women's Work, Women's Space, and Women's Status Among the Classic-Period Maya Elite of the Copan Valley, Honduras. In *Women in Prehistory: North America and Mesoamerica*, ed. Cheryl Claassen and Rosemary A. Joyce. 33–46. Philadelphia: University of Pennsylvania Press.

————. 1999. Multiple Sources of Prestige and the Social Evaluation of Women in Prehispanic Mesoamerica. In *Material Symbols: Culture and Economy in Prehistory*, ed. John Robb. 257–76. Carbondale: Center for Archaeological Investigations, Southern Illinois University.

————. 2002. Household and State in Prehispanic Maya Society: Gender, Identity, and Practice. In *Ancient Maya Gender Identity and Relations*, ed. Lowell S. Gustafson and Amelia M. Trevelyan. 75–92. Westport, Conn.: Greenwood Press.

Hesse-Biber, Sharlene Nagy and Michelle L. Yaiser, eds. 2004. *Feminist Perspectives on Social Research*. Oxford: Oxford University Press.

Hollimon, Sandra E. 1997. The Third Gender in Native California: Two-Spirit Undertakers Among the Chumash and Their Neighbors. In *Women in Prehistory: North America and Mesoamerica*, ed. Cheryl Claassen and Rosemary A. Joyce. 173–88. Philadelphia: University of Pennsylvania Press.

Hollimon, Sandra E. 2000. Archaeology of the 'Aqi: Gender and Sexuality in Prehistoric Chumash Society. In *Archaeologies of Sexuality*, ed. Robert A. Schmidt and Barbara L. Voss. 179–96. London: Routledge.

————. 2001. Warfare and Gender in the Northern Plains: Osteological Evidence of Trauma Reconsidered. In *Gender and the Archaeology of Death*, ed. Bettina Arnold and Nancy L. Wicker. 179–93. Walnut Creek, Calif.: AltaMira Press.

Holy, Ladislav. 1996. *Anthropological Perspectives on Kinship*. London: Pluto Press.

Hoodfar, Homa. 1992. Feminist Anthropology and Critical Pedagogy: The Anthropology of Classrooms' Excluded Voices. *Canadian Journal of Education* 17: 303–20.

hooks, bell. 1989. *Talking Back: Thinking Feminist, Thinking Black*. Boston: South End Press.

————. 1994. *Teaching to Transgress: Education as the Practice of Freedom*. New York: Routledge.

————. 2000. *Feminist Theory: From Margin to Center*. 2nd ed. Boston: South End Press.

Hooton, Earnest A. 1926. Methods of Racial Analysis. *Science* 8: 376–81.

Horrocks, Roger. 1995. *Male Myths and Icons: Masculinity in Popular Culture*. Basingstoke: Macmillan.

Howard, Melanie and Sue Tibballs. 2003. *Talking Equality: What Women and Men Think About Equality in Britain Today* [online]. London: Equal Opportunities Commission. *http://www.eoc.org.uk/pdf/talking%20equality%20report.pdf* (accessed 28 October 2005).

Hoyme, L. H. 1957. The Earliest Use of Indices for Sexing Pelves. *American Journal of Physical Anthropology*. 15: 537–46.

Hrdy, Sarah Blaffer. 1981. *The Woman That Never Evolved*. Cambridge, Mass.: Harvard University Press.

Hurcombe, Linda. 2000. Time, Skill and Craft Specialization as Gender Relations. In *Gender and Material Culture in Archaeological Perspective*, ed. Moira Donald and Linda Hurcombe. 88–109. Chippenham: Macmillan.

Igarashi, S., Y. Tanno, O. Onodera, M. Yamazaki, S. Sato, A. Ishikawa, N. Miyatani, M. Nagashima, Y. Ishikawa, K. Sahashi, et al. 1992. Strong Correlation Between the Number of CAG Repeats in Androgen Receptor Genes and the Clinical Onset of Features of Spinal and Bulbar Muscular Atrophy. *Neurology* 42: 2300–2302.

Illouz, Eva. 1998. The Lost Innocence of Love: Romance as a Postmodern Condition. *Theory, Culture and Society* 15 (3–4): 161–86.

Ingolds, Tim. 2000. *The Perception of the Environment: Essays in Livelihood, Dwelling and Skill*. London: Routledge.

Isaac, Glynn L. 1983. Aspects of Human Evolution. In *Evolution from Molecules to Men*, ed. D. S. Bendall. 509–43. New York: Cambridge University Press.

Isbell, William H. 2000. What We Should Be Studying: The "Imagined Community" and the "Natural Community." In *The Archaeology of Communities: A New World Perspective*, ed. Marcello A. Canuto and Jason Yaeger. 243–66. London: Routledge.

Jackson, Michael. 1989. *Paths Toward a Clearing: Radical Empiricism and Ethnographic Inquiry*. Bloomington: Indiana University Press.

Jagose, Annamarie. 1996. *Queer Theory: An Introduction*. New York: New York University Press.

Jakobsen, Janet R. 1998. *Working Alliances and the Politics of Difference: Diversity and Feminist Ethics*. Bloomington: Indiana University Press.

Jameson, Frederic. 1991. *Postmodernism, or the Cultural Logic of Late Capitalism*. Durham, N.C.: Duke University Press.

———. 1998. Notes on Globalization as a Philosophical Issue. In *The Cultures of Globalization*, ed. Frederic Jameson and Masao Miyoshi. 54–77. Durham, N.C.: Duke University Press.

Jameson, John. 2003. *Ancient Muses: Archaeology and the Arts*. Birmingham: University of Alabama Press.

Jayaratne, Toby E. 1983. The Value of Quantitative Methodology in Feminist Research. In *Theories of Women's Studies*, ed. Gloria Bowles and Renata Duelli Klein. 140–62. London: Routledge.

Jones, Sian. 1991. The Female Perspective. *Museums Journal* 91 (2): 24–27.

Jones, Sian and Sharon Pay. 1990 The Legacy of Eve. In *The Politics of the Past*, ed. Peter Gathercole and David Lowenthal. 160–71. London: Unwin Hyman.

Jones, Stephen, Robert D. Martin, and David R. Pilbeam. 1992. *The Cambridge Encyclopedia of Human Evolution*. Cambridge: Cambridge University Press.

Jordan, Brigitte. 1993. *Birth in Four Cultures: A Crosscultural Investigation of Childbirth in Yucatan, Holland, Sweden, and the United States*. Montreal: Eden Press Women's Publications.

Joyce, Rosemary A. 1992. Images of Gender and Labor Organization in Classic Maya Society. In *Exploring Gender Through Archaeology: Selected Papers from the. 1991 Boone Conference*, ed. Cheryl Claassen. 63–70. Madison, Wis.: Prehistory Press.

———. 1993. Women's Work: Images of Production and Reproduction in Prehispanic Southern Central America. *Current Anthropology* 34: 255–74.

———. 1996. The Construction of Gender in Classic Maya Monuments. In *Gender and Archaeology*, ed. Rita P. Wright. 167–95. Philadelphia: University of Pennsylvania Press.

———. 1998. Performing the Body in pre-Hispanic Central America. *Res: Anthropological Aesthetics* 33: 147–65.

———. 2000a. Girling the Girl and Boying the Boy: The Production of Adulthood in Ancient Mesoamerica. *World Archaeology* 31: 473–83.

———. 2000b. A Precolumbian Gaze: Male Sexuality Among the Ancient Maya. In *Archaeologies of Sexuality*, ed. Robert A. Schmidt and Barbara L. Voss. 263–83. London: Routledge.

———. 2001a. *Gender and Power in Prehispanic Mesoamerica*. Austin: University of Texas Press.

———. 2001b. Negotiating Sex and Gender in Classic Maya Society. In *Gender in Pre-Hispanic America: A Symposium at Dumbarton Oaks, 12 and 13 October 1996*, ed. Cecilia F. Klein. 109–41. Washington, D.C.: Dumbarton Oaks Research Library and Collection.

———. 2001c. Personhood, Agency, and Individuality: The Case of Classic Maya Names. Paper presented at the 66th Annual Meeting of the Society for American Anthropology. April 2001, New Orleans.

———. 2002. Desiring Women: Classic Maya Sexualities. In *Ancient Maya Gender Identity and Relations*, ed. Lowell S. Gustafson and Amelia M. Trevelyan. 329–44. Westport, Conn.: Greenwood Press.

———. 2004. Embodied Subjectivity: Gender, Femininity, Masculinity, Sexuality. In *A Companion to Social Archaeology*, ed. Lynn M. Meskell and Robert W. Preucel. 82–95. Malden, Mass.: Blackwell.

Joyce, Rosemary A. and Cheryl Claassen. 1997. Women in the Ancient Americas: Archaeologists, Gender, and the Making of Prehistory. In *Women in Prehistory: North America, and Mesoamerica*, ed. Cheryl Claassen and Rosemary A. Joyce. 1–14. Philadelphia: University of Pennsylvania Press.

Joyce, Rosemary A., Robert W. Preucel, Jeanne Lopiparo, Carolyn Guyer, and Michael Joyce. 2002. *The Languages of Archaeology: Dialogue, Narrative, and Writing.* Malden, Mass.: Blackwell.

Kahn, Joel S. 1980. *Minangkabau Social Formations: Indonesian Peasants and the World Economy.* Cambridge: Cambridge University Press.

Kakaliouras, Ann M. 2003. Biological Distance and the Ethnolinguistic Classification of Late Woodland (800–1650 AD) Native Americans on the Coast of North Carolina. Ph.D. dissertation, Department of Anthropology, University of North Carolina.

Kato, Tsuyoshi. 1982. *Matriliny and Migration: Evolving Minangkabau Traditions in Indonesia.* Ithaca, N.Y.: Cornell University Press.

Keller, Evelyn Fox. 1985. *Reflections on Gender and Science.* New Haven, Conn.: Yale University Press.

Kennedy, Elizabeth and Madeline Davis. 1994. *Boots of Leather, Slippers of Gold: The History of a Lesbian Community.* New York: Routledge.

Kent, Suan, ed. 1998. *Gender in African Prehistory.* Walnut Creek, Calif.: AltaMira Press.

Kidder, Alfred. 1949. Introduction to Charles A. Amsden, *Prehistoric Southwesterners from Basketmaker to Pueblo.* xi–xiv. Los Angeles: Southwest Museum.

Kirsch, Max H. 2000. *Queer Theory and Social Change.* London: Routledge.

Kitzinger, Sheila. 1972. *The Experience of Childbirth.* 3rd ed. Baltimore: Penguin.

Klein, Cecelia F. 2001. Conclusions: Envisioning Pre-Columbian Gender Studies. In *Gender in Pre-Hispanic Mesoamerica,* ed. Cecelia F. Klein. 363–85. Washington, D.C.: Dumbarton Oaks Research Library and Collection.

Knapp, A. B. 1998a. Boys Will Be Boys: Masculinist Approaches to a Gendered Archaeology. In *Redefining Archaeology: Feminist Perspectives,* ed. Mary Casey, Denise Donlon, Jeannette Hope, and Sharon Wellfare. 32–36. Research Papers in Archaeology and Natural History 29. Canberra: ANH Publications, Australian National University.

———. 1998b. Who's Come a Long Way, Baby? Masculinist Approaches to a Gendered Archaeology. *Archaeological Dialogues* 5 (2): 91–125.

Knapp, A. B. and Lynn M. Meskell. 1997. Bodies of Evidence on Prehistoric Cyprus. *Cambridge Archaeological Journal* 7 (2): 183–204.

Kohl, Philip. 1993. Limits of a Post-Processual Archaeology (or, The Dangers of New Scholasticism). In *Archaeological Theory: Who Sets the Agenda?* ed. Norman Yoffee and Andrew Sherrat. 11–19. Cambridge: Cambridge University Press.

Kohlstedt, Sally G. and Helen E. Longino. 1997. The Woman, Gender, and Science Question: What Do Research on Women in Science and Research on Gender and Science Have to Do with Each Other? *Osiris* 12: 3–15.

Krier, Jennifer. 2000. The Marital Project: Beyond the Exchange of Men in Minangkabau Marriage. *American Ethnologist* 27 (4): 877–97.

Kristeva, Julia. 1982. *Powers of Horror: An Essay on Abjection.* New York: Columbia University Press.

Krogman, Wilton. 1951. The Scars of Human Evolution. *Scientific American* 18: 554–57.

Kus, Susan. 1992. Toward an Archaeology of Body and Soul. In *Representations in Archaeology,* ed. Jean-Claude Gardin and Christopher S. Peebles. 168–77. Bloomington: Indiana University Press.

La Spada, A. R., E. M. Wilson, D. B. Lubahn, A. E. Harding, and K. H. Fischbeck. 1991. Androgen Receptor Gene Mutations in X-Linked Spinal and Bulbar Muscular Atrophy. *Nature* 352: 77–79.

Lakoff, George and Mark Johnson. 1980. *Metaphors We Live By.* Chicago: University of Chicago Press.

Lakoff, George and Mark Johnson. 1999. *Philosophy in the Flesh: The Embodied Mind and Its Challenge to Western Thought.* New York: Basic Books.

Lambek, Michael and Andrew Strathern, eds. 1998. *Bodies and Persons: Comparative Perspectives from Africa and Melanesia.* Cambridge: Cambridge University Press.

Lamphere, Louise. 1974. Strategies, Cooperation, and Conflict Among Women in Domestic Groups. In *Woman, Culture, and Society,* ed. Michelle Z. Rosaldo and Louise Lamphere. 97–112. Stanford, Calif.: Stanford University Press.

Lamphere, Louise. 1977. *From Working Daughters to Working Mothers: Immigrant Women in a New England Industrial Community.* Ithaca, N.Y.: Cornell University Press.

Lamphere, Louise. 1987. Feminism and Anthropology: The Struggle to Reshape Our Thinking About Gender. In *The Impact of Feminist Research in the Academy,* ed. Christie Farnham. 11–33. Bloomington: Indiana University Press.

Lancaster, Roger N. 1992. *Life Is Hard: Machismo, Danger, and the Intimacy of Power in Nicaragua.* Berkeley: University of California Press.

Landau, Misia. 1984. Human Evolution As Narrative. *American Scientist* 72: 262–68.

———. 1991. *Narratives of Human Evolution.* New Haven, Conn.: Yale University Press.

Laqueur, Thomas W. 1990. *Making Sex: Body and Gender from the Greeks to Freud.* Cambridge, Mass.: Harvard University Press.

Lasch, Christopher. 1979. *The Culture of Narcissism: American Life in an Age of Diminishing Expectations.* New York: Norton.

Lash, Scott and John Urry. 1987. *The End of Organized Capitalism.* Madison: University of Wisconsin Press.

Lavelle, M. 1995. Natural Selection and the Development of Sexual Variation in the Human Pelvis. *American Journal of Physical Anthropology* 98: 59–72.

Lee, Richard B. 1980. Lactation, Ovulation, and Women's Work. In *Biosocial Mechanisms of Population Regulation,* ed. Mark N. Cohen, Roy S. Malpass, and Harold G. Klein. 321–48. New Haven, Conn.: Yale University Press.

———. 1968. What Hunters Do for a Living, or, How to Make Out on Scarce Resources. In *Man the Hunter,* ed. Richard B. Lee and Irven De Vore. 30–48. New York: Aldine.

Lee, Richard B. and Irven DeVore, eds. 1968. *Man the Hunter.* New York: Aldine.

Lévi-Strauss, Claude. 1969. *The Raw and the Cooked.* New York: Harper and Row.

Levine, Mary A. 1991. An Historical Overview of Research on Women in Anthropology. In *The Archaeology of Gender: Proceedings of the 22nd Annual Chacmool Conference,* ed. Dale Walde and Noreen D. Willows. 177–86. Calgary: Archaeological Association of the University of Calgary.

Lewin, Ellen. 1993. *Lesbian Mothers: Accounts of Gender in American Culture.* Ithaca, N.Y.: Cornell University Press.

Lewin, Ellen and William L. Leap. 1996. *Out in the Field: Reflections of Gay and Lesbian Anthropologists.* Urbana: University of Illinois Press.

———. 2002. *Out in Theory: The Emergence of Lesbian and Gay Anthropology.* Urbana: University of Illinois Press.

Lloyd, Elisabeth A. 1995. Objectivity and the Double Standard for Feminist Epistemologies. *Synthèse* 104: 351–81.

———. 1996. Science and Anti-Science: Objectivity and Its Real Enemies. In *Feminism, Science, and the Philosophy of Science,* ed. Lynn Hankinson Nelson and Jack Nelson. 217–59. Dordrecht: Kluwer Academic.

Loffreda, Beth. 2000. *Losing Matt Shepard: Life and politics in the Aftermath of Anti-Gay Murder.* New York: Columbia University Press.

Longino, Helen E. 1987. Can There Be a Feminist Science? *Hypatia* 2: 51–64.

———. 1994. In Search of Feminist Epistemology. *Monist* 77 (4): 472–85.

———. 1998. Values and Objectivity. In *Philosophy of Science: The Central Issues,* ed. Martin Curd and J. A. Cover. 170–91. New York: Norton.

Lopez, Iris. 1997. Agency and Constraint: Sterilization and Reproductive Freedom Among Puerto Rican Women in New York City. In *Situated Lives: Gender and Culture in Everyday Life,* ed. Louise Lamphere, Helena Ragoné, and Patricia Zavella. 157–71. New York: Routledge.

Lorde, Audre. 1984a. The Master's Tools Will Never Dismantle the Master's House. In Lorde, *Sister Outsider: Essays and Speeches.* 110–13. Freedom, Calif.: Crossing Press.

———. 1984b. The Uses of Anger: Women Responding to Racism. In Lorde, *Sister Outsider: Essays and Speeches.* 124–33. Freedom, Calif.: Crossing Press.

Lovejoy, C. O. 1981. The Origin of Man. *Science* 211: 341–50.

Lovibond, Sabina. 1989. Feminism and Postmodernism. *New Left Review* 178: 5–28.

Lowe, Marian and Ruth Hubbard. 1983. *Women's Nature: Rationalization of Inequality.* New York: Pergamon Press.

Luhmann, Niklas. 1986. *Love as Passion: The Codification of Intimacy.* Cambridge, Mass.: Harvard University Press.

Lurie, Nancy O. 1966. Women in Early American Anthropology. In *Pioneers of American Anthropology: The Uses of Biography,* ed. June Helm. 31–71. Seattle: University of Washington Press.

Lyotard, Jean-François. 1984. *The Postmodern Condition: A Report on Knowledge.* Minneapolis: University of Minnesota Press.

MacCormack, Carol P. 1994. *Ethnography of Fertility and Birth.* Prospect Heights, Ill.: Waveland Press.

Mahmood, Saba. 2001. Feminist Theory, Embodiment, and the Docile Agent: Some Reflections on the Egyptian Islamic Revival. *Cultural Anthropology* 16 (2): 202–36.

Majewski, Teresita. 2000. "We Are All Storytellers": Comments on Storytelling, Science, and Historical Archaeology. *Historical Archaeology* 34: 7–19.

Malinowski, Bronislaw. 1984 [1922]. *Argonauts of the Western Pacific.* Prospect Heights, Ill.: Waveland Press.

———. 1929. *The Sexual Life of Savages in North Western Melanesia.* London: Routledge.

Manalansan, Martin F. I. 2003. *Global Divas: Filipino Gay Men in the Diaspora.* Durham, N.C.: Duke University Press.

Manderson, Lenore. 1999. Social Meanings and Sexual Bodies: Gender Sexuality and Barriers to Women's Health Care. In *Sex, Gender, and Health,* ed. Tessa M. Pollard and Susan Brin Hyatt. 75–93. Cambridge: Cambridge University Press.

Martin, Biddy. 1994. Sexualities Without Genders and Other Queer Utopias. *Diacritics* 24 (2–3): 104–21.

Martin, Debra L. 1997. Violence Against Women in the La Plata River Valley (A.D. 1000–1300). In *Troubled Times: Violence and Warfare in the Past,* ed. Debra L. Martin and David W. Frayer. 45–76. Amsterdam: Gordon and Breach.

———. 2000. Bodies and Lives: Biological Indicators of Health Differentials and Division of Labor by Sex. In *Women and Men in the Prehispanic Southwest: Labor, Power, and Prestige,* ed. Patricia L. Crown. 267–300. Santa Fe, N.M.: School of American Research Press.

Martin, Emily. 1991. The Egg and the Sperm: How Science Has Constructed a Romance Based on Stereotypical Male-Female Roles. *Signs* 16 (3): 485–501.

———. 2001. *The Woman in the Body: A Cultural Analysis of Reproduction.* Rev. ed. Boston: Beacon Press.

Martin, Robert D. and L. A. MacLarnon. 1990. Reproductive Patterns in Primates and Other Mammals: The Dichotomy Between Altricial and Precocial Offspring. In *Primate Life History and Evolution*, ed. C. Jean DeRousseau. 47–79. New York: Wiley-Liss.

Martindale, Kathleen. 1992. Theorizing Autobiography and Materialist Feminist Pedagogy. *Canadian Journal of Education* 17: 321–40.

Martorell, Reynaldo. 1989. Body Size, Adaptation, and Function. *Human Organization* 48 (1): 284–90.

Mauss, Marcel. 1985. A Category of the Human Mind: The Notion of Person, the Notion of Self. In *The Category of the Person: Anthropology, Philosophy, History*, ed. Michael Carrithers, Steven Collins, and Steven Lukes. 1–25. Cambridge: Cambridge University Press.

Mauss, Marcel. 1992. Techniques of the Body. In *Incorporations*, ed. Jonathan Crary and Sanford Kwinter. 454–77. New York: Zone Books.

McCafferty, Sharisse D. and Geoffrey G. McCafferty. 1988. Powerful Women and the Myth of Male Dominance in Aztec Society. *Archaeological Review from Cambridge* 7 (1): 45–59.

McCaughey, Martha. 1996. Perverting Evolutionary Narratives of Heterosexual Masculinity—Or Getting Rid of the Heterosexual Bug. *GLQ: A Journal of Lesbian and Gay Studies* 3 (2–3): 261–87.

McClaurin, Irma. 1996. *Women in Belize: Gender and Change in Central America.* New Brunswick, N.J.: Rutgers University Press.

———. 2001. *Black Feminist Anthropology: Theory, Politics, Praxis, and Poetics.* New Brunswick, N.J.: Rutgers University Press.

McLaren, Margaret A. 2002. *Feminism, Foucault, and Embodied Subjectivity.* Albany: State University of New York Press.

Medicine, Beatrice. 1983. "Warrior Women": Sex Role Alternatives for Plains Indian Women. In *The Hidden Half: Studies of Plains Indian Women*, ed. Patrice Albers and Beatrice Medicine. 267–80. Norman: University of Oklahoma Press.

Meighan, Clement W. 1992. Some Scholars' Views on Reburial. *American Antiquity* 57 (4): 704–10.

Mengerts, William F. 1948. Estimation of Pelvic Capacity. *Journal of the American Medical Association* 138: 169–74.

Merleau-Ponty, Maurice. 1962. *Phenomenology of Perception.* 10th ed. London: Routledge.

Mervis, Jeffrey. 2002. Can Equality in Sports Be Repeated in the Lab? *Science* 298: 356.

Meskell, Lynn M. 1995. Goddess, Gimbutas and "New Age" Archaeology. *Antiquity* 69: 74–86.

———. 1996. The Somatisation of Archaeology: Discourses, Institutions, Corporeality. *Norwegian Archaeological Review* 29: 1–16.

———. 1998. The Irresistible Body and the Seduction of Archaeology. In *Changing Bodies, Changing Meanings: Studies on the Human Body in Antiquity*, ed. Dominc Montserrat. 139–61. London: Routledge.

———. 1999. *Archaeologies of Social Life: Age, Sex, Class et Cetera in Ancient Egypt.* Oxford: Blackwell.

———. 2000. Re-em(bed)ding Sex: Domesticity, Sexuality, and Ritual in New Kingdom Egypt. In *Archaeologies of Sexuality*, ed. Robert A. Schmidt and Barbara L. Voss. 253–62. London: Routledge.

———. 2002. *Private Life in New Kingdom Egypt.* Princeton, N.J.: Princeton University Press.

Meskell, Lynn M. and Rosemary A. Joyce. 2003. *Embodied Lives: Figuring Ancient Maya and Egyptian Experience.* London: Routledge.

Mies, Maria. 1983. Towards a Methodology for Feminist Research. In *Theories of Women's Studies*, ed. G. Bowles and R. D. Klein. 117–139. London: Routledge.

Mihesuah, Devon A., ed. 2000. *Repatriation Reader: Who Owns American Indian Remains?* Lincoln: University of Nebraska Press.

Miller, Barbara Diane. 1993. The Anthropology of Sex and Gender Hierarchies. In *Sex and Gender Hierarchies*, ed. Barbara Diane Miller. 3–31. Cambridge: Cambridge University Press.

Mithlo, Nancy. 1993. Native American Artists. Ph.D dissertation, Stanford University.

Mohammed, Patricia. 1986. The Caribbean Family Revisited. In *Gender in Caribbean Development: Papers Presented at the Inaugural Seminar of the University of the West Indies, Women and Development Studies Project*, ed. Patricia Mohammed and Catherine Shepherd. 170–82. Mona, Jamaica: University of the West Indies.

Mohanty, Chandra Talpade. 1988. Under Western Eyes: Feminist Scholarship and Colonial Discourses. *Feminist Review* 30: 61–88.

Mohanty, Chandra Talpade, Anna Russo, and Lourdes Torres, eds. 1991. *Third World Women and the Politics of Feminism.* Bloomington: Indiana University Press.

Moi, Toril. 1985. *Sexual/Textual Politics: Feminists Literary Theory.* London: Routledge.

Moir, J. C. 1946. The Use of Radiology in Predicting Difficult Labour. *Journal of Obstetrics and Gynaecology* 53: 487.

Monagan, Alfrieta P. 1985. Rethinking "Matrifocality." *Phylon* 46: 353–62.

Moore, Henrietta L. 1988. *Feminism and Anthropology.* Cambridge: Polity Press.

———. 1993. The Differences Within and the Differences Between. In *Gendered Anthropology*, ed. Teresa del Valle. 193–204. London: Routledge.

———. 1994. *A Passion for Difference: Essays in Anthropology and Gender.* Bloomington: Indiana University Press.

———. 1996. *The Future of Anthropological Knowledge.* London: Routledge.

———. 1997. Interior Landscapes and External Worlds: The Return of Grand Theory in Anthropology. *Australian Journal of Anthropology* 8 (2): 125–44.

———. 1999. Whatever Happened to Women and Men? Gender and Other Crises in Anthropology. In *Anthropological Theory Today*, ed. Henrietta L. Moore. 151–71. Cambridge: Polity Press.

———. 2000. Ethics and Ontology: Why Agents and Agency Matter. In *Agency and Archaeology*, ed. by M.-A. Dobres and J. Robb. 259–63. New York: Routledge.

———. 2004. Global Anxieties: Concept-Metaphors and Pre-Theoretical Commitments in Anthropology. *Anthropological Theory* 4 (1): 71–88.

Morgan, Robin, ed. 1984. *Sisterhood Is Global: The International Women's Movement Anthology.* Garden City, N.Y.: Anchor/Doubleday.

Morgan, Robin. 2001. *The Demon Lover.* New York: Washington Square Press.

Morgen, Sandra, ed. 1989a. *Gender and Anthropology: Critical Reviews for Research and Teaching.* Washington, D.C.: American Anthropological Association.

———. 1989b. Gender and Anthropology: Introductory Essay. In *Gender and Anthropology: Critical Reviews for Research and Teaching*, ed. Sandra Morgen. 1–20. Washington, D.C.: American Anthropological Association.

Morris, Rosalind C. 1995. All Made Up: Performance Theory and the New Anthropology of Sex and Gender. *Annual Review of Anthropology* 24: 567–92.

Moser, Stephanie. 1998. *Ancestral Images: The Iconography of Human Origins*. Ithaca, N.Y.: Cornell University Press.

Moussa, Ahmed and Hartwig Altenmüller. 1977. *Das grab des Nianchchnum und Chnumhotep*. Mainz: Deutches Archäologisches Institut.

Mukhopadhyay, Carol C. and Patricia J. Higgins. 1988. Anthropological Studies of Women's Status Revisited: 1977–1987. *Annual Review of Anthropology* 17: 461–95.

Mullings, Leith and Alaka Wali. 2001. *Stress and Resilience: The Social Context of Reproduction in Central Harlem*. New York: Kluwer Academic.

Naim, Mochtar. 1985. Implications for Merantau for Social Organization in Minangkabau. In *Change and Continuity in Minangkabau: Local, Regional, and Historical Perspectives on West Sumatra*, ed. Lynn L. Thomas and Franz von Benda-Beckmann. 111–17. Athens: Ohio University Center for International Studies.

Napier, John. 1967. The Antiquity of Human Walking. *Scientific American* 21: 665–66.

Needham, Rodney, ed. 1971. *Rethinking Kinship and Marriage*. London: Tavistock.

Nelson, Sarah M. 1990. Diversity of the Upper Paleolithic "Venus" Figurines and Archeological Reality. In *Powers of Observation, Alternative Views in Archaeology*, ed. Sarah M. Nelson and Alice B. Kehoe. 11–22. Archaeological Papers of the American Anthropological Association 2. Washington, D.C.: American Anthropological Association.

———. 1997. *Gender in Archaeology: Analyzing, Power, and Prestige*. Walnut Creek, Calif.: AltaMira Press.

———, ed. 2003. *Ancient Queens: Archaeological Explorations*. Walnut Creek, Calif.: AltaMira Press.

———. 2003. COSWA Concerns. *SAArchaeological Record* 3(4): 6–7.

———. 2004. *Gender in Archaeology: Analyzing Power and Prestige*. 2nd ed. Walnut Creek, Calif.: AltaMira Press.

Nelson, Sarah M. and Margaret C. Nelson. 1994. Conclusion. In *Equity Issues for Women in Archaeology*, ed. Margaret C. Nelson, Sarah M. Nelson, and Alison Wylie. 229–35. Archaeological Papers of the American Anthropological Association 5. Washington, D.C.: American Anthropological Association.

Nelson, Margaret C., Sarah M. Nelson, and Alison Wylie, eds. 1994. *Equity Issues for Women in Archaeology*. Archaeological Papers of the American Anthropological Association 5. Washington, D.C.: American Anthropological Association.

Nelson, Sarah M. and Myriam Rosen-Ayalon, eds. 2002. *In Pursuit of Gender: Worldwide Archaeological Approaches*. Walnut Creek, Calif.: AltaMira Press.

Newton, Ester. 1972. *Mother Camp: Female Impersonators in America*. Chicago: University of Chicago Press.

Ng, Cecilia S. H. 1987. The Weaving of Prestige: Village Women's Representations of the Social Categories of Minangkabau Society. Ph.D. dissertation, Australian National University.

Nussbaum, Martha C. 1999. The Professor of Parody: The Hip Defeatism of Judith Butler. *New Republic*, February 22, 37–45.

Oakley, Ann. 1981. Interviewing Women: A Contradiction in Terms. In *Doing Feminist Research*, ed. Helen Roberts. 30–61. London: Routledge.

———. 1984. *The Captured Womb: A History of the Medical Care of Pregnant Women*. New York: Blackwell.

O'Donnell, Emer. 2004. Birthing in Prehistory. *Journal of Anthropological Archaeology* 23: 163–71.

Okruhlik, Kathleen. 1998. Gender and the Biological Sciences. In *Philosophy of Science: The Central Issues*, ed. Martin Curd and J. A. Cover. 192–208. New York: W.W. Norton.

Olwig, Karen F. 1981. Women, "Matrifocality," and Systems of Exchange: An Ethnohistorical Study of the Afro-American Family on St. John, Danish West Indies. *Ethnohistory* 28 (1): 59–78.

Omolade, Barbara. 1987. A Black Feminist Pedagogy. *Women's Studies Quarterly* 15 (3–4): 32–39.

Ortman, Scott G. 1998. Corn Grinding and Community Organization in the Pueblo Southwest, A.D. 1150–1550. In *Migration and Reorganization: The Pueblo IV Period in the American Southwest*, ed. Katherine A. Spielmann. 165–92. Tempe: Arizona State University Anthropological Research Papers No. 51.

Ortner, Sherry B. 1974. Is Female to Male as Nature Is to Culture? In *Woman, Culture, and Society*, ed. Michelle Zimbalist Rosaldo and Louise Lamphere. 67–88. Stanford, Calif.: Stanford University Press.

———. 2003. *New Jersey Dreaming: Capital, Culture and the Class of '58*. Durham, N.C.: Duke University Press.

Ortner, Sherry B. and Harriet Whitehead, eds. 1981a. *Sexual Meanings: The Cultural Construction of Gender and Sexuality*. Cambridge: Cambridge University Press.

———. 1981b. Introduction: Accounting for Sexual Meanings. In *Sexual Meanings: The Cultural Construction of Gender and Sexuality*, ed. Sherry B. Ortner and Harriet Whitehead. 1–28. Cambridge: Cambridge University Press.

Osborne, Peter and Lynne Segal. 1994. An Interview with Judith Butler. *Radical Philosophy: A Journal of Socialist and Feminist Philosophy* 67: 32–39.

Ottino, Paul. 1974. *Madagascar, les Comores et Sud-Ouest de l'Océan Indien*. Antananarivo: Centre d'anthropologie culturelle et social, Université de Madagascar.

Owsley, Douglas and Richard Jantz. 2001. Archaeological Politics and Public Interest in Paleoamerican Studies: Lessons from Gordon Creek Woman and Kennewick Man. *American Antiquity* 66 (4): 565–75.

Parezo, Nancy J., ed. 1993. *Hidden Scholars: Women Anthropologists in the Native American Southwest*. Albuquerque: University of New Mexico Press.

Parkinson, R. B. 1995. "Homosexual" Desire and Middle Kingdom Literature. *Journal of Egyptian Archaeology* 81: 57–76.

Parsons, Elsie C. 1916. The Zuni La'mana. *American Anthropologist* 18 (4): 521–528.

———. 1929. *The Social Organization of the Tewa of New Mexico*. Menasha, Wis.: American Anthropological Association.

———. 1939. *Pueblo Indian Religion*. Chicago: University of Chicago Press.

Patterson, Thomas C. 2005. *The Theory and Practice of Archaeology: A Workbook*. 3rd ed. Upper Saddle River, N.J.: Prentice-Hall.

Peletz, Michael. 1987. The Exchange of Men in Nineteenth-Century Negeri Sembilan (Malaya). *American Ethnologist* 14 (3): 449–69.

———. 1994. Comparative Perspectives on Kinship and Cultural Identity in Negeri Sembilan. *Sojourn* 9 (1): 1–53.

———. 1996. *Reason and Passion: Representations of Gender in a Malay Society.* Berkeley: University of California Press.

Pennsylvania Department of Education. 2004. *Academic Standards for Reading, Writing, Speaking, and Listening.* http://www.pde.state.pa.us/stateboard_ed/cwp/view.asp?a=3&Q=76716&stateboard_edNav=|5467|&pde_internetNav=| (accessed 3 September 2004).

Perry, Elizabeth M. and Rosemary A. Joyce. 2001. Providing a Past for *Bodies That Matter*: Judith Butler's Impact on the Archaeology of Gender. *International Journal of Sexuality and Gender Studies* 6 (1/2): 63–76.

Peterson, Jane. 2002. *Sexual Revolutions: Gender and Labor at the Dawn of Agriculture.* Walnut Creek, Calif.: AltaMira Press.

Phillips, Anne. 1997. From Inequality to Difference: A Severe Case of Displacement. *New Left Review* 224 (July/August): 142–53.

———. 1999. *Which Equalities Matter?* Cambridge: Polity Press.

Pollock, Susan. 1991. Women in a Men's World: Images of Sumerian Women. In *Engendering Archaeology: Women and Prehistory*, ed. Joan M. Gero and Margaret W. Conkey. 366–87. Cambridge, Mass.: Blackwell.

Pomeroy, Sarah. 1974. *Goddesses, Whores, Wives, and Slaves in Classical Antiquity.* New York: Schocken.

Potter, James M. 2004. The Creation of Person, the Creation of Place: Hunting Landscapes in the American Southwest. *American Antiquity* 69 (2): 322–338.

Potter, James M. and Scott G. Ortman. 2002. Community and Cuisine in the Prehispanic Southwest. Paper presented at the symposium "Feasting in the Southwest" at the 8th Southwest Symposium, Tucson, Arizona, January 10–12, 2002.

Praetzellis, Adrian. 2000. *Death by Theory: A Tale of Mystery and Archaeological Theory.* Walnut Creek, Calif.: AltaMira Press.

Preucel, Robert W. 1991. The Philosophy of Archaeology. In *Processual and Postprocessual Archaeologies: Multiple Ways of Knowing the Past*, ed. Robert W. Preucel. 17–29. Carbondale: Center for Archaeological Investigations, Southern Illinois University.

———. 1995. The Postprocessual Condition. *Journal of Archaeological Research* 3: 147–75.

Price, T. D. and Anne Birgitte Gebauer. 2002. *Adventures in Fugawiland: A Computer Simulation in Archaeology.* 3rd ed. Columbus, Ohio: McGraw-Hill.

Prindiville, Joanne. 1985. Mother, Mother's Brother, and Modernization: The Problems and Prospects of Minangkabau Matriliny in a Changing World. In *Change and Continuity in Minangkabau: Local, Regional, and Historical Perspectives on West Sumatra*, ed. Lynn L. Thomas and Franz von Benda-Beckmann. 29–43. Athens: Ohio University Press.

Prine, Elizabeth. 2000. Searching for Third Genders: Towards a Prehistory of Domestic Space in Middle Missouri Villages. In *Archaeologies of Sexuality*, ed. Robert A. Schmidt and Barbara L. Voss. 197–219. London: Routledge.

Proust, Marcel. 1981. *Remembrance of Things Past.* New York: Random House.

Quinn, Naomi. 1977. Anthropological Studies on Women's Status. *Annual Review of Anthropology* 6: 181–225.

Rapp, Rayna. 2001. Gender, Body, and Biomedicine: How Some Feminist Concerns Dragged Reproduction to the Center of Social Theory. *Medical Anthropology Quarterly* 15 (4): 466–77.

Rasmussen, Susan. 1996. Tent as Cultural Symbol and Field Site: Social and Symbolic Space, "Topos," and Authority in a Tuareg Community. *Anthropological Quarterly* 69 (1): 14–26.

Rautman, Alison E., ed. 2000. *Reading the Body: Representations and Remains in the Archaeological Record.* Philadelphia: University of Pennsylvania Press.

Rautman, Alison E. and Lauren Talalay. 2000. Introduction: Diverse Approaches to the Study of Gender. In *Reading the Body: Representations and Remains in the Archaeological Record,* ed. Alison E. Rautman. 1–12. Philadelphia: University of Pennsylvania Press.

Reeder, Greg. 1993. United for Eternity. *KMT, a Modern Journal of Ancient Egypt* 41 (1): 22–31.

Reeder, Greg. 2000. Same-Sex Desire, Conjugal Constructs, and the Tomb of Niankhknum and Khnumhotep. *World Archaeology* 32 (2): 193–208.

Reenen, Joke van. 1996. *Central Pillars of the House: Sisters, Wives, and Mothers in a Rural Community in Minangkabau, West Sumatra.* Leiden: Research School CNWS.

Reinharz, Shulamit. 1992. *Feminist Methods in Social Research.* New York: Oxford University Press.

Reischer, Erica and Kathryn S. Koo. 2004. The Body Beautiful: Symbolism and Agency in the Social World. *Annual Review of Anthropology* 33: 297–317.

Reiter, Rayna R., ed. 1975. *Toward an Anthropology of Women.* New York: Monthly Review Press.

Renfrew, Colin and Paul Bahn. 2004. *Archaeology: Theories, Methods, and Practice.* 4th ed. London: Thames and Hudson.

Rich, Adrienne. 1983. Compulsory Heterosexuality and Lesbian Existence. In *Powers of Desire: The Politics of Sexuality,* ed. Ann Snitow, Christine Stansell, and Sharon Thompson. 227–54. New York: Monthly Review Press.

Riding In, James. 1992. Without Ethics and Morality: A Historical Overview of Imperial Archaeology and American Indians. *Arizona State Law Journal* 24 (1): 11–34.

Rieff, David. 1993. Multiculturalism's Silent Partner: It's the New Globalized Consumer Economy, Stupid. *Harper's* 287 (August): 62–72.

Righard, L. and M. O. Alade. 1990. Effect of Delivery Room Routines on Success of First Breast-Feed. *Lancet* 336 (8723): 1105–7.

Robb, John. 2002. Time and Biography: Osteobiography of the Italian Neolithic Lifespan. In *Thinking Through the Body: Archaeologies of Corporeality,* ed. Yannis Hamilakis, Mark Pluciennik, and Sarah Tarlow. 153–71. New York: Kluwer Academic.

Robertson, Roland. 1992. *Globalization: Social Theory and Global Culture.* London: Sage.

Romanowicz, Janet V. and Rita P. Wright. 1996. Gendered Perspectives in the Classroom. In *Gender and Archaeology,* ed. Rita P. Wright. 199–223. Philadelphia: University of Pennsylvania Press.

Roof, Judith. 1997. The Girl I Never Want to Be: Identity, Identification, and Narrative. In *A Queer World: The Center for Lesbian and Gay Studies Reader,* ed. Martin Duberman. 9–16. New York: New York University Press.

Rooks, Judith P. 1997. *Midwifery and Childbirth in America.* Philadelphia: Temple University Press.

Rosaldo, Michelle Zimbalist. 1974. Woman, Culture, and Society: A Theoretical Overview. In *Woman, Culture, and Society,* ed. Michelle Zimbalist Rosaldo and Louise Lamphere. 17–42. Stanford, Calif.: Stanford University Press.

———. 1980. The Use and Abuse of Anthropology: Reflections on Feminism and Cross-Cultural Understanding. *Signs* 5: 389–417.

Rosaldo, Michelle Zimbalist and Louise Lamphere, eds. 1974. *Woman, Culture, and Society.* Stanford, Calif.: Stanford University Press.

Roscoe, Will. 1991. *The Zuni Man-Woman.* Albuquerque: University of New Mexico Press.

Roscoe, Will. 1996. How to Become a Berdache: Toward a Unified Analysis of Gender Diversity. In *Third Sex, Third Gender: Beyond Sexual Dimorphism in Culture and History,* ed. Gil Herdt. 329–72. New York: Zone Books.

———. 1998. *Changing Ones: Third and Fourth Genders in Native North America.* Basingstoke: Macmillan.

Rosen, Ruth. 2000. *The World Split Open: How the Modern Women's Movement Changed America.* New York: Viking.

Rosenberg, Karen R. 1986. The Functional Significance of Neanderthal Pubic Morphology. Ph.D. dissertation. University of Michigan.

———. 1992. The Evolution of Modern Human Childbirth. *Yearbook of Physical Anthropology* 35: 89–124.

Rosenberg, Karen R. and Wenda Trevathan. 1996. Bipedalism and Human Birth: The Obstetrical Dilemma Revisited. *Evolutionary Anthropology* 4: 161–68.

Rosenberg, Karen R. and Wenda Trevanthan. 2001. The Evolution of Human Birth. *Scientific American* 285 (5): 72–77.

———. 2002. Birth, Obstetrics, and Human Evolution. *British Journal of Obstetrics and Gynecology* 109 (11): 1199–1206.

Rothman, Barbara K. 1982. *In Labor: Women and Power in the Birthplace.* New York: W.W. Norton.

Rousham, Emily K. 1999. Gender Bias in South Asia: Effects on Child Growth and Nutritional Status. In *Sex, Gender, and Health,* ed. Tessa M. Pollard and Susan Brin Hyatt. 37–52. Cambridge: Cambridge University Press.

Rubin, Gayle. 1975. The Traffic in Women: Notes on the "Political Economy" of Sex. In *Toward an Anthropology of Women,* ed. Rayna R. Reiter. 157–210. New York: Monthly Review Press.

———. 1984. Thinking Sex: Notes for a Radical Theory of the Politics of Sexuality. In *Pleasure and Danger: Exploring Female Sexuality,* ed. Carole S. Vance. 267–319. New York: Routledge.

Ruff, C. B. 1995. The Biomechanics of the Hip and Birth in Early *Homo. American Journal of Physical Anthropology* 98: 527–74.

Rush, David. 2000. Nutrition and Maternal Mortality in the Developing World. *American Journal of Clinical Nutrition* 72: 212S–240S.

Sacks, Karen. 1974. Engels Revisited: Women, the Organization of Production, and Private Property. In *Woman, Culture, and Society,* ed. Michelle Zimbalist Rosaldo and Louise Lamphere. 205–22. Stanford, Calif.: Stanford University Press.

Sanday, Peggy Reeves. 1974. Female Status in the Public Domain. In *Woman, Culture, and Society,* ed. Michelle Zimbalist Rosaldo and Louise Lamphere. 189–206. Stanford, Calif.: Stanford University Press.

———. 1981. *Female Power and Male Dominance: On the Origins of Sexual Inequality.* New York: Cambridge University Press.

———. 1990a. Androcentric and Matrifocal Gender Representations in Minangkabau Ideology. In *Beyond the Second Sex: New Directions in the Anthropology of Gender,* ed. Peggy Reeves Sanday and Ruth Gallagher Goodenough. 139–68. Philadelphia: University of Pennsylvania Press.

———. 1990b. Introduction. In *Beyond the Second Sex: New Directions in the Anthropology of Gender*, ed. Peggy Reeves Sanday and Ruth Gallagher Goodenough. 1–20. Philadelphia: University of Pennsylvania Press.

———. 1998. Matriarchy as a Sociocultural Form: An Old Debate in a New Light. Paper presented at the 16th Congress of the Indo-Pacific Prehistory Association, July 1–7.

———. 2002. *Women at the Center: Life in a Modern Matriarchy*. Ithaca, N.Y.: Cornell University Press.

Schacht, Steven. 2000. Using a Feminist Pedagogy as a Male Teacher: The Possibilities of a Partial and Situated Perspective. *Radical Pedagogy* 2 (2). http://radicalpedagogy.icaap.org/content/issue2_2/ (accessed 10 December 2004).

Schildkrout, Enid. 2004. Inscribing the Body. *Annual Review of Anthropology* 33: 319–44.

Schmidt, Robert A. 2000. Shamans and Northern Cosmology: The Direct Historical Approach to Mesolithic Sexuality. In *Archaeologies of Sexuality*, ed. Robert A. Schmidt and Barbara L. Voss. 220–35. London: Routledge.

Schmidt, Robert A. and Barbara L. Voss, eds. 2000a. *Archaeologies of Sexuality*. London: Routledge.

———. 2000b. Archaeologies of Sexuality: An Introduction. In *Archaeologies of Sexuality*, ed. Robert A. Schmidt and Barbara L. Voss. 1–34. London: Routledge.

Schneider, David. 1984. *A Critique of the Study of Kinship*. Ann Arbor: University of Michigan Press.

Schneider, David M. and Kathleen Gough. 1961. *Matrilineal Kinship*. Berkeley: University of California Press.

Schultz, A. H. 1949. Sex Differences in the Pelves of Primates. *American Journal of Physical Anthropology* 7: 887–964.

Scott, D. T. 1997. Le Freak, C'est Chic! Le Fag, Quelle Drag! In *PoMoSexuals: Challenging Assumptions About Gender and Sexuality*, ed. Carol Queen and Lawrence Schmiel. 62–69. San Francisco: Cleis Press.

Scott, J. R., P. J. Di Saia, C. B. Hammond, and W. N. Spellacy. 1999 *Danforth's Obstetrics and Gynecology*. New York: Lippincott, Williams and Wilkins.

Scott, Joan W. 1999 [1986]. *Gender and the Politics of History*. New York: Columbia University Press.

Scully, Diana. 1980. *Men Who Control Women's Health: The Miseducation of Obstetrician-Gynecologists*. Boston: Houghton Mifflin.

Sedgwick, Eve K. 1990. *Epistemology of the Closet*. Berkeley: University of California Press.

Sefton, Tom. 2004. What We Want from the Welfare State. In *British Social Attitudes: Continuity and Change over Two Decades*, ed. Alison Park, John Curtice, Katarina Thomson, Lindsey Jarvis, and Catherine Bromley, eds. 1–28. London: Sage.

Sennett, Richard. 1998. *The Corrosion of Character: The Personal Consequences of Work in the New Capitalism*. New York: W.W. Norton.

Serenius F., A. T. Elidrissy, and P. Dandona. 1984. Vitamin D Nutrition in Pregnant Women at Term and in Newly Born Babies in Saudi Arabia. *Journal of Clinical Pathology* 37 (4): 444–47.

Shanks, Michael and Ian Hodder. 1995. Processual, Postprocessual and Interpretive Archaeologies. In *Interpreting Archaeology: Finding Meaning in the Past*,

ed. Ian Hodder, Michael Shanks, Alexandra Alexandri, Victor Buchli, John Carman, Jonathan Last, and Gaving Lucas. 3–29. London: Routledge.
Shaw, Caroline M. 1995. *Race, Sex, and Class in Kenya*. Minneapolis: University of Minnesota Press.
Shaw, Nancy S. 1974. *Forced Labor: Maternity Care in the United States*. New York: Pergamon Press.
She, 2000. Sex and a Career. *World Archaeology* 32 (2): 166–72.
Shih, Chuan-Kang. 2001. Genesis of Marriage Among the Moso and Empire-Building in Late Imperial China. *Journal of Asian Studies* 60 (2): 381–412.
Shildrick, Margrit and Janet Price. 1999. Openings on the Body: A Critical Introduction. In *Feminist Theory and the Body: A Reader*, ed. Janet Price and Margrit Shildrick. 1–14. New York: Routledge.
Shimkin, Demitri B., Edith M. Shimkin, and Dennis A. Frate. 1978. *The Extended Family in Black Societies*. The Hague: Mouton.
Silvera, Makeda. 1992. Man-Royals and Sodomites: Some Thoughts on the Invisibility of Afro-Caribbean Lesbians. *Feminist Studies* 18 (3): 521–32.
Sinfield, Alan. 1998. *Gay and After*. London: Serpent's Tail.
Skokic, Tea. 2001. Feministicka antropoloska kritika: od univerzalizma do razlike. *Ethnoloska Tribina* 31 (24): 5–20.
Slocum, Sally. 1975. Woman the Gatherer: Male Bias in Anthropology. In *Toward an Anthropology of Women*, ed. Rayna R. Reiter. 36–50. New York: Monthly Review Press.
Small, Meredith F., ed. 1984. *Female Primates: Studies by Women Primatologists*. New York: Alan R. Liss.
Smith, Dorothy. 1974. Women's Perspective as a Radical Critique of Sociology. *Sociological Inquiry* 44: 7–13.
Smith, M. G. 1962. *Kinship and Community in Carriacou*. New Haven, Conn.: Yale University Press.
Smith, Raymond T. 1956. *The Negro Family in British Guiana*. London: Routledge.
———. 1996. *The Matrifocal Family: Power, Pluralism, and Politics*. New York: Routledge.
Soper, Kate. 1990. Feminism, Humanism and Postmodernism. *Radical Philosophy: A Journal of Socialist and Feminist Philosophy* 55 (Summer): 11–17.
Sørensen, Mary Louise Stig. 2000. *Gender Archaeology*. Cambridge: Polity Press.
Spargo, Tamsin. 1999. *Foucault and Queer Theory*. Cambridge: Icon Books.
Spector, Janet D. 1993. *What This Awl Means: Feminist Archaeology at a Wahpeton Dakota Village*. St. Paul: Minnesota Historical Society Press.
Spector, Janet D. and Mary K. Whelan. 1989. Incorporating Gender into Archaeology Courses. In *Gender and Anthropology: Critical Reviews for Research and Teaching*, ed. Sandra Morgen. 41–94. Arlington, Va.: American Anthropological Association.
Sperling, Susan and Yewoubdar Beyene. 1997. A Pound of Biology and a Pinch of Culture or a Pinch of Biology and a Pound of Culture? The Necessity of Integrating Biology and Culture in Reproductive Studies. In *Women in Human Evolution*, ed. Lori D. Hager. 137–52. London: Routledge.
Spivak, Gayatri Chakravorty. 1988. Can the Subaltern Speak? In *Marxism and the Interpretation of Culture*, ed. Cary Nelson and Lawrence Grossberg. 271–313. Urbana: University of Illinois Press.
Stacey, Judith. 1988. Can There Be a Feminist Ethnography? *Women's Studies International Forum* 11 (1): 21–27.

Stack, Carol B. 1974. *All Our Kin: Strategies for Survival in a Black Community.* New York: Harper and Row.

Stivens, Maila. 1996. *Matriliny and Modernity: Sexual Politics and Social Change in Rural Malaysia.* St. Leonard's, New South Wales: Allen and Unwin.

Strathern, Andrew. 1996. *Body Thoughts.* Ann Arbor: University of Michigan Press.

Strathern, Marilyn. 1988. *The Gender of the Gift: Problems with Women and Problems with Society in Melanesia.* Berkeley: University of California Press.

———. 1991. *Partial Connections.* Savage, Md.: Rowman and Littlefield.

———. 1992. Parts and Wholes: Refiguring Relationships in a Post-Plural World. In *Conceptualizing Society,* ed. Adam Kuper. 75–103. London: Routledge.

Strum, S. C. and L. M. Fedigan. 1997. Changing images of Primate Societies. *Current Anthropology* 38 (4):677–681.

Stuart-Macadam, Patricia. 1989. Nutritional Deficiency Diseases. In *Reconstruction of Life from the Skeleton,* ed. Mehmet Ya,sar I,scan and Kenneth A. R. Kennedy. 210–22. New York: Alan R. Liss.

Sörensen, Mary Louise Stig. 2000. *Gender Archaeology.* Cambridge: Polity Press.

Tanner, Nancy. 1971. Minangkabau Disputes. Ph.D. dissertation, Department of Anthropology, University of California, Berkeley.

———. 1974. Matrifocality in Indonesia and Africa and Among Black Americans. In *Woman, Culture, and Society,* ed. Michelle Zimbalist Rosaldo and Louise Lamphere. 129–56. Stanford, Calif.: Stanford University Press.

———. 1981. *On Becoming Human.* Cambridge: Cambridge University Press.

Tanner, Nancy and Adrienne Zihlman. 1976. Women in Evolution. Part I. Innovation and Selection in Human Origins. *Signs* 1 (3): 585–608.

Tarlow, Sarah. 1999. *Bereavement and Commemoration: An Archaeology of Mortality.* Malden, Mass.: Blackwell.

Tavris, Carol. 1992. *The Mismeasure of Woman.* New York: Simon and Schuster.

Terborg-Penn, Rosalyn. 1998. *African American Women in the Struggle for the Vote, 1850–1920.* Bloomington: Indiana University Press.

Thomas, David. 1999. *Archaeology: Down to Earth.* Fort Worth, Tex.: Harcourt Brace College Publishers.

Thomas, Julian. 1990. Monuments from the Inside: The Case of Irish Megalithic Tombs. *World Archaeology* 22: 168–78.

———. 1993. The Hermeneutics of Megalithic Space. In *Interpretative Archaeology,* ed. Christopher Tilley. 73–97. Oxford: Berg.

———, ed. 2000. *Interpretive Archaeology: A Reader.* London: Leicester University Press.

———. 2002. Archaeology's Humanism and the Materiality of the Body. In *Thinking Through the Body: Archaeologies of Corporeality,* ed. Yannis Hamilakis, Mark Pluciennik, and Sarah Tarlow. 29–45. New York: Kluwer Academic.

Thoms, H. 1941. The Clinical Application of Roentgen Pelvimetry and a Study of the Results in 1,100 White Women. *American Journal of Obstetrics and Gynecology* 42: 957–75.

Tilley, Christopher. 1994. *A Phenomenology of Landscape.* Oxford: Berg.

To, W. W. and I. C. Li. 2000. Occipital Posterior and Occipital Transverse Positions: Reappraisal of the obstetric risks. *Australian and New Zealand Journal of Obstetrics and Gynecology* 40 (3):275–79.

Tong, Rosemarie. 1998. *Feminist Thought: A More Comprehensive Introduction.* 2nd ed. Boulder, Colo.: Westview Press.

Toynbee, Polly. 2003. *Hard Work: Life in Low-Pay Britain.* London: Bloomsbury.

Trevathan, Wenda. 1987. *Human Birth: An Evolutionary Perspective.* Chicago: Aldine.

————. 1988. Fetal Emergence Patterns in Evolutionary Perspective. *American Anthropologist* 90: 19–26.

————. 1996. An Evolutionary Perspective on Authoritative Knowledge About Birth. In *Childbirth and Authoritative Knowledge: Cross-Cultural Perspectives*, ed. Robbie E. Davis-Floyd and Carolyn F. Sargent. 80–90. Berkeley: University of California Press.

Tringham, Ruth E. 1991. Households with Faces: The Challenge of Gender in Prehistoric Architectural Remains. In *Engendering Archaeology: Women and Prehistory*, ed. Joan M. Gero and Margaret W. Conkey. 93–131. Cambridge, Mass.: Blackwell.

Trinkaus, Erik. 1984. Neandertal Pubic Morphology and Gestation Length. *Current Anthropology* 25: 509–14.

Trivers, Robert L. 1972. Parental Investment and Sexual Selection. In *Sexual Selection and the Descent of Man, 1871–1971*, ed. Bernard Campbell. 136–79. Chicago: Aldine-Atherton.

Turner, Bryan S. 1984. *The Body and Society: Explorations in Social Theory*. Oxford: Blackwell.

————. 1991. Recent Developments in the Theory of the Body. In *The Body: Social Process and Cultural Theory*, ed. Mike Featherstone, Mike Hepworth, and Bryan S. Turner. 1–35. London: Sage.

United States Department of Labor. 1981. *The Negro Family: The Case for National Action* (the Moynihan Report). Westport, Conn.: Greenwood Press.

VanPool, Christine S. and Todd L. VanPool. 1999. The Scientific Nature of Postprocessualism. *American Antiquity* 64: 35–53.

Visweswaran, Kamala. 1997. Histories of Feminist Ethnography. *Annual Review of Anthropology* 26: 591–621.

————. 1998. "Wild West" Anthropology and the Disciplining of Gender. In *Gender and American Social Science: The Formative Years*, ed. Helene Silverberg. 86–123. Princeton, N.J.: Princeton University Press.

Voss, Barbara L. 2000. Feminisms, Queer Theories, and the Archaeological Study of Past Sexualities. *World Archaeology* 32 (2): 180–92.

Wadley, Lyn. 1998. The Invisible Meat Providers: Women in the Stone Age of South Africa. In *Gender in African Prehistory*, ed. Susan Kent. 69–82. Walnut Creek, Calif.: AltaMira Press.

Walde, Dale and Noreen D. Willows, eds. 1991. *The Archaeology of Gender: Proceedings of the 22nd Annual Chacmool Conference*. Calgary: Archaeological Association of the University of Calgary.

Walrath, Dana. 1997. Sexual Dimorphism of the Pelvis and Its Relationship to Birth in Human Evolution. Ph.D. dissertation. Department of Anthropology, University of Pennsylvania.

————. 2003. Rethinking Pelvic Typologies and the Human Birth Mechanism. *Current Anthropology* 44 (1): 5–31.

Walrath, Dana and P. Bingham. 2003. Tri-Nucleotide CAG Repeat Number in the Androgen Receptor Gene as a Mechanism for Inter-Specific Variation of Sexual Dimorphism in primates. *American Journal of Physical Anthropology*. Supplement 36: 219.

Walrath, Dana and Mica Glantz. 1996. Sexual Dimorphism in the Pelvic Midplane and Its Relationship to Neandertal Reproductive Patterns. *American Journal of Physical Anthropology* 100 (1): 89–100.

Warner, Michael. 1993. *Fear of a Queer Planet: Queer Politics and Social Theory*. Minneapolis: University of Minnesota Press.

Washburn, Sherwood L. 1951. The New Physical Anthropology. *Transactions of the New York Academy of Sciences* 13 (2): 258–304.
———. 1960. Tools and Human Evolution. *Scientific American* 203 (3): 62–75.
Washburn, Sherwood L. and C. S. Lancaster. 1968. The Evolution of Hunting. In *Man the Hunter*, ed. Richard B. Lee and Irven DeVore. 293–303. New York: Aldine.
Watson, Patty J. and Mary C. Kennedy. 1991. The Development of Horticulture in the Eastern Woodlands of North America: Women's Role. In *Engendering Archaeology: Women in Prehistory*, ed. Joan M. Gero and Margaret W. Conkey. 255–75. Cambridge, Mass.: Blackwell.
Weed, Elizabeth. 1997. Introduction. In *Feminism Meets Queer Theory*, ed. Elizabeth Weed and Naomi Schor. vii–xiii. Bloomington: Indiana University Press.
Weed, Elizabeth and Naomi Schor, eds. 1997. *Feminism Meets Queer Theory*. Bloomington: Indiana University Press.
Weiler, Kathleen. 1991. Freire and a Feminist Pedagogy of Difference. *Harvard Educational Review* 61 (4): 449–74.
Weiner, Annette B. 1976. *Women of Value, Men of Renown: New Perspectives in Trobriand Exchange*. Austin: University of Texas Press.
———. 1995. Culture and Our Discontents. *American Anthropologist* 97 (1): 14–21.
Weismantel, Mary. 1995. Making Kin: Kinship Theory and Zumbagua Adoptions. *American Ethnologist* 22 (4): 685–709.
Wekker, Gloria. 1999. What's Identity Got to Do with It? Rethinking Identity in Light of the Mati Work in Suriname. In *Female Desires: Same-Sex Relations and Transgender Practices Across Cultures*, ed. Evelyn Blackwood and Saskia E. Wieringa. 119–38. New York: Columbia University Press.
———. 2006. *The Politics of Passion: Women's Sexual Culture in the Afro-Surinamese Diaspora*. New York: Columbia University Press.
Weston, Kath. 1993. Lesbian/Gay Studies in the House of Anthropology. *Annual Review of Anthropology* 22: 339–67.
———. 1998. *Long Slow Burn: Sexuality and Social Science*. New York: Routledge.
Whalley, Lucy A. 1998. Urban Minangkabau, Muslim Women: Modern Choices, Traditional Concerns in Indonesia. In *Women in Muslim Societies: Diversity Within Unity*, ed. Herbert L. Bodman and Nayereh Tohidi. 229–49. Boulder, Colo.: Lynne Rienner.
Whannel, Garry. 2001. *Media Sport Stars: Masculinities and Moralities*. London: Routledge.
Whitehead, Harriet. 1981. The Bow and the Burden Strap: A New Look at Institutionalized Homosexuality in Native North America. In *Sexual Meanings: The Cultural Construction of Gender and Sexuality*, ed. Sherrie B. Ortner and Harriet Whitehead. 80–115. Cambridge: Cambridge University Press.
Whitridge, Peter. 2002. Landscapes, Houses, Bodies, Things: "Place" and the Archaeology of the Inuit Imaginary. Paper presented at the 67th Annual Meeting of the Society of American Archaeology, Denver, March 20–24, 2002.
Wood, J. W., G. R. Milner, H. C. Harpending, and K. M. Weiss. 1992. The Osteological Paradox: Problems of Inferring Prehistoric Health from Skeletal Samples. *Current Anthropology* 33: 343–70.
Worthman, Carol M. 1995. Hormones, Sex, and Gender. *Annual Review of Anthropology* 24: 593–616.
Wouters, Cas. 1998. Balancing Sex and Love Since the 1960s Sexual Revolution. *Theory, Culture and Society* 15 (3–4): 187–214.

Wylie, Alison. 1991. Gender Theory and the Archaeological Record: Why Is There No Archaeology of Gender? In *Engendering Archaeology: Women and Prehistory*, ed. Joan M. Gero and Margaret W. Conkey. 31–54. Cambridge, Mass.: Blackwell.

———. 1992. The Interplay of Evidential Constraints and Political Interests. *American Antiquity* 57: 15–35.

———. 1995. Doing Philosophy as a Feminist: Longino on the Search for a Feminist Epistemology. *Philosophical Topics* 23 (2): 345–58.

———. 1997a. The Engendering of Archaeology: Refiguring Feminist Science Studies. *Osiris* 12: 80–99.

———. 1997b. Good Science, Bad Science, or Science as Usual? Feminist Critiques of Science. In *Women in Human Evolution*, ed. Lori D. Hager. 29–55. London: Routledge.

———. 2000. Questions of Evidence, Legitimacy, and the (Dis)unity of Science. *American Antiquity* 65: 227–37.

———. 2001. Doing Social Science as a Feminist: The Engendering of Archaeology. In *Feminism in Twentieth-Century Science, Technology, and Medicine*, ed. Angela N. H. Creager, Elizabeth A. Lunbeck, and Londa Schiebinger. 23–45. Chicago: University of Chicago Press.

———. 2002. *Thinking from Things: Essays in the Philosophy of Archaeology*. Berkeley: University of California Press.

Wylie, Alison, Lorraine Greaves, and Staff of the London Battered Women's Advocacy Center. 1995. Women and Violence: Feminist Practice and Quantitative Method. In *Changing Methods: Feminists Transforming Practice*, ed. Sandra Burt and Lorraine Code. 301–25. Peterborough, Ont.: Broadview Press.

Yanagisako, Sylvia J. 1977. Women-Centered Kin Networks in Urban Bilateral Kinship. *American Ethnologist* 4 (2): 207–26.

———. 1979. Family and Household: The Analysis of Domestic Groups. *Annual Review of Anthropology* 8: 161–205.

Yanagisako, Sylvia Junko and Jane Fishburne Collier. 1987. Toward a Unified Analysis of Gender and Kinship. In *Gender and Kinship: Essays Toward a Unified Analysis*, ed. Jane Fishburne Collier and Sylvia Junko Yanagisako. 14–50. Stanford, Calif.: Stanford University Press.

Young, Iris M. 1994. Gender as Seriality: Thinking About Women as a Social Collective. *Signs* 19 (3): 713–38.

Yuval-Davis, Nira. 2003. Nationalist Projects and Gender Relations. *Naroda Umjetnost* 40 (1): 9–36.

Zavella, Patricia. 1987. *Women's Work and Chicano Families: Cannery Workers of the Santa Clara Valley*. Ithaca, N.Y.: Cornell University Press.

Zernicke, Kate. 1999. MIT Women Win Fight Against Bias. *Boston Globe*, March 21, A01.

Zihlman, Adrienne. 1978. Women in Evolution. Part II. Subsistence and Social Organization Among Early Hominoids *Signs* 4 (1): 4–20.

Zihlman, Adrienne. 1981. Women as the Shapers of Human Adaptation. In *Woman the Gatherer*. Frances Dahlberg. 75–120. New Haven, Conn.: Yale University Press.

———. 1987. American Association of Physical Anthropologists Annual Luncheon Address, April 1985: Sex, Sexes and Sexism in Human Origins. *Yearbook of Physical Anthropology* 30: 11–19.

———. 1997. The Paleolithic Glass Ceiling: Women in Human Evolution. In *Women in Human Evolution*, ed. Lori D. Hager. 91–113. London: Routledge.

Zihlman, Adrienne and Nancy Tanner. 1978. Gathering and Hominid Adaptation. In *Female Hierarchies*, ed. Lionel Tiger and Heather Fowler. 163–94. Chicago: Beresford Book Service.

Žižek, Slavoj. 1999. *The Ticklish Subject: The Absent Centre of Political Ontology*. London: Verso.

Contributors

Evelyn Blackwood is Associate Professor in Anthropology and Women's Studies at Purdue University. She has produced a number of works in an Native American female two-spirits, *tombois* in Indonesia, gender and power, matrilineal kinship, and theories of sexualities. She has published a monograph on the Minangkabau of West Sumatra entitled *Webs of Power: Women, Kin and Community in a Sumatran Village*. She is coeditor with Saskia Wieringa *of Female Desires: Same-Sex Relations and Transgender Practices Across Cultures* and editor of *The Many Faces of Homosexuality: Anthropology and Homosexual Behavior*.

Thomas A. Dowson is an archaeologist whose research includes shamanism and the interpretation of rock art, theory and methodology of archaeological approaches to art, and the popular representation of prehistoric and ancient artistic traditions. He is also committed to an examination of archaeology's sexual politics. His publications include *Rock Engravings of Southern Africa* and, with David Lewis-Williams, *Images of Power: Understanding San Rock Art*. He also edited the *Queer Archaeologies* volume of *World Archaeology*.

Pamela L. Geller currently teaches at American University in Washington, D.C. She received her Ph.D. in anthropology from the University of Pennsylvania in 2004. As an anthropological archaeologist, Geller's investigations of the past are enriched by intra- and interdisciplinary engagement. Her recent research has implemented a humanistic bioarchaeological framework to examine the body and the meanings encoded in its modification and manipulation. It is through a study of the body that she is able to best bring together her diverse research interests—pre-Columbian Mesoamerican cultures, feminist and social theories, bioarchaeology, and repatriation. She has conducted fieldwork in Belize, Honduras, Israel, and Hawai'i.

Julia A. Hendon is Associate Professor of Anthropology in the Department of Sociology and Anthropology at Gettysburg College. A specialist in Mesoamerican archaeology with interests in household archaeology, gender, economic specialization, landscape, and the development of complex societies, her fieldwork and research has concentrated on the Classic period Maya and neighboring complex societies in northern Honduras. She is coeditor with Rosemary A. Joyce of *Mesoamerican Archaeology: Theory and Practice* and has published articles in *American Anthropologist, Annual Review of Anthropology, Latin American Antiquity,* and *Cambridge Archaeological Journal.*

Rosemary A. Joyce, Professor of Anthropology at the University of California, Berkeley, has engaged in archaeological fieldwork in Honduras since 1977. She received a Ph.D. from the University of Illinois-Urbana in 1985. At Harvard University from 1985 to 1994, she served as Assistant Director and Curator at the Peabody Museum and Assistant and Associate Professor of Anthropology. She moved to Berkeley in 1994 as Associate Professor of Anthropology and was Director of the Phoebe Apperson Hearst Museum of Anthropology from 1994 to 1999. Her recent books include *Gender and Power in Prehispanic Mesoamerica, The Languages of Archaeology, Embodied Lives* (2003), and the hypertext *Sister Stories.*

Ann M. Kakaliouras teaches anthropology at Appalachian State University in Boone, North Carolina. She received her Ph.D. in Anthropology from the University of North Carolina at Chapel Hill in 2003 and she is continuing to explore questions she pursued in her dissertation regarding biocultural relationships between Late Woodland (A.D. 800–1650) coastal North Carolina Native peoples. Also, she is currently working on a historical project to document the ways early twentieth-century physical anthropologists constructed a uniquely disciplinary "Indian" through articulating their quantitative analyses (anthropometric and skeletal studies) with their qualitative statements about Native Americans.

Susan Kus is Associate Professor of Anthropology at Rhodes College in Memphis, Tennessee. Her early and continuing interest as an archaeologist is in state origins and the symbolic organization of space. This interest has led her most recently into ethnographic fieldwork with ritual specialists in Madagascar who orient houses and tombs in space and time, seeking to appreciate how local systems of knowledge are created, recreated, and found convincing.

Louise Lamphere is Distinguished Professor of Anthropology at the University of New Mexico and past president of the American Anthropological Association. She began her writing in feminist anthropology with the publication in 1974 of *Woman, Culture, and Society*, coedited with Michelle Zimbalist Rosaldo. She has studied issues of women and work for 25 years, beginning with her study of women workers in Rhode Island industry, *From Working Daughters to Working Mothers*. She also coauthored a study of working women in Albuquerque entitled *Sunbelt Working Mothers: Reconciling Family and Factory* with Patricia Zavella, Felipe Gonzales, and Peter Evans. She has coedited with Helena Ragoné and Patricia Zavella a collection of articles entitled *Situated Lives: Gender and Culture in Everyday Life*. She is currently completing a biography of three Navajo women entitled *Weaving Together Women's Lives: Three Generations in a Navajo Family*.

Henrietta L. Moore is Deputy Director and Professor of Social Anthropology at the London School of Economics. She has published extensively on social and feminist theory, and on Africa. Her writings include *A Passion for Difference: Essays in Anthropology and Gender* and *Cutting Down Trees*, coauthored with Megan Vaughan. The latter won the American African Studies Association 1995 Herskovits Prize. She has also edited *The Future of Anthropological Knowledge* and coedited with Todd Sanders *Contemporary Anthropological Theory*. She is currently completing a book on anthropology and psychoanalysis.

Sarah M. Nelson is John Evans Professor of Archaeology at the University of Denver. She specializes in the archaeology of China and Korea, as well as early complex societies and gender. She also writes fiction about archaeology. She has written *Gender in Archaeology: Analyzing Power and Prestige*, edited *In Pursuit of Gender: Worldwide Archaeological Approaches* with Myriam Rosen-Ayalon, edited *Equity Issues for Women in Archaeology* with Margaret Nelson and Alison Wylie, and edited *Denver: An Archaeological History*, also available from the University of Pennsylvania Press.

Elizabeth M. Perry received a BA in Anthropology from Arizona State University and an MA and Ph.D. in anthropology from the University of Arizona. Her interests include gender and sexuality theory, social power, and bioarchaeology. She is currently the lead osteologist for the Animas-La Plata Archaeology Project in Southwest Colorado and the Director of Cultural Resources for SWCA Environmental Consultants in Utah, Nevada and Idaho.

James M. Potter received a B.A. in anthropology from Berkeley and an M.A. and Ph.D. in Anthropology from Arizona State University. His interests include landscape and metaphor theory, gender issues, the archaeology of the American Southwest, and faunal analysis. He is currently the Principal Investigator of the Animas-La Plata Archaeology Project in Southwest Colorado.

Miranda K. Stockett received a Ph.D. in Anthropology from the University of Pennsylvania in 2005. Her research focuses on the juncture of identity, community, and settlement patterns in pre-Columbian Mesoamerica, as well as on the development of feminist theory in anthropology. She is currently a Penn Writing Fellow at the University of Pennsylvania, a Research Associate at the University of Pennsylvania Museum of Archaeology and Anthropology, and codirector of the Proyecto Arqueologico Valle de Jesus de Otoro in central Honduras.

Dana Walrath teaches medicine and is a Women's Studies affiliated faculty member at the University of Vermont. She earned a Ph.D. in 1997 from the University of Pennsylvania in medical and biological anthropology. Her doctoral research developed novel synthetic techniques and theories for the interpretation of the evolution of human childbirth. Her interests span biocultural aspects of reproduction, genetics, and evolutionary medicine. Walrath's publications have appeared in *Current Anthropology*, *American Anthropologist*, and *American Journal of Physical Anthropology*. Her work and writings often focus upon the conceptual relationship between evolutionary research and feminism. For the University of Vermont's College of Medicine she has developed an innovative program that brings anthropological perspectives into the study of medicine.

Alison Wylie is Professor in the Departments of Philosophy and Anthropology at the University of Washington. She is a philosopher of science with longstanding interests in feminist philosophy of science and in epistemic and normative issues raised by archaeology. *Thinking from Things* presents her analysis of evidential reasoning in archaeology, and her feminist essays appear in *Hypatia*, for which she coedited a 2004 special issue on "Feminist Science Studies," as well as in *Science and Other Cultures* and *The Cambridge Companion to Feminism in Philosophy*.

Index

Abject, 117–19, 122, 123, 125
Academy, xi, 4, 5, 18, 23, 25, 41, 42, 56, 59, 69, 70, 100–101, 106, 129, 132, 136–37, 140, 145, 166, 169, 171
Accessibility, 13–15
Activity areas, 120–21
Africa, xii, xv, 105–6. *See also* Afro-Caribbean societies; South Africa
African Americans, xii, 73, 76, 78, 178 n.8. *See also* Women
Afro-Caribbean societies, 74–79, 86, 171, 178 n.8
Age, xvi, 2, 11, 18, 43, 111, 125, 160, 163, 164
Agency, xi, xiv–xvi, 9, 11, 13, 14, 17, 26, 29–31, 41, 53–54, 56, 68, 81, 84–86, 108–9, 117, 134, 138, 170–72, 175
Alberti, Benjamin, 52, 92
Alcoff, Linda, 167, 174
All American Women (Cole), xii
Alonso, Ana, 115, 116
Altriciality, 61–62
Ambiguity, 23–24, 27, 35, 40, 42, 89, 125, 151, 171, 172
American Anthropological Association, xiii, 114, 130, 143, 179 n.4
American Association of Physical Anthropology, 59, 180 n.3
American Southwest, xi, 116, 119–24
Androcentrism, x, 4–7, 9, 12, 17, 18, 94, 131, 145, 159–61
Antifeminism, 15, 54
Antiracism, 143
Appadurai, Arjun, 26
Applied anthropology, xi, 15

Archaeological Institute of America, 130
Association for Feminist Anthropology, xii–xiii

Barbin, Herculine, 125
Beck-Gernsheim, Elizabeth, 29
Behar, Ruth, xii
Bem, Sandra, 159–60
Benedict, Ruth, xi
Berdache. *See* Native American, two-spirit
Betsileo, 111–13
Binary oppositions, x, 1, 5–7, 10, 16, 52, 92, 101, 109, 123, 162, 167, 168, 177 n.1, active : passive, 6, 64, 65; civilized : primitive, 6; dominance : subjugation, 5, 44; heterosexual : homosexual, 101; male : female, 117–21, 165, 167; man : woman, 5, 7, 16, 161; masculine : feminine, 93, 160; mind : body, 6, 46–48; culture : nature, 6, 44, 51; public : private, 6, 33–34; sex : gender, 6, 7, 10, 44, 46, 51, 121, 123
Bioarchaeology, 144, 146, 180 nn.3, 4
Bipedalism, 57–58, 62, 69
Bisexuality, 35, 93, 100–101. *See also* Men, bisexual; Sexuality; Women, bisexual
Biomedicine, 46, 59–63, 69, 171
Black Feminist Anthropology (McClaurin), xii
Borneman, John, 74
Bottom line maxim, 134, 170
Braidotti, Rosi, 47
Brumfiel, Elizabeth, 109–10, 179 n.4
Butler, Judith, x, xv, 8, 13, 15–16, 42, 50–53, 115–18
Bynum, Caroline Walker, 46

Naim, Mochtar, 80
Napier, John, 58
National Organization for Women, 4
Nationalism, 95
Native American Graves Protection and
   Repatriation Act (NAGPRA). *See*
   Repatriation
Native Americans, xi, 129, 144; two-spirit,
   179 nn.2, 1, 180 n.3. *See also*
   Pueblo culture
Natural selection, 60, 153
Neanderthals, 154
Neoliberalism, xii
New Archaeology. *See* Processual
   archaeology
Newton, Ester, xii
Not One of the Boys: Living Life as a Feminist
   (Feigen), 157–58
Nussbaum, Martha C., 115

Obstetrics, 58–63, 69; obstetrical dilemma,
   58–65, 68–70, 171
Oppression, 5, 14, 16, 123, 124, 125, 134,
   167, 169
Origin story: Christian, 147–49; evolution,
   149; Zuni, 122–23
Ortman, Scott G., 124
Ortner, Sherry, 6, 44
Other, 144, 154
Osteology, 10, 59, 124, 144, 146, 180 n.4;
   osteobiography, 49. *See also* Human
   remains

Paleoanthropology, xv, 55–58
Parsons, Elsie Clews, xi, 122
Patriarchal Man, 74, 77–79, 81, 84, 86–87
Patriarchy, 5, 134. *See also* Patriarchal Man
Patterson, Thomas, 138
Pedagogy, xii, 14, 145–46, 148, 155; class-
   room, xii, xiii, 2, 15, 17, 19, 129, 131,
   132, 134, 136, 137, 143, 145–49, 152,
   154, 172, 173, 181 n.9; engaged, 145;
   feminist, xiii, xvi, 15, 131, 135–37, 141,
   146–48, 154, 147, 172
Peletz, Michael, 80, 85
Performance, xv, xvi, 8, 9, 30, 50–52, 108,
   110, 116–18, 120–24, 163, 171. *See also*
   Butler; Performativity
Performativity, xvi, 14, 23, 42, 50, 52,
   113, 115–25, 171. *See also* Butler;
   Performance

Personhood, 29, 45–46, 48, 49
Phenomenology, 17, 47, 49–50
Philosophy, 25, 40, 42, 45–46, 49, 140, 167,
   179 n.2
Planned Parenthood, 4
Political activism, 3–4, 13–14, 19, 115, 125,
   168–70, 174
Political economy, x, xvii, 9, 26, 28–30
Popular media, 15, 91, 156, 158, 179 n.1
Postmodernism, xvi, 17, 24, 27, 28, 41–42,
   107, 146
Postprocessual archaeology, 13, 17, 107,
   110, 130, 131, 137–39, 141, 159, 165,
   179 n.3
Poststructuralism, xvi, 93, 146
Potter, Elizabeth, 167
Poverty, xii, xiv, 31, 37, 42, 69, 73, 75,
   178 n.8
Praxis, 25, 26, 113, 173
Pregnancy. *See* Reproduction
Price, Janet, 117, 119
Primate Visions (Haraway), 149.
Primates, 59, 60, 61, 62, 65, 66, 67, 150,
   151; primatology, 12, 55, 65, 145
Processual archaeology, 106, 108, 130,
   131, 138. *See also* Postprocessual
   archaeology
Psychoanalysis. *See* Psychology
Psychology, 32, 36, 40, 45, 47, 117, 174,
   179 n.2; evolutionary, 145, 153, 180 n.5,
   181 n.11
Public : private. *See* Binary oppositions
Public policy, xiii, 34, 73, 147, 148
Pueblo culture, 119–23

Queer archaeology, 89, 90, 99
Queer identity, 7, 90, 181 n.10; anthropol-
   ogist, 89, 99,145. *See also* Homosexuality;
   Men, gay; Same-sex relations; Sexuality;
   Women, lesbian
Queer theory, xii, 7, 14–18, 23, 25, 30, 35,
   44, 89–90, 95–97, 99, 143

Race, xiii, xv, xvi, 3, 10, 11, 23–28, 30, 43,
   60, 95, 119, 134, 145, 152, 153, 170, 172,
   174; interracial relationships, 91
Racism, 60, 131, 145, 146, 152, 178 n.8.
   See also Antiracism
Reeder, Greg, 97–99
Rieff, David, 27
Relationalism, 175

Acknowledgments

We have incurred many debts, both personal and professional, during the course of our work on this volume. First and foremost, we would like to thank the contributors to this volume for their hard work, patience, and innovative scholarship. The authors' contributions represent the current, though ever-evolving, state of feminist anthropology. In introducing a portion of the varied discourses that comprise anthropological feminist theorizing today, they recognize that multivocality and debate are what keep feminist anthropology fresh, interesting, and self-reflexive. Our contributors are also united in the belief that feminist theory facilitates social, intellectual, and political changes inside and outside of the discipline, but present many different perspectives on how to operationalize these changes in professional and classroom settings. Furthermore, all contributors are committed to grounding the all-too-often ethereal and abstract in empirical evidence and practical case studies from their current work. We would like to extend our thanks both for these insights, and for all the authors' hard work and dedication in seeing this book through to publication.

In addition to volume contributors, we would also like to thank those people who participated in the AAA session from which this volume emerged. Furthermore, we must acknowledge Peter Agree at the University of Pennsylvania Press, who was a champion of this project from the outset. Peter, as well as Laura Miller, Alison Anderson, and Laura Young of Penn Press, have been encouraging, helpful, and patient throughout the publication process. For planting the seeds of feminist anthropology so many years ago that bore fruit with this volume, we are beholden to Bob Preucel and Wendy Ashmore. Also, no thanks would be complete without acknowledging our families. For their unfailing encouragement, Pamela extends her eternal gratitude to Brian, Sidney,

Barbara, and Abbie, while Miranda wishes to thank Steve, Cindy, Amy, Jeff, and Siddharth for their staunch and very valued support. Finally, we would like to tip our hats to each other. Indeed, we are each other's biggest fans and critics, and this has allowed us to flourish as friends, archaeologists, and scholars.